Coventry and Warwickshire's Footballing Greats

Introduction

Welcome to Coventry and Warwickshire's Footballing Greats! It is a celebration of players from the area, from the early days of professional football in the 1870s to the present day. This book is about players from the modern city of Coventry and county of Warwickshire boundaries post 1974. Historically part of Warwickshire, the city of Coventry became part of the new West Midlands metropolitan county along with parts of Birmingham in 1974. We are going to look at players who have played for Coventry City and others who are from the area and who have played for other teams. The journey begins with "Early Greats" and subsequent chapters will take us up to the present era. We are also going to celebrate our non-league players and teams, players who have won international recognition and schoolboy and youth team football. I hope that you will enjoy reading this book as I have writing it. I thank everyone who has helped me along the way.

Chapter One – Early Greats

In this chapter we are going to look at some of the most successful early players. Some of them played for Coventry City, others achieved success elsewhere. From the 1870s to the 1940s Coventry and Warwickshire has produced some great players.

Charlie Wilson

Charlie was a centre forward who was born in Atherstone on 30th March 1895. He began his career with local team Atherstone Town before joining Coventry City of the Southern League in 1914. Some sources of information indicate that Charlie played in the 1918/19 season for Coventry City and also Tottenham Hotspur under pseudonyms. Charlie went on to have a great career for Huddersfield Town winning the First Division title in 1924 and 1925 under legendary manager Herbert Chapman. In March 1926 he joined Stoke City then played for Stafford Rangers, Wrexham, Shrewsbury Town and Alfreton. Charlie, for some reason, was overlooked by England even though he was scoring goals for the best team in the country at the time, Huddersfield Town! He passed away in 1971 aged seventy six.

Josiah (Joe) Barratt

Joe was a right winger who was born in Bulkington on 21st February 1895. He played local football for Nuneaton Town; Joe was spotted by James McIntyre and played for Southampton as wartime guest player in March 1919. Joe, who liked playing with a piece of straw in his mouth, joined Southampton permanently in 1919. He would go on to make 102 appearances and score 8 goals for the Saints. Surprisingly Joe was transferred to Birmingham in

March 1922. Southampton would go on to become champions of Third Division South. Joe played twenty two league matches that season and contributed towards Southampton's success. Joe also played for Lincoln City, Bristol Rovers and Pontypridd (winning the Welsh Football League). In 1928 he joined Nuneaton Town and played for them for two seasons. Joe finished his playing career with Coventry Colliery. In the late 1940s he was junior coach at Coventry City. He sadly passed away in April 1968 aged seventy three. His son Harry played for Coventry City in the 1930s and 1940s.

Harry Barratt

Harry was born in Headington, Oxfordshire on 25th December 1918. He attended Ash Green School and played for Coventry Boys and Salem Baptists before progressing to Herbert's Works side. In December 1935 Coventry City signed Joe's son Harry aged seventeen. Harry, an inside-right, had been playing for Herbert's A.F.C, living with his parents at 132, Coventry Road, Exhall. A versatile player, Harry played in nine different positions for Coventry City including goalkeeper. Harry made his reserves debut against his dad's old team Southampton in 1936 which City won 2-1. He made his full debut on 9th April 1938 at Outside-Right in a 3-2 win over Blackburn Rovers at Highfield Road. Harry was a decent cricketer and played for Bedworth CC with former Bantams teammate Jack Pritchard. Harry played 178 times for Coventry City scoring thirteen goals. In addition Harry played for Coventry City during the war time seasons and was a regular scorer. He played for Leicester City, he helped the Foxes win the Regional Championship in 1942. He retired after getting injured in 1951. He was manager of Rugby Town and Snowdon Colliery (Kent) before returning to Coventry City as Chief scout in

December 1955. Harry was responsible for George Curtis moving to Coventry City having been his manager in Kent. Between 1958 and 1962 Harry was manager of Gillingham, a total of 195 games with a win ratio of 37.44% from 73 wins. In the 1960s Harry was Secretary/Manager of Tunbridge Wells United and Social secretary of Morris Motors in Coventry. For many years he was National Coach for the British Crown Green Bowls Association. He passed away on 25th September 1989.

Harry Kent

Harry was a centre half who was born on 22nd of October 1879 in Bedworth. Harry began his career at Notts County but never played for the first team. In the early 1900s he played for Newark, Heanor Town and Ilkeston Town before joining Southern League Brighton & Hove Albion. In 1908 he signed for First Division Middlesbrough. A year later he would join Watford of the Southern League. Harry would become Watford player-manager in 1910, the beginning of a long reign as Watford's manager. In the 1914/15 season he would lead the club to the Southern League championship. Five years later in 1920 Watford were founder members of Football League Division Three. Harry remained at Vicarage Road until 1926; he is the club's longest serving manager. Graham Taylor has managed more games but Harry has the record for consecutive seasons as manager. Harry was also a pub landlord in Watford. He passed away on 22nd December 1948.

Charles Griffiths

Charles was born in Rugby the year unknown. He had a modest playing career as an inside forward. Some sources of information say that he played for Coventry City. I was however unable to find any match data. Charles is more famous as a coach and a manager. In 1910 he worked for German team Karlsruher KV. During Charles's time with them they won the Southern German championship. In August 1911 Charles would make history becoming Bayern Munich's first full time manager. Despite being only in charge of Bayern for seven months he developed modern training methods which paved the way for those who followed. It was probably a premature decision by Bayern to dismiss Charles; the club finished second therefore missing out on qualification to the German Championship. Charles next worked for Stuttgarter Kickers whom he led to the Southern German championship. After World War One Charles was part of was part of the coaching staff for the Belgium national team in 1920. They won the Olympic gold medal in the summer games which were held in Antwerp, Belgium. Charles also went on to coach Vitesse Arnhem, Lille, France (Olympic). He worked in football until he passed away in 1936.

Arthur "Nat" Robinson

Nat was a goalkeeper who was born in Coventry on 28th February 1878. He began his career with local teams Allesley, Coventry Stars and Singers FC. In 1898 he joined Small Heath / Birmingham FC then going on to play 306 times for them. During his time in Birmingham he twice played for Football League XI and he also played in two England trials. Nat went onto play for Chelsea and Coventry City. He passed away on 15th May 1929.

Arthur Johnson

Arthur was an outside left who was born in Atherstone on 16th December 1903. He began his career with local team Atherstone

Town before joining Huddersfield Town 1924. The Terriers were champions under legendary manager Herbert Chapman. Arthur never played for them and moved to Barnsley in 1925. Spells at Birmingham and Bristol City followed, he then finishing off his career with Coventry City. Arthur played 5 times for Coventry City. Sadly he passed away in June 1987.

John (Jack) Henry Kearns

Jack was a full back from Nuneaton. He played for Hartshill United before joining Coventry City in 1903. Jack also played for Birmingham, Bristol City and Aston Villa winning the League with them in 1910. Jack's great nephew is Mick Kearns who you will read about later in the book.

Frederick (Fred) Herbert

One of the first local greats to play for The Bantams, Fred was born in Bedworth but the year is unknown. Nicknamed "Cute" he worked at Exhall Colliery whilst enjoying a good career in local football for Foxford United, Bedworth Town and Exhall Colliery. Fred joined Coventry City in 1922; an inside left or left winger his goal scoring record for The Bantams is impressive. In 199 appearances he scored 86 goals which put him joint fourth with Ted Roberts in Coventry City's all time goal scoring list. Fred made his Coventry City debut on 18th November 1922 against Stockport County in Division Two. On the 17th March 1923 he scored his first goal for the club in a 2-1 defeat against Leicester City. In the next five seasons he would become a regular in the team. He had a benefit match against Luton Town on 12th November 1927 which City won 4-2. On 25th September 1929 it was announced that Fred would be joining Brierley Hill Alliance in the Birmingham and District League.

Fred was a publican at The Beehive Inn on High Street in Bedworth. A newspaper article from March 1936 said that Fred was residing at the pub with his father-in-law. He passed away in 1945.

Memorable Match

Coventry City 7-0 Rotherham United – Division Three (North) 7th November 1925.

Fred Herbert scored three goals playing at inside left as The Bantams thrashed Rotherham. William Patterson scored two goals and one each for Jimmy Dougall and William Poole. Paterson (centre forward) and Dougall (outside right) were fine Scottish players.

Coventry City – Best, Houldey, Randle, Watson, McIvanney, Rowley, Walker, Dougall, Paterson, Poole, Herbert

Henry Arthur (Harry) Boileau

A wing half who was born in Bedworth in 1910, Harry played for Bedworth Town prior to signing professional forms with Coventry City in August 1931. He played 165 league and FA Cup matches for The Bantams in the 1930s. Harry was nick named "Old Philosopher" because of his enjoyment of smoking a pipe. In January 1941 Harry joined Notts County with three other Coventry players – Morgan, Elliott and Davidson. In May 1942 he lined up for Birmingham alongside George Mason against West Bromwich Albion. During the war years Harry also guested for Northampton

Town and continued to play for Coventry City up until May 1946 when he was given a free transfer.

A very fine cricketer too, Harry played for Humber-Hillman and Coventry City. In August 1938 he took three wickets in one over against GEC. In May the same year Coventry City played in a benefit match at Humber cricket club. Harry, along with Tom Crawley, Billy Frith and Harry Barratt all played in the match. In August 1943 he hit a very good sixty two not out for GEC against Morris.

In August 1965 Harry became manager of Bedworth Town. He was previously a scout for Birmingham City and owned a café in Wyken. Harry resigned from the post in April 1966 after eight months in charge. Harry passed away in 1981 aged seventy one.

Memorable Match

Coventry City 2-0 Thames - Division Three (South) 5th September 1931

Harry made his Coventry City debut in a 2-0 win with Clarrie Bourton scoring both goals.

Coventry City – Allen, Watson, Tilford, Baker, Boileau, O'Brien, Johnson, White, Bourton, Lake, Lauderdale

John (Jackie) Randle

Jackie was born in Bedworth on 23rd August 1902. He was a full back who made over 150 appearances for Coventry City between 1923 and 1927. Signed from local team Exhall Colliery, Jackie followed a similar path to fellow Bedworth player Fred Herbert. From 1927 to 1933 Jackie played for Birmingham, who were in the First Division, playing over 100 times. Jackie also played for Southend United, Bournemouth & Boscombe Athletic and Guildford City. Jackie sadly passed away in 1990.

Stan Keeley

Stan was born in Foleshill on 14th June 1920, a left back he joined Coventry City from Herbert's Athletic. In September 1942 he played against Aston Villa, deputising for Walter Metcalf. Stan made 4 official appearances in the 1946/47 season plus his war time appearances. He later played for Bedworth Town; in September 1952 he had a benefit match along with other long serving players Owen Woolley and Jack Kirkaldie. Bedworth beat Derby County Colts 1-0 at The Oval. Stan also became player /manager of Bedworth Town. A good cricketer too, he hit 121 for Herbert's in July 1938. Stan also played for Longford Cricket Club. Stan passed away in 1993 aged seventy three.

Ron O'Brien

Ron was a half back from Coventry who made fifty eight appearances for Coventry City in the early 1930s. Ron joined Watford in the 1933/34 season; he also played for local teams Morris Motors and Bedworth Town. During the war years he played regularly for Coventry City.

Harvey John (Jack) Pritchard

Jack was born in Meriden on 30th January 1913 and he lived in Birmingham Road in Allesley. He was an outside right and played five times for Coventry City in the 1936/37 season. He joined Coventry City from Exhall Colliery who were a good team in local football. On 6th January 1934 they beat Bermuda WMC 5-0. It was the Birmingham Junior Cup Third Round: Jack scored in the second half. It was a good month for Jack as he scored again as Humber-Hillman were beaten 3-0 in the Midland Daily Telegraph Cup. In December 1934 Jack scored twice as Bedlam Lane was beaten 3-0.

Jack's first game for Coventry City was for the reserve team against Clapton Orient Reserve's in 1935. Manager Harry Storer secured Jack's services after a private trial at Highfield Road. Birmingham and Bristol City had expressed an interest in him.

Coventry City Reserves Team – Morgan, Brook, Wilmot, Birtley, Elliott, Frith, Pritchard, Wilson, Bacon, Lake, Crisp

On 14th October 1935, Jack signed professional forms for Coventry City. The twenty year old was one of the best talents in local football. Jack made his first team debut in a 1-1 draw against Fulham on 14th of September 1936, Arthur Fitton scoring for the Bantams.

Coventry City – Morgan, Astley, Smith, Mason, Boileau, Frith, Fitton, Pritchard, Bourton, Lauderdale, Jones

In March 1936 Jack played for England in a junior international against Scotland at Tynecastle, Edinburgh. England fielded a side that was represented by Birmingham County FA; Jack was the only player from Coventry City. England won 4-2 with Jack scoring one of the goals in the first half.

Jack had a decent career after he left Highfield Road, playing for Crystal Palace, Manchester City and Southend United. When Jack was at Manchester City he played with legendary keeper Frank Swift, England forward Eric Brook and Northern Ireland forward Peter Doherty. City won the First Division in 1937 but were bizarrely relegated the next season despite being the division's top scorers. Jack scored his first goal for Manchester City in a 1-0 win over Chelsea on 2nd April 1938. In the same month he scored goals as Charlton Athletic, Leeds United and West Bromwich Albion were thrashed. Maybe if Jack had played for them earlier they might have stayed up as they picked up some form when he was included at the end of the season. Jack made thirteen appearances in the 1938/39 season in which Manchester City finished fifth in the Second Division.

In December 1939 Jack played for Leicester City against Wolverhampton Wanderers at Molineux. He played for a few teams during the war years including West Ham United and Leyton Orient.

In May 1943 Coventry City beat an RAF XI 2-1; Jack guested for a strong RAF team that included England international Neil Franklin and former Bantams favourite Leslie Jones.

In November 1943 Jack scored for Northampton Town against Coventry City. He was guesting for the Cobblers. Crawley and Gardner scored two goals each in a 4-1 win for The Bantams. In August 1945 Jack helped Coventry City beat Arsenal 2-0 at Highfield Road, Gardner and Lowrie scoring the goals.

Jack had some very good seasons during the war years he played 47 times in total for Manchester City scoring 9 goals. His best season for the Maine Road team was in the 1940/41 season where he played 30 times scoring 5 times. Jack was a very good player for Northampton Town making 113 appearances scoring 27 goals during the war time seasons. In the 1941/42 season he played 26 times for the Cobblers scoring 11 times. Jack continued to be a good player for them for the next three seasons. He made one appearance for West Ham United in the 1944/45 season. Jack made 9 appearances for Coventry City during the war time seasons scoring twice,

I contacted Jack's granddaughter Deborah Pritchard on twitter. Deborah is an award winning composer; she has been very helpful on finding out information about Jack.

Jack served in the Royal Army Medical Corps and was a Physical Training Instructor (PTI) at Aldershot. He played for the RAMC team, and also guested for other teams throughout the war years. After the war he played for Southend United from 1947 to 1956. He then joined Folkestone as a player in 1956 and was manager from 1957 to 1962. In September 1958 he was praised for being a shrewd manager as he signed ex-football league players Dennis Churms and Frank Dudley for Folkstone.

Jack went to Chelmsford as a trainer for just 6 months in 1962 and was also a FA Coach. From 1962 onwards he returned to Folkestone as manager, also helping with training, and ran a cafe with wife Eva. He also took on various roles such as steward at the social club as well as some coaching.

In later life he retired and lived in Folkestone and then Hythe, Kent. He then moved to live with his daughter Julie in Ringsfield,

Beccles for the last few years of his life. Jack sadly passed away on the 16th of April 2000 in Beccles, Suffolk. Jack was physically fit throughout his whole life and died of Alzheimer's aged 87.

Charles (Charlie) Henry Cross

A left half who signed for Coventry City in September 1919 from Siddeley Deasy FC, Charlie only played thirteen times for his hometown club before a move to Crystal Palace in 1922. He spent six seasons with Crystal Palace playing over 230 times, and then finished his career with Wolverhampton Wanderers and Merthyr Town.

Les Bruton

Born in Foleshill, Coventry on 1st of April 1903, Les began his career with Bell Green Wesleyans. In November 1922 he was spotted by Second Division Southampton, however only made seven appearances in nearly four years. Les played as a centre forward or inside left. He joined Peterborough & Fletton United in 1926. A spell in Scotland with Raith Rovers was followed by a move to First Division Blackburn Rovers. Les played the best football of his career at Ewood Park scoring twenty three times in thirty eight appearances. In February 1932 Les joined Liverpool, playing six times and scoring once, against Chelsea. In July 1933 he joined Birmingham Combination team Leamington Town, and then he was a coach at Coventry City. Les sadly passed away on 2nd April 1989.

Fred Keeble

An inside forward, Fred was born in Coventry on 30th August 1919. Fred was at Coventry City but only played for the first team in war time matches. Fred also played for Scottish team Albion Rovers, A team mate of Fred in Scotland was Celtic legend Jock Stein. A return to England in 1946 saw him at Grimsby Town. Then he played for Notts County with another football legend Tommy Lawton. Fred subsequently played for Bedworth, Nuneaton Borough and Lockheed Leamington winning the 1951 Birmingham Senior Cup with Lockheed. In 1953 Fred was player-Manager of Leamington team Flavels. Fred passed away on 8th May 1987; his grandson is Jai Stanley a talented midfielder who played for Bedworth, Atherstone and Leamington.

Francis (Frank) White

Born in Warwick on 30th June 1910, Frank was an outside right. He began his career with local teams St Paul's and Warwick Town. In 1929 he signed for West Bromwich Albion, playing for their reserve team. Coventry City signed Frank in May 1931; he would be a great success at Highfield Road. In his four years at the club he played 126 times scoring 26 goals, however assisting many goals. Fellow forwards Clarrie Bourton, Jock Lauderdale and Billy Lake benefited from Frank's excellent wing play. Frank later played for Newport County, Peterborough United and Racing Club de Paris. In 1946 he was back in his home town playing for Warwick West End and then played for Central Hospital.

Jack Townsend

Jack was an outside left who was born in Nuneaton in 1906. He played thirty two games for Coventry City between 1927 and 1929. In November 1928 he scored as Coventry City beat Crystal Palace 3-0 in a Division Three (South) match. Jack played for a few local teams including Griff Colliery, Nuneaton Town and Hinckley United.

Fred Gardner

Born in Coventry on 4th of June 1922, Fred was a talented sportsman. He was an outside right for Birmingham and guested for Northampton and Port Vale before signing for Coventry City in 1945. Fred played thirteen games scoring three goals in four years at Highfield Road. He faced competition from Warner and Simpson for a place in the first team so he joined Newport County in May 1949. Fred then played for Rugby Town and Lockheed Leamington in the early 1950s. In 1949 he became a regular for Warwickshire County Cricket Club; Fred was a fine opening batsman. In 1953 he scored 110 for Warwickshire against Australia, which was the first by a Warwickshire player against an Australian touring side. In July 1950 he scored a superb 215 not out against Somerset in Taunton. Fred scored 17,826 runs for Warwickshire, with an average of 33.83, and made 29 centuries. Fred finished playing cricket in 1961. He passed away on 12th January 1979.

Stan Smith

A wing half born in Coventry on 24th February 1925, Stan played for the club during the war years signing professional in 1942. He joined from local team Nuffield Mechanisation. Stan was a regular for Coventry City in the 1947/48 season. In total he made thirty one appearances for the club before joining Swansea Town in 1950. Stan never made a first team appearance for Swansea. He then went into non-league football with Stafford Rangers, Nuneaton Borough and Bedworth Town. In the late 1950s he was a coach of Coventry City's A team and was also a physiotherapist. Stan sadly passed away on 6th of October 2012 aged eighty seven. There is more about Stan in a later chapter telling of when he was part of a Nuneaton Borough team that had a great FA Cup run.

Ernie Boston

Ernie was a centre forward who was born in Coventry on 11th January 1888. He began his career with local teams Lord Street Juniors and Victoria Swifts. Ernie played 54 times for Coventry City scoring 3 goals.

Joe Hewett

Joe was a goalkeeper from Coventry who played for Coventry Motors before signing for Watford in 1927. After four years and over 100 matches he joined Coventry City in 1931 playing 5 games for the club.

Joe Mitchell

Born in Coventry, Joe was a forward who began his career with Lord Street Juniors. In 1912 he signed for Coventry City playing twenty four times scoring four goals. Joe's most famous goal was against Manchester United in the FA Cup in January 1913. He later played for Nuneaton Town and also played Rugby.

Horace Matthews

Horace was an outside left who was born in Handsworth on 26th of March 1913. He moved to Coventry at a very young age. I had the genuine pleasure of meeting Horace's daughter Gloria, his son in law Geoff and grandson Steve. Horace's mum and dad owned a sweet shop in Far Gosford Street which was sadly bombed during the war. In March 1937 he married Frances McKnight in All Saints' Church, Bedworth. Charles Butler was the best man. At the time Horace was a player for Newdigate Colliery. Horace lived most of his life in Nicholls Street which was next to the Highfield Road ground. By trade an Electrician, Horace was also a talented footballer who played local football for Gosford Street Baptists, Newdigate Colliery and AWA Baginton. During the war years AWA Baginton were a strong team who included Bob Ward who played one official match for Coventry City in the FA Cup. Bob later assisted Jimmy Knox at AP Leamington and VS Rugby. Billy Beaufoy was also a prominent player in local football. In 1944 and 1945 Horace won the "Midland Daily Telegraph Cup" with AWA Baginton. Horace joined Coventry City in 1945; he made four appearances in the 1944/45 season. Horace played five times in the 1945/46 season scoring against Fulham. His only recognised matches were against Aston Villa in the FA Cup in January 1946. The Bantams lost to Aston Villa 3-2 over two legs but City beat them 2-1 at Highfield Road. In total he played nine times for Coventry City between 1945 and 1946. Horace's team mates at Coventry City included George Mason, Tommy Crawley, George Lowrie, "Plum" Warner and Emilio Aldecoa. On 6th of May 1945 Horace played for a Combined Services XI against a Belgian Army XI at the Windmill Ground in Leamington. Coventry City team mates Tommy Crawley, Bob Ward and Aston Villa's Bob Iverson also played; unfortunately I wasn't able to find out the result. In March 1946 Horace was part of Coventry City's A team who had quite a strong squad of players. Team mates included Harry Boileau, Alf Setchell and Tommy Dougall who was the son of 1920s Coventry City winger Jimmy Dougall. Horace also played for Darlaston, Halesowen, Hinckley, Rootes, Rugby Town and Nuneaton Borough. In August 1960 it was announced that Horace would be coaching a Humber team of apprentices in the Coventry and North Warwickshire Works League.

Horace's son Johnny was on Coventry City's books in the 1960s. More about Johnny later in the book. Sadly Horace passed away in 1989 aged seventy six.

Alf Setchell

Alf was an outside right who was born in Coventry on 29th October 1924. I asked Alf's son John about his dad's career. John was also a good player and is featured later in the book.

Could you be able to tell me a little bit about your dad's football career?

Yes. My dad, made his debut for Coventry at a very young age but sadly his career got disturbed by the War. During this period teams had guest players, so my dad played for Portsmouth (as he was in the Navy), then also Glasgow Rangers. Post war he joined Kidderminster (for more money than Coventry!!), then eventually went to a very successful Bedworth Town team.

On 10th of December 1942 Alf was named in Coventry City's team to play Walsall -Coventry City lined up as follows.

Wood,Elliott,Metcalf,Smith,Mason,Bond,Simpson,Simmonds,Crawley,Lowrie,Setchell.

On 22nd of April 1943 Alf guested for Portsmouth in a match against Southampton. In November 1943 he played for Southport against Liverpool, unfortunately Liverpool won 9-0. On 17th of April 1948 it was announced that Alf was being released by

Coventry City who had a big squad of players so his chances of first team football were going to be limited.

In January 1950 Alf was the man of the match as he scored a hat trick for Hereford United Reserves over Gloucester City Reserves. In April 1950 Alf helped Bedworth Town beat Lockheed Leamington 1-0. They included former Coventry City player Norman Smith. Lockheed were a strong team and were captained by Les Latham who was also a former Bantams player. Alf worked at Dunlop Aviation Division and was Secretary of the Unicorn Social Club in Holbrooks. He sadly passed away in 2011 aged eighty seven.

Eric Betts

Eric was an outside left who was born in Coventry on 27th of July 1925. He played one match for Coventry in September 1947 but went on to have a long football career. Eric played for a number of teams including West Ham United, Walsall, Wrexham, Crewe Alexandra and Rochdale. Eric sadly passed away on 16th of March 1990.

Johnny (Jack) Lovering

Jack was a half back who was born in Nuneaton on 10th December 1922. He began his early career with Nuneaton Griff and Holbrooks Old Boys FC then spent time with Coventry City and Birmingham. Jack re-joined Coventry City in 1946 but only made six first team appearances in three years. In the summer of 1949 he joined Bedworth then played for Atherstone, Nuneaton Borough and Bermuda. He sadly passed away on 21st of September 2017 aged ninety four.

Ken Watkins

Ken was right-half from Coventry who played for works football Humber FC and for Coventry City during the war time seasons. He often played for Coventry and District Works XI's against a Birmingham and District Works teams. In April 1945 Ken played for Coventry City against a Polish Air Force XI. The match finished 2-2 with Tommy Crawley scoring both goals for City.

Coventry City – Carey, Ward, Elliott, Watkins, Boileau, Mason, Faulkner, Setchell, Crawley, Edwards, Matthews.

In November 1945 Ken signed professional forms for Coventry City. Most of his games were in the 1945/46 transitional season therefore do not count as official matches. Ken also guested for Port Vale, after the war he played for Rugby Oakfield and Rootes FC. In May 1950 Oakfield played a Combined XI in a benefit match for Ken. George Mason of Coventry City lined up for the Combined XI.

He was also a good batsman for Humber and GEC; he played alongside Harry Storer who was also Coventry City manager. Ken's father was Harry Watkins a former Humber grounds man, cricketer and coach at Henry XIII School. Ken also played for Warwickshire CCC second XI in the Minor Counties' Championship. In May 1952 Ken scored a brilliant 105 not out for Rootes"A" v Morris "B" in 55 minutes. I spoke to Ken's son Ken Watkins junior, his dad was born in the pavilion at Rootes Cricket Club. Ken Watkins senior played with Tom Cartwright for Rootes, Tom would go on to play for Warwickshire and England. Ken's best man was Fred Gardner who he played with for Coventry City; Fred was a very good cricketer also. Ken's best remembered match for Coventry City was when he got man of the match against

Arsenal. Ken Watkins junior told me that he got "ten woodbines" for being named man of the match. Ken Watkins senior played cricket well into his fifties, he achieved a century at the age of fifty five!

Ken lived in who lived in Coventry all of his life, sadly passed away on 26th November 2009 aged eight six.

His grandson Kenny was also a local footballer for Coventry Marconi and Stratford Town. There is more about Ken Watkins junior and his son Kenny later in the book.

Herbert (Harry) Mann

Herbert was born in Nuneaton on 30th December 1907. A forward / outside left, he began his career with Griff Colliery then joined Derby County making 4 appearances. Herbert then played non-league football for Grantham Town. In May 1931 he joined Second Division Manchester United making 13 appearances and scoring goals against Notts County and Oldham Athletic. In November 1933 he joined Ripley Town. He passed away on 24th April 1977.

Leamington Spa and Warwick's Football Legends.

William Garbutt

William was born in Hazel Grove, Cheshire on 9th January 1883. As a young man he joined the army and played for the Royal Artillery. William played at outside right. He joined Southern League team Reading in 1903. In December 1905 he joined Woolwich Arsenal going onto make 65 appearances scoring 14 goals. William then played for Blackburn Rovers between 1908 and 1911 before having a brief second spell with Woolwich

Arsenal. He retired from playing in 1912 aged 29 and moved to Italy. William was appointed manager of Genoa in 1912. During the First World War he served as an officer in France. He is considered the father of Italian football. Genoa won the Italian Championship in 1915, 1923 and 1924. He was ground-breaking in his methods of introducing physical development in football with dribbling practice and jumping exercises. William also won La Liga with Athletic Bilbao in 1936. He also managed AS Roma, Napoli, Milan and had two more spells with Genoa. In 1949 aged 65 and not in good health he moved to Leamington Spa to live with his sister in law in Regent Street in the town centre. In 1960 he moved to Priory Road in neighbouring Warwick. William sadly passed away on 16th February 1964 aged 81. He was cremated at Canley Crematorium in Coventry. In Italy his passing was covered in great detail by newspapers but in his country of birth there was only a small obituary in a local newspaper.

Edris (Eddie) Albert Hapgood

Eddie was born in Bristol on 24th September 1908. He played football in Bristol and for Kettering Town prior to joining Arsenal in October 1927. Eddie was a left back who would become Arsenal captain. The Gunners were the team of the 1930s under legendary manager Herbert Chapman. They had great players like Alex James, Ted Drake and Cliff Bastin. Eddie won the Football League in 1931, 1933, 1934, 1935 and 1938, the FA Cup in 1930 and 1936 and the FA Charity Shield in 1930, 1931, 1933, 1934 and 1938. He also played 30 times for England in which 21 were as captain. Eddie's most famous matches were against Italy and Germany. On 14th November 1934 England hosted World Cup winners Italy which was to be known as "The Battle of Highbury.". England were regarded as one of the world's best teams and the match was billed as the clash of the world's best. Eddie suffered a broken nose in an ill-tempered match which England won 3-2. On 14th May 1938 Eddie captained England in a 6-3 win over Germany in Berlin. Surely England would have won the World Cup in the 1930s but they didn't enter the competition until 1950. Eddie served in the RAF during the Second World War. He guested for Chelsea and Luton Town. During the war years he continued to play for Arsenal and England in unofficial matches. Eddie also played for Shrewsbury Town and managed Blackburn Rovers, Watford and Bath City. After football he fell on hard times and when he asked Arsenal for help they sent him £30! Eddie and his wife ran a YMCA hostel in Weymouth. He was a season ticket holder for Coventry City when he was retired living in Leamington Spa. On Good Friday, 20 April 1973 at Honiley Hall, near Kenilworth he sadly passed away aged 64. He was helping at a sports forum with former England team mate Stan Cullis. Eddie was living at Heath Terrace in the Milverton area of Leamington Spa, at the time of his death. He was buried in Brunswick Street Cemetery, Leamington, following a service at St. Mark's Church.

Foleshill Football

In Coventry City's Southern League days of the 1900s and 1910s a number of players came from local clubs Foleshill Great Heath, Foleshill St Paul's and Foleshill St George's. We are now going to look at some notable players from that era.

Thomas (Tommy) Arnold

A forward who began his career with Foleshill Great Heath, Tommy made over 50 appearances, scoring 19 goals for Coventry City in two spells between 1904 and 1911. In 1904 Tommy signed for Second Division Woolwich Arsenal making a couple of first team appearances before returning to Coventry. Tommy later became coach and, later, a director at Coventry.

Richard (Dick) Barnacle

A full back signed from Foleshill St Georges in 1908, Dick went onto play 138 times for Coventry City from 1908 to 1915. He got into the first team whilst working full time as a miner. Dick played one game for Newport County in 1919.

Alfred (Freddy) Chaplin

A wing half who attended Bablake School, Freddy played for Foleshill Great Heath and Foleshill St Paul's prior to joining Coventry City in 1902. Freddy then played for Small Heath and Woolwich Arsenal before a second spell with Coventry City from 1907 to 1912. In his second spell Coventry played in The Southern League, Freddy played over 140 times for his home team.

Reg Dalton

A centre half who signed for Coventry City in 1919 from Edgwick, Reg played fifty four times for Coventry City in the league. However Reg suffered a bad cartilage injury which ended his time at Coventry. A brief spell at Halifax Town was followed by a return to local football with Foleshill Great Heath and Nuneaton Town.

Harry Demming

An outside left born in Bedworth, Harry only made one appearance for Coventry City, in May 1925. A promising young player who played for Collycroft Stars, Leamington Town, Exhall Colliery, Nuneaton Town and Foleshill Great Heath, Harry once represented Birmingham FA in a Junior International match against Scotland.

Herbert Gilbert

A centre half who played for Foleshill St Paul's and Herbert's Athletic prior to joining Coventry City in 1905, Herbert played in the Birmingham League and Southern League for Coventry City.

Clem Warren

Clem was an inside right from Nuneaton who played for Edgwick FC and Herbert's Athletic before joining Coventry City in 1922. Clem played 18 times for Coventry City scoring 3 goals. He later played for Yeovil Town, Walsall and Worcester City.

Harold Welch

Harold was a forward who played for Foleshill Great Heath. He joined Coventry City who were a Southern League First Division team and made his debut on 27th December 1910. Harold scored on his debut in a 5-2 win over New Brompton. In total he made 50 appearances scoring 9 goals for Coventry City. Harold played in some famous FA Cup matches: in January 1913 he played against Manchester United in a 1-1 draw at Old Trafford. It was a famous result for the Bantams. United included the legendary Billy Meredith in their team. The match would also be memorable for the wrong reasons. Harold collapsed after the match after receiving several blows to the chest. He was taken to hospital but in the evening he was feeling better. He missed the replay at Highfield Road which Manchester United won 2-1. Harold retired from football during the years of World War One. In October 1948

Harold passed away aged 59 when he was living in Rugby and was the proprietor of a fish and chip shop in Lawford Road, Rugby. Harold had lived in the town for about ten years having previously been the licensee of the Spittlemoor Inn, Hillfields, Coventry.

Final Thoughts

Some of the information available was quite sketchy for some of the players, but I hope that you have enjoyed reading about them. I have thoroughly enjoyed researching these players via old newspaper archives and reference books.

Chapter Two – England Internationals from Coventry and Warwickshire

In this chapter we are going to look at players from Coventry and Warwickshire who have represented England at various levels.

Arthur Brown

With much gratitude to Coventry City FC historian Lionel Bird, it has now been confirmed that Arthur Brown was the first Coventry born player to play for England. Arthur was born on 3rd December 1858 at Broomfield Place, Spon End, Coventry, Warwickshire. It was previously recorded that he was born on 15th of March 1859 in Birmingham. Arthur played for Aston Villa in two spells and spent time with a number of amateur teams in the Aston area. Arthur's younger brother Albert also played for Aston Villa. On the 18th of February 1882 Arthur scored four goals on his England debut playing as a centre forward against Ireland in Belfast. It was England's first ever match against Ireland and also the first time an England player scored a hat rick. England won 13-0. Howard Vaughton also of Aston Villa scored five goals and Arthur Brown scored four. It is unknown which player got his hat rick first, so it is very possible that the first England player to score three or more goals in a match was from Coventry.

Arthur passed away on 1st of July 1909 in Aston at the age of fifty years. Information about Arthur was obtained on englandfootballonline.com, an excellent website.

Kenneth Edward "Jackie" Hegan

Jackie is the second Coventry born player to play for England. He was born in Coventry on 24th January 1901 attending Bablake School. Jackie lived in Ellys Road and Widdrington Road which are in the Radford area of Coventry. In 1925 he married Eveline McGowran and they had two children. Jackie was an outside-left who played for the Royal Military College football team, The Army, Collyhurst United and Corinthians FC. An England Amateur international who made twenty three appearances between 1920 and 1932, Jackie appeared in Charity Shield matches between Amateurs and Professionals XIs. He was runners-up with Amateurs. In 1920 Jackie was part of Great Britain's Olympic team in Antwerp, Belgium. In 1923 Jackie played four times for England (full internationals) making his debut in a 6-1 win over Belgium on 19th March 1923 scoring two goals. The Belgium match was played at Arsenal's stadium, Highbury in Islington London. It was a friendly international in which Henry Chambers, Norman Bullock, James Seed and David Mercer also scored.

England Win in Paris

France 1-4 England – 10th May 1923, friendly match

Hegan playing at outside left scored two goals. Buchan and Creek also scored for England. Dewaquez scored a consolation goal for France. Norman Creek was a team mate of Jackie Hegan at Corinthians FC.

England – Alderson, Cresswell, Jones, Plum, Seddon, Barton, Osbourne, Buchan, Creek, Hartley, Hegan

Jackie's military career saw him serve in The Royal Dublin Fusiliers and The Royal Army Service Corps. Jackie later earned the rank of Lieutenant Colonel and was awarded the OBE in September 1943. In 1949 he retired from the army. On 3rd March 1989 he passed away aged eighty eight.

George Henry ('Daddy') Green

George Henry Green was born on 2nd of May 1901 in Shrubland Street, Royal Leamington Spa. George was brought up by his Grandmother in Eagle Street, Leamington Spa. A left half (midfield), George played for Leamington Town and Nuneaton Town which attracted the interest of many league clubs. On 3rd of May 1923 he signed for Division One team Sheffield United. George would become a legend at Bramhall Lane playing over 400 times between 1923 and 1934. His father was also called George 'Daddy' senior and he played for Leamington Town too. This is where the nickname Daddy possibly came from.

George represented The Professionals as they beat The Amateurs to win the 1924 FA Charity Shield. A year later he would be part of the Sheffield United team that won the FA Cup in 1925 after they beat Cardiff City 1-0, Fred Tunstall scoring the winning goal. George played eight times for England between 1925 and 1928, making his England debut on 21st May 1925 in a 3-2 win against France in Paris. England team mates included fellow Blade Vincent Matthews and the legendary Dixie Dean. George returned to Leamington Town in 1934 and retired in 1937 after the club folded. After his retirement from football he worked at Benford's factory and was landlord of the Ranleigh Inn in Leamington. During the war he was a Physical Training Instructor and he was later landlord of the Cottage Tavern in Ashorne village. George passed away on 1st of March 1980.

Memorable Match

France 1-5 England – Friendly match, 27th May 1928

Marcel Langiller gave France an early lead; however England would score five goals to win comfortably with a goal for David Jack and two each for Dixie Dean and George Stephenson.

England – Olney, Goodall, Blenkinsopp, Edwards, Matthews, Green, Bruton, Jack, Dean,Stephenson, Barry

Final Thoughts on Jackie and George

Jackie and George were two years apart from being England team mates. They did however play against each other in the 1924 Charity Shield. George, representing The Professionals, beat Jackie's team The Amateurs 3-1 at Highbury on the 6th of October 1924. Both George and Jackie were at a different standard of football to that of Coventry City in the 1920s so they didn't slip The Bantams' net as such. There is an excellent article about George on Leamington history.co.uk – Leamington's Greatest Footballer.

Both players would have been 'worth a few quid' in today's transfer market, Coventry and Warwickshire legends.

Nigel Winterburn

A Warwickshire lad who became a Gunners legend! Nigel was born in the village of Arley in North Warwickshire on 11th December 1963. Nigel played for Alderman Smith school team, Nuneaton Schoolboys under 15s and Attleborough Mills. In the early 1980s he was on the books of Birmingham City and Oxford United but never made the first team. In September 1983 Nigel joined Wimbledon, breaking into the first team aged nineteen. Wimbledon were a club on the rise and achieved promotion to the First Division in 1986. In the summer of 1987 Arsenal manager signed Nigel for £350.000 as a long term replacement for Kenny Sansom. Once Kenny left in November 1988, Nigel became first choice left back forming the famous Arsenal back four with Lee Dixon, Tony Adams and David O'Leary. Nigel made his full England debut against Italy in November 1989. Unfortunately for him Stuart Pearce and Tony Dorigo were preferred choices for England. Nigel's second cap came against Germany in June 1993.

Nigel would become a club legend for Arsenal. He would remain at Highbury until 2000. At Arsenal he won the league three times, FA Cup twice, League Cup and European Cup Winners' Cup with an incredible 584 appearances for Arsenal which makes him fifth in the all-time list of appearances for the club. In June 2000 he joined West Ham United serving them well for three years before retiring in 2003. Since retiring he has worked as a coach for Blackburn Rovers and has worked in the media for BT Sport.

In a different era Nigel would have been an England regular. He however faced tough competition from Stuart Pearce and Graeme Le Saux. He is a Warwickshire player of whom to be very proud and one of the best left backs of the modern era.

Tim Flowers

Tim was born in Kenilworth on 3 February 1967. He went to Park Hill and Kenilworth School. He was the same age as Graham Rodger and both Kenilworth lads began their career at Wolverhampton Wanderers. Tim became Wolves goalkeeper aged seventeen in 1984. It was a bleak time for Wolves as they suffered successive relegations. In June 1986 Tim joined First Division Southampton initially as an understudy to Peter Shilton. Tim had a loan spell with Swindon Town and eventually became first choice goalkeeper at Southampton. He was one of the best goalkeepers in the country in the early 1990s. Tim made his England debut against Brazil on 13th June 1993 in Washington DC. In November 1993 he moved to Blackburn Rovers for £2.4million making him the most expensive British goalkeeper. Rovers finished second in the 1993/94 Premier League but went one better the next season. Tim joined Leicester City in 1999 winning the League Cup in his first season. Towards the end of his career he had loan spells with Stockport County, Manchester City and Coventry City. Tim was assistant manager to Iain Dowie at Coventry City from February 2007 to February 2008. He has recently enjoyed success as manager of Solihull Moors, In August 2020 he was appointed manager of Macclesfield Town but the club was wound up in September 2020. Tim won 11 England caps from 1993 to 1998: if he had not faced competition from David Seaman he would have won a lot more. A modern day Warwickshire great, he enjoyed a good career in the top level of English football.

Ben Foster

Still a Premiership regular at the age of thirty seven, Ben is a local player who has done extremely well. Ben was born in Royal

Leamington Spa on 3rd of April 1983. He attended North Leamington School. At sixteen Ben worked in a restaurant and went to college in Stratford to train as a chef. In 2000 the young goalkeeper broke into Racing Club Warwick's first team and was spotted by Stoke City scout Colin Dobson. Ben signed for Stoke City in April 2001 and would remain on the club's books for four years but never made a first team appearance. In June 2003 he suffered a cruciate ligament injury which kept him out for six months. Upon his recovery he broke into the Potters' first team squad. During his four years in Staffordshire he had various loan moves, one of which would be a turning point in his career. Whilst on loan with Wrexham he was spotted by Manchester United manager Alex Ferguson who was watching his son Darren. Ben signed for Manchester United in July 2005, but not considered ready for first team football was sent on loan to Watford. It would be a great move as Watford won promotion to the Premiership via the playoffs. Ben remained at Vicarage Road for the Hornets' first season back in the top flight. In June 2007 Ben returned to Old Trafford and had knee surgery. He finally made his United debut in March 2008. By then Ben was already an England international having made his debut in February 2007. Ben was never a regular for Manchester United due to competition for the goalkeeping jersey and injuries. In the summer of 2010 in order to play first team football he moved to Birmingham City. Ben did well at Birmingham winning the League Cup but they were relegated to the Championship. In the summer of 2011 he joined West Bromwich Albion on loan then signed permanently for them in 2012. Ben remained with the Baggies until they got relegated in 2018 when he joined Watford. There is no reason why he can't continue to play at a good level for he is still a very good goalkeeper. At the time of writing he is still first choice at Vicarage Road as Watford look to return to the Premiership following relegation to the Championship. Ben has played eight times for England and probably should have won more caps but suffered injuries and Joe Hart was in good form. His last appearance for England was on 24th June 2014 in the World Cup against Costa Rica a 0-0 draw.

Laura Bassett

Laura is a former England international defender born in Nuneaton on 2nd of August 1983. She grew up in Bulkington and joined Bedworth Girls at the age of nine. Her dad and brother both played football. In 1997 Laura joined Coventry City Ladies playing in the FA Women's National League North. At the age of seventeen she joined Birmingham City Ladies: this would be a great move for her. Laura would become Birmingham captain and represent England at youth and senior level. In February 2003 she made her senior debut against Italy, which would be the first of her 61 caps. In 2006 Laura played for New York Magic on loan. On an interview on you tube Laura said that she enjoyed living in Manhattan. In 2008 Laura joined Arsenal who won the treble whilst she was at the club. Laura also played for Leeds United Ladies, Chelsea Ladies, had a second spell with Birmingham City Ladies and also played for Notts County and Canberra United. Laura scored an unfortunate own goal in the 2017 World Cup semi-final v Japan. It was one of those bizarre moments that happen sometimes in football. A cross came from the right hand side. Laura attempted to clear the ball and it went in the goal. Nine times out of ten the ball would have gone out for a throw in or corner. Laura was absolutely devastated and showed great courage to put it behind her. It was one of those things that happen. We are still proud of you, Laura! In June 2019 Laura announced her retirement at the age of thirty five.

Scott Garner

Scott was born in Coventry on the 20th of September 1989 and attended Woodway Park School. I was keen to contact Scott as not many players get the chance to captain their country. Scott had the honour of captaining England C (Semi-Professional) team in 2009. He is a leader, an old fashioned centre half, who has enjoyed a good career in non-league football. I asked Scott a few questions via Facebook and email.

How did you get spotted by Leicester City?

I was playing for Bedworth United under 9s playing in an attacking midfield/striker role. In a summer tournament I was scoring a lot of goals and winning tournaments. I then got spotted by Leicester City and I was soon developed into a defender. I was there from under 9s to under19s: I had a fantastic time there! We won the under 18s Premier League beating Arsenal in the semis and Sunderland on penalties at the Stadium of Light , the only disappointment being not to have done better in the Youth Cup.

Did you play for Coventry City school boys?

I played two games for school boys when I was twelve. It wasn't the same level as the academy and I started to cross paths, so my parents knew the academy was the main focus.

Representing England and to captain England C is a true honour. What are your memories of those matches?

Absolutely amazing memories and really proud of doing so. I remember being called up at nineteen to go to Hungary. It was

*fantastic from the minute they pick you up in a private car.
Wearing your England tie makes you feel special, a great
experience and then to captain the side in Hungary and then
Russia huge occasions are things I'll never forget and great to tell
future generations about.*

Who are the best players that you played with or against?

*Hard question sometimes as they are not always just the biggest
names now, but I played against Daniel Sturbridge, James Milner,
Jordan Henderson and Jamie Vardy (before he was well known). I
got booked for pulling him back he was lightning quick.*

*I played with some great players in the academy team the likes of
Andy King (Leicester City legend), Max Gradel, Joe Mattock,
Jeffery Schlupp and Billy Kee. Most of the squad have gone on to
have careers in the game.*

**Having previously played for Boston it must have been great to
be able to return. It looks like you have a special connection
with the club?**

*Absolutely. It's a team I always wanted to go back to at some point
and finish off something I felt I'd started. I have always had a
great connection with the fans, staff, and the club as a whole. It
was hard to leave when I did but I think justified it with achieving
promotion with Halifax the next season. I am now back with
Boston and lining up for the play-off final next Saturday will mean
the world to me to help win the club promotion especially with it
being the last game at York Street before we move into the new
stadium.*

Scott has also played for Ilkeston Town, Mansfield Town, Grimsby Town, Lincoln City, Alfreton Town, Cambridge United. FC Halifax Town and Guiseley. Unfortunately Boston United lost in the play-off final. They will be looking for another promotion challenge in the 2020/21 season.

Nikki Miles

Nikki is a central defender for Coventry United. She played locally for Binley Woods and was scouted by Coventry City. Nikki represented England at under 15 level and an England Further Education Students team.

Could you tell me how you first got into football?

My older brother played with his mates in the street and up the field. I used to join them daily and came home battered and bruised usually in tears and they were extremely rough and would kick me a lot. However I believe it gave me such a strong character and allowed me to be the player I am today.

I believe that you have represented England at a couple of levels, which must have been such an honour for you?

It was a huge honour especially at such a young age. It was a difficult time and hard to adapt at such a young age from country to club but it is something that I will forever be grateful for.

Where did the nickname the General come from?

Our Marketing manager Robbie Woodward gave me the name. I believe he named me due to my being extremely loud and commanding on the pitch. I also think it's down to my many years at Coventry, nineteen in total.

Coming from Coventry it must be fantastic to have played for Coventry City Ladies and Coventry United Ladies. Do you have any favourite matches for both?

Yes being from Coventry and being able to represent my city for pretty much my whole life has been an honour. Each week I'm proud to put on my shirt. However I take more satisfaction where I have made a difference to other young girls and inspire them to play or giving more girls the opportunity to play.

However my favourite game in a Coventry United shirt has to be against Cardiff where we had to win to get ourselves promoted into the women's Championship. It was an unreal day, being 2-1 all game which was a tight game but two last minute goals saw us all go crazy with a 4-1 win to finish and celebrate our way into the Championship.

For Coventry City I must say it could be my debut appearance at sixteen. I was coming back from a school skiing trip and then playing against Wolves. What a crazy experience that was! Another great experience was when we won the Midland Combination league to gain promotion into the National League. So many incredible players I have played with over the years and I am forever grateful.

Could you tell me a little bit how you got into coaching?

When I was at school I never really knew what I wanted to do. As football was not a full time job at the time, I knew I needed a plan

B. At fourteen or fifteen I started to volunteer and by the time I got to sixteen I was involved in running after school clubs. It expanded from there and I achieved a UFEA B licence. This saw me work with hundreds of young girls and boys as well as older groups. I have been extremely lucky to work with so many incredible young people and give back the opportunities I had growing up.

How good is Shannon O'Brien, a great prospect?

What a great talent! I have known Shannon since she was about ten. She was part of the Coventry centre of excellence when I first got into coaching. She was a talented footballer then and I am now playing with her in the first team. It is an honour and it's great to see her grow and I fully believe she has an extremely bright future ahead.

Shannon now plays for FA Women's Championship 2020/21 winners Leicester City Ladies.

Chapter Three – International players

In this chapter we are going to look at players from Coventry and Warwickshire who have represented different countries at international level.

Louisa Bisby (Australia)

One of Warwickshire's greatest ladies players, Louisa was born in Royal Leamington Spa on 1st of June 1979. She went to Brookhurst Primary School in Leamington. Aged eleven Louisa was wanted by both Coventry City and Aston Villa. Louisa chose Villa because she would be selected for the ladies' team whereas at Coventry she would have been a mascot. At the age of fifteen she moved to Australia. Louisa played in defence initially then developed into a midfielder. In 2007 she played for the Matildas (Australia ladies' team) and also played in China and Germany. Louisa is now team manager of successful W-League team Melbourne City.

Emma Lipman (Malta)

Emma is currently a defender for Lazio and a full international for Malta. She was born in Nuneaton on 23rd February 1989. Emma began her career at Coventry City Ladies from the age of ten then playing for the first team aged fourteen. She went to university in Leeds for three years playing for the university team then played for Leeds United Ladies. Emma then joined Manchester City. On 16th October 2014 she was part of the team that won the FAWSL Continental Cup. Manchester City beat Arsenal 1-0 which was a fantastic result. Arsenal included players like Rachel Yankey, Alex Scott and Danielle Carter all England internationals. Manchester City also had good players including current England captain Steph

Houghton and Isobel Christensen who scored the winning goal. Emma's first team chances were limited when City signed Lucy Bronze and Emma Stokes and she joined Sheffield FC. Since 2017 Emma has played in Italy for AGSM Verona, Roma, Fiorentina and Lazio. In October 2019 Emma made her official international debut for Malta, she previously having played in an unofficial friendly against Bolton Wanderers. Malta earned a 1-1 draw against Israel in November 2019. Emma plays for Lazio with Maltese team mate Rachel Cuschieri. Emma has done really well in her football career and she should be proud of what she has achieved so far.

Leon Pitchaya James (Thailand)

Leon is a Thailand under 19 international footballer who plays as a midfielder for Sukhothai FC who compete in the Thai League. He previously played for Ratchaburi Mitr Phol Football Club. Leon was born in Coventry on 29th August 2001. I asked Leon a few questions via Facebook.

Did you grow up in Coventry? And how did you get spotted by Leicester City?

I was born and bred In Coventry and I have been playing football ever since I was four. That is when I started playing Saturday league football for Coventry Jaguars. When I was six, I got scouted for Coventry City. A few days after both Birmingham City and Leicester City showed interest in me. At that time I was training with all three teams: therefore I had to choose between the three so I chose Leicester City.

Have you played for the full international team?

I've represented Thailand under 19s in two tournaments and have been in a number of camps.

Rikki Bains (Panjab)

Rikki was a central defender who was born in Coventry on 3rd February 1988. Rikki played for Coventry City's youth team then went onto play for a number of clubs including Accrington Stanley, Darlington and Tamworth. He being an international player for Panjab, I asked Rikki a few questions about his career.

How did you get spotted by Coventry City?

I was ten years old and playing for Bedworth United in the local leagues. I joined the first academy team put together at Coventry after youth teams were moved into academies. After a successful trial game I was asked to join the team.

Do you have a favourite match for the youth team?

There were a lot of good games because we competed with Premier League academies. A game in the semi-finals of the league playoffs against Newcastle United stands out. It was one of the last games at Highfield Road. We played really well and won. Also a game against Arsenal at the Ryton training ground was good. It was Cesc Fabregas's first game and we totally dominated the game.

How did the call up to play for Panjab come about?

The founder of the national team contacted me many times to try and get me involved. I had a lot on my plate at the time so was unsure but it turned to be a great experience.

Did you play in the ConIFA World Cup for Panjab? So unlucky in the 2016 tournament. Penalties can be a cruel way to lose.

Yes I did, it was crazy, in a place called Abkhazia that was still recovering from years of war but the stadiums were packed. Everyone stopped working in order to come and watch the football. The ground was shaking after some of the goals!

Are you still playing for Bedworth?

No I gave up playing several years ago. It was too difficult to manage with a family and career. Also it can be extremely frustrating! I still hadn't mastered the mental strength to acknowledge the different standards and levels of football I had seen and been involved in and how to adjust.

Rikki played for Panjab who are a representative football team formed in 2014. They were formed in UK and represent the Punjabi diaspora (Punjabi community in the UK). Panjab are members of ConIFA (Confederation of Independent Football Associations) which is for teams not affiliated to FIFA. There have been three ConIFA World Cups and are made up of teams that represent states, minorities, stateless peoples and regions. Panjab were drawn in Group D for the ConIFA World Cup. They beat Sapmi 1-0 and Somaliland 5-0 to progress to the knockout stage. Panjab beat Western Armenia 3-2 in the quarter finals, striker

Amar Purewal with his second hat rick of the tournament. Padania were beaten 1-0 in the semi-final to set up a final against host team Abkhazia. Panjab were very unlucky as they were beaten 6-5 on penalties after the match finished one goal each. In the 2018 tournament played in England, Panjab reached the quarter finals the next one due to be played in 2022.

Michael Brady (USA)

A former United States international midfielder originally from Coventry, Michael was born in Coventry on 7th July 1964. He is currently a coach at Duke University soccer team. I asked Michael a few questions about his career via email.

Could you tell me about your junior and school football teams?

My first memories of playing were for my junior school which was St. Thomas More. We had a full orange kit and my true love for the game began on the nights before game days. I did the usual lying of my kit on the bedroom floor before bed and dreamed all night about the game. I am/was the youngest of four kids and the two eldest were boys so they taught me everything I know about being tough and having to fight for playing time. As is the norm I became a good goalkeeper as I was always the first one in goal when the three of us went to the park for a kick around.

We had rolled up socks everywhere in the house and somehow created really physical and competitive games in small rooms all around the house much to mum's disdain.

I played for a local youth club (Coundon Cockerels) towards the end of my tenure at St. Thomas More and the one thing I remember vividly is we played in Tottenham Hotspur kits.

Once at Bishop Ullathorne for secondary school I was lucky enough to meet the man who would convince me that I was actually pretty good. His name is Tony Kiely and at the time he was an English teacher and volunteered to coach my year's football team. He immediately named me as the team captain (a position I held right through the end of high school) and turned out that the only class I ever got decent grades in was English! My school team was a really good one and just an amazing part of my childhood. At some point I was recruited by Wolves and signed schoolboy forms with them at fourteen. Most school holidays were spent at Lilleshall and such places for week long training camps with the club. At this time I was also becoming an accomplished tennis player and was ranked in the top five nationally at the U15 age group. Any times not at Lilleshall with Wolves I was there with I believe it was BP who sponsored the best youth tennis players in England. I loved football and found tennis frustrating as when things weren't going well I couldn't take my frustrations out on someone with a committed and robust challenge! I was not interested in academics and only wanted to play football. I left school at sixteen with a few O levels, and then I went to Wolves as a trial apprentice staying in an hotel in Birmingham. I missed home terribly and was not mature or tough enough emotionally to compete with the grown men in the locker room. I t was not a very nurturing environment back then and my lack of mental toughness affected my performance and after six months I was released.

As a side story here my best friend in the neighbourhood was Jamie Hill (son of Jimmy Hill and his ex-wife Heather who was a teacher at Cardinal Newman I believe). From probably eight years old to sixteen we were best mates and therefore I went to every

Coventry City game and always had access to the team and the visiting team post game. I was a massive Leeds United fan at the time but loved going to Highfield Road every other Saturday regardless of who was playing. When the new training ground opened we were lucky enough to go and have the occasional kick around there.

I then had a trial with Blackburn Rovers and did well enough to be put in digs right by the stadium and had another month's long trial apprenticeship. Same story as with Wolves unfortunately and again I would like to believe that as a player I was good enough to play at that level but emotionally not even close.

How did the move to USA come about?

As we were family friends with Heather Hill we at some point were introduced to Noel Cantwell who at the time was the manager of Peterborough United. Our families all got along very well and lifelong friendships were forged. As my dreams of playing pro in England were fading Noel had moved to the States and was now coaching the Jacksonville Tea Men in the NASL. I was born to Irish immigrant parents in Chicago (along with my three siblings) and therefore had a US passport. We visited family in Chicago on several summer vacations growing up. My dad contacted Noel and asked if he would take a look at me and the fact that I had a US passport made it easy for Noel as I would not have to take a foreigner spot if he liked me. My dad and I travelled to Jacksonville for a three week visit/try-out in 1982. I did really well and everyone liked the story of this young kid with an American passport who was ready to play at the top level. Noel offered me a contract but confided in my dad that the league was going under any day (which happened as he predicted). His assistant coach at the time was Dennis Violet (Man United legend) who went to The

Washington Diplomats before the League shut its doors. While in DC he met Pete Mehlert who was volunteering with the Diplomats whilst being the head coach of the American University Men's Soccer programme in DC. I returned to England with no solid plans and Dennis told Pete about me. I got a call from Pete and he invited me to travel to DC and play for American University and go to school at the same time. Fortunately our knowledge of the US at the time allowed us to understand that universities actually paid for kids to go to school and to play soccer at the same time. I arrived in DC in the summer with my second eldest brother as my minder. We worked soccer camp to make a few bucks and then took a road trip to visit an American friend of ours who had spent a couple of years in Coventry and was now living in St. Louis. My plan was to stay for the fall and toughen up a little emotionally and hopefully become a better athlete as we all looked at Americans as the best athletes in the world at the time.

I returned in January for the second term and I can't I say never looked back but at least I stuck it out. I was recruited to the youth national Team and played in the FIFA U20 World Cup Finals in Mexico in 1983.

One of your matches for USA was against England, which must have been a great experience?

As you mentioned a highlight was playing against England in LA when they were preparing for the World Cup Finals. I came on as a substitute and we got smoked. The head coach at the time said in the locker room after the game that the fastest I ran all day was when the final whistle blew and I chased Glenn Hoddle to get his shirt. I still have the shirt and it was the only time I had ever or since experienced a guy who wore cologne on his game shirt.

Do you get over to visit Coventry?

I have not been to Coventry for 20 years at least but did get to see Tony Kiely last year. It was great to see him despite the fact that unfortunately it was at my brother's funeral. I hope to one day get back to Coventry to show my wife and two children where I spent many of my formative years.

Are you still involved with soccer?

I am currently still in the game as the Associate Head Coach at Duke University in Durham NC.

Memorable Match

USA 0-5 England – 16th June 1985, Los Angeles, Memorial Coliseum – Friendly International

Scorers: Gary Lineker 2, Kerry Dixon 2, Trevor Steven

USA: Arnie Mausser (Tim Harris), Kevin Crow, Mike Windischmann, Dan Canter (Michael Brady), Paul Caligiuri, Perry van der Beck, Ed Radwanski (Steve Snyder), Rick Davis, Bruce Murray (Jacques Ladouceur), John Kerr (Jeff Hooker), Hugo Pérez

England: Chris Woods, Viv Anderson, Kenny Sansom (Dave Watson), Glenn Hoddle (Trevor Steven), Terry Fenwick, Terry Butcher, Brian Robson (Peter Reid), Paul Bracewell, Kerry Dixon, Gary Lineker, Chris Waddle (John Barnes)

Bernie James (USA)

Bernie was born on 25th November 1958 in Coventry. In his playing days he was a defender. I asked Bernie a few questions about his playing and coaching career.

Do you remember much about your childhood in Coventry? How old were you when you moved to Washington?

I don't remember much about Coventry. I moved to the LA area when I was about three. I remember the house and yard.

Who would you say were the best players that you played with and against?

The best player I played against was George Best. Even at the age he was he was remarkable! Given the current rules and how good the fields are I can't imagine him not being as effective as Messi is today. Best player I have played with is Alan Hudson a great player and a great guy. I didn't play much with him at that time because I was a reserve.

If you could pick one match during your career as your favourite what would it be?

It has to be beating Mexico 3- 0 in the LA Coliseum. I think it was an under 23 game but 30, 000 fans attended. For Mexico fans in LA it was an away game at home.

It must have been a great honour to represent the USA's Olympic and national teams. What are your memories of those matches?

Played in the 1979 Pan Am games in Puerto Rico and was in the pool for the 1980 Olympics which were boycotted in Russia. A few times for the National team which was a great honour. I owe a lot to Harry Redknapp who kept pushing me. I wasn't that good when I signed by English standards and boy did he let me know it. Also Jimmy Gabriel and Alan Hinton all guys that were great along the way.

Are you still coaching soccer?

Yes still coaching and running a club called Crossfire in the Seattle area, love coaching and lucky to be involved in a great sport like soccer. I ended up playing in four decades and twenty-four years of professional soccer and loved every minute of it. I would play today if anyone was stupid enough to pay me.

Have you ever visited Coventry as an Adult?

I am proud to be from Coventry and of England have been back a few times. My mom moved back to England to be with her sister and still lives there.

Luke Rowe (New Zealand)

A Left Back who plays for Bedworth United and played for New Zealand at full international level, I had the pleasure of speaking to Luke and I asked him about his career. Born in Coventry on the 16th of September 1991, a few sources say that he was born in Royal Leamington Spa but this is not true. Luke went to Foxford

School and was scouted by both Birmingham City and Coventry City at the age of thirteen. The young defender decided to join the Blues and would stay with them until he was nineteen. Luke was in the same age group as Jake Jervis and Jordan Mutch and the year below were Jack Butland and Nathan Redmond. Coventry lads Callum Wilson, Jamie Patterson and Cyrus Christie were in Luke's age group. Luke had one year as a professional at Birmingham City often playing for the reserves. One time a couple of lads were on trial from New Zealand and they told Luke he must be the lad for the under 20s. This was a bit of a surprise but then he got a call from the under 20s' manager who wanted to watch him. This was fantastic news as Luke's dad is a proud New Zealander. In 2011 Luke went to the Under 20 World Cup in Colombia, which was a great experience. New Zealand drew two matches but lost to Portugal which meant they missed out the knock out stage. Luke had trials for the 2012 New Zealand Olympic team but only made the standby players. Between 2011 and 2013 Luke played in New Zealand for Team Wellington and Wellington Phoenix. He made two appearances for Wellington Phoenix who compete in the A-League; a team mate was Paul Ifill who previously played for Millwall, Crystal Palace and Sheffield United. In March 2013 Luke made his full international debut against Soloman Islands which New Zealand won 2-0. Luke recalls it was very hot! The stadium is built into the hillside, a unique experience. Luke got a chance because a few of the senior players like Chris Wood and Winston Reid were unavailable. Marco Rojas is a New Zealand player who Luke rates highly: they call him the "Kiwi Messi" now playing for Melbourne Victory. I asked Luke who is toughest opponent was and he told me it was Alessandro Diamanti when he played against West Ham's reserves. A horrible game Luke recalls: "I was chasing shadows. I couldn't get anywhere near him". Luke decided to move back to England in 2013. At first he struggled to find a team. He then met Stuart Storer through his sister at college. Stuart was manager of Hinckley but by the time Luke waited for international clearance Hinckley went under. Then Stuart took over at Bedworth United in 2013 and signed Luke and both have been there ever since. There is a good bunch of lads at Bedworth and hopefully they will win promotion next season.

James Quinn (Northern Ireland)

Born in Coventry on 15th December 1974, James attended Cardinal Wiseman School. A forward who began his career with Birmingham City, he played four times for the Blues. In 1993 James joined Blackpool of the Second Division. His time there was a success and he scored a decent amount of goals. In April 1996 he won his first full cap for Northern Ireland, both his parents being from Belfast. James would serve his country well, winning 50 caps over ten years scoring 4 goals. In 1998 he joined West Bromwich Albion playing 114 times for The Baggies. James then played for a number of clubs including Dutch team Willem II, Sheffield Wednesday, Peterborough United and both Bristol teams on loan. His last club was Northampton Town. He retired from playing in 2007. James took up coaching after playing and in 2012 he obtained a UEFA Pro Licence then becoming head coach of development team Central Jersey Spartans. James has worked as a first team coach with Tranmere Rovers and is currently in the same role at Solihull Moors. Never a prolific goal scorer in his career he was though a good ball player who could play out wide. Players like David Healy would have benefited playing with James for Northern Ireland.

James Collins (Republic of Ireland)

James is a striker who currently plays for Championship team Luton Town. He was born in Coventry on 1st of December 1990 and attended Sacred Heart and Cardinal Wiseman Schools. James began his career with Aston Villa academy and remained on their books until 2011. The young striker spent time on loan with Darlington and Burton Albion before a permanent move to Shrewsbury Town. James then played for Swindon Town, Hibernian, Shrewsbury, Northampton Town and Crawley Town. In 2017 he joined Luton Town, enjoying success as they won promotion to the Championship. James qualified to play for Republic of Ireland through his parents: he represented them at under 19 and 21 levels. He finally made his full debut on the 10th September 2019 in a 3-1 win over Bulgaria scoring the third goal. James has now played four times for the Republic of Ireland at senior level. Still only twenty nine, James should hopefully win more international caps and add to his only goal. Growing up James was a Coventry City fan and is often a player who is talked of as slipping the net. James has been linked with the club before so you never know we might see him play for the City one day. He has had his controversies but he has always scored goals wherever he has played, a Coventry kid who has done well.

Chris Dawson (Seychelles)

I had the pleasure of speaking to Chris. He was a midfielder who was born in Coventry on 22nd August 1979. Chris spent his early years in Coventry but due to his parents' work commitments the family did a lot of travelling and spent time in Asia. Chris and his family settled in Aberdeen and he got into football, playing for a junior team called Albion Rangers. Chris played with Baldur Bett son of Aberdeen and Scotland midfielder Jim Bett who also became a professional footballer. Chris recalls one match when he scored three goals against top young Scottish goalkeeper Ryan Esen which impressed Kenny Black a professional footballer and coach. Chris played for Scotland schoolboys and he attracted the attention of the big clubs in Scotland. Tommy Burns (Celtic) Roy Aitken (Aberdeen) and Kenny Dalglish (Blackburn Rovers) all expressed an interest in him. However it was Bolton Wanderers' manager Colin Todd who signed him. They invited Chris's family down. The late 1990s were exciting times at Bolton. They had won promotion to the Premiership. Chris spent five years at the club through the academy to the first team squad. He played in a few friendlies for them. During his time there he played with Kevin Nolan and Eidur Gudjohnsen and he was Andy Todd and Per Frandsen's boot boy. When his time at Bolton came to an end a few teams come in for him, Crewe Alexandra, Aberdeen and Dundee United but he decided to move to Malaysia. Chris joined Kula Lumpar FA where the money was very good. A few high profile players played in Malaysia in the late 1990s/early 2000s like Tony Cottee, Chris Kiwomya and Niall Quinn. Chris stayed longer and did very well. He played in an attacking role behind the front two. At times in Malaysia Chris didn't feel safe: in one match he scored and the crowd turned on him and started throwing things! They lost the match 3-1. It was the time of the Bali bombing in 2002 so it was a scary part of the world in which to be. Chris came back to England where he had a trial with Worcester City and played for Bromsgrove Rovers and Oldbury. By this time Chris was in his late 20s but he had enough of football: he often felt targeted by opposition players because he was a former professional. The teams expected wonders off him because he had played at a higher level. Just because he was an ex pro didn't make him another Messi! Chris had enough of football and is now successful in business. What Chris said reminded me a bit about when Tim Sherwood was at Coventry City where some fans got on his back and booed. Tim said: "If I could beat ten men and score a screamer I would be playing at the top!"

Chris was also an international footballer for the Seychelles. He played in Africa Cup of Nations qualifiers. He recalls playing against Zimbabwe whom the Seychelles beat 2-1. Peter Ndlovu was in the Zimbabwe team. Another match was against Mali who had a strong team with players who played in Europe's top leagues. One of those players was Mahamadou Diarra who introduced himself to Chris on the plane. Chris was unaware who he was. His team mates were saying, "That's Mahamadou Diarra!!" At the time Diarra was playing for Lyon but would go on to play for Real Madrid. When the players got off the plane the press pushed past them to greet the stars from Mali. In the match itself Mahamadou was not so friendly and said, "We are going to beat you," which they did, 3-0!

Graham Alexander (Scotland)

The best Coventry born player never to play for Coventry City, Graham has enjoyed a fantastic career making over 1000 senior appearances. Graham was born in Coventry on the 10th of October 1971. He grew up in Canley. At the age of nine Graham and his mate went to a football trial for Coventry Sporting. He got picked and played with them until he was sixteen and being a Canley lad it was local for him. A Coventry City scout decided that Graham wasn't quite at the level they were looking for so he ended up at Scunthorpe United. Between 1988 and 1990 he was a youth team player at Scunthorpe, breaking into the first team in April 1991. Graham would become the club's first choice right back for the next four years. In July 1995 he joined Luton Town becoming a dependable right back at Kenilworth road. Graham's next move in 1999 to Preston North End would be the turning point in his career. At Deepdale he became a modern day legend, making over 400 appearances for The Lilywhites. Graham was appointed club captain and was a set-piece specialist. Preston were a good team and were unfortunate not to win promotion to the Premiership. In April 2002 Graham got international recognition and at the age of thirty one he made his Scotland debut. Eligible for Scotland through his Scottish father, he would go on to win forty caps. In August 2007 Graham made a surprise move to Lancashire rivals Burnley. It would be a great move for in two seasons Burnley won promotion to the Premiership. Graham now in his mid-thirties was by now an accomplished defensive midfielder and he thoroughly deserved his chance to play in the top flight. So close with Preston North End for many years, Graham made his Premiership debut for Burnley on 15th August 2009. At thirty seven he became the oldest player to make a Premier League debut. He was also Burnley's player of the season. In 2011 he made a return to Preston North End. He even scored in his last game for the club. Graham also became joint-caretaker manager, alongside David Unsworth after Phil Brown was sacked. Fast forward to 2020 he is now manager of League Two Salford City who have ambitions to climb the football pyramid. Graham has also managed Fleetwood Town and Scunthorpe United and did well. One day I can see Graham managing at Premiership or Championship level.

Daniel Nardiello (Wales)

Daniel was born in Coventry on 22 October 1982. He was a forward for Manchester United, Barnsley and Queens Park Rangers. He being the son of former Coventry City and Wales striker Donato Nardiello, I asked Daniel a few questions about his career.

Could you tell me about your junior career? Did you grow up / go to school in Coventry?

I left Coventry at the age of six. All the family still lived in Coventry and we were back regularly but I went to school in Stourbridge and played for the local district there. I still watched CCFC on a regular basis at Highfield Road.

You come from a football family did it help as a young player that your dad and uncle were both players?

Yes it was a massive help. My Dad and uncle had a great understanding of the game and always helped and guided me through my youth and full career. Football was a huge part of our family life.

It must have been amazing to play for Wales like your dad; I believe that you played for England youth too?

Yes it was an incredible honour to represent Wales and follow in my father's footsteps, something I am very proud of. Also very proud to of represented England at youth level. I was very lucky on both counts and got to play with some unbelievably talented players.

A tough one maybe, do you reckon that you could name a best XI that you played with?

I have been asked this many times and although I played a handful of games for MUFC and Wales I don't like to include the superstars there as I didn't play a huge amount of games with them. The like of Keane, Scholes, Bale were just phenomenal players and it was great to play with them on a few occasions but I usually go with players who I played with over a number of seasons, I recently did this team:

GK - Nick Pope
LB - Chris Hussey
CB - Craig Morgan
CB - Anthony Kay
RB - Bobby Hassell
CM - Brian Howard
CM - Kari Arnason
AM - Dean Gorre
LW - Ben Pringle
RW - Chris Shuker
ST - Alex Revell

What are your favourite matches in your career?

I suppose you always remember the big games but three that spring to mind are the 2-2 draw with Leeds at Elland Road where I scored two for Barnsley; the play-off semi- final vs Huddersfield where I scored the winner in the last five minutes and the play-off final itself against Swansea where we won on penalties, again both for Barnsley.

Final Thoughts

It is fantastic that so many Coventry and Warwickshire players have played international football for so many different countries. Some of these players are still playing and I wish them all continued success.

Chapter Four – 1950s' Greats

In this chapter we are going to look at players from Coventry and Warwickshire who played for Coventry City in the 1950s.

Reginald Derrick Matthews (Reg Matthews)

One of the greatest goalkeepers to play for Coventry City, Reg is a true Coventry legend. Born on 20th December 1933, Reg attended Barkers' Butts School in Coundon and lived in Brightmere Road. Reg Played for Coventry Schools and signed for Coventry City when he was fourteen years old, He became part of the ground staff at Highfield Road whilst playing for Modern Machine Tools FC who were a nursery team. Reg signed professional forms for Coventry City in May 1950. On 21st of March 1953 Reg made his Coventry City debut in a Division Three (South) 1-0 defeat at Southend United.

Coventry City – Matthews, Dick Mason. Kirk, McDonnell, Cook, Simpson, Johnson, Warner, Brown, Hill, Waldock

Reg played 116 times for Coventry City before signing for Chelsea in November 1956 for a record £22.500 for a goalkeeper. At Stamford Bridge he played with famous players Jimmy Greaves, Terry Venables, John and Peter Sillett. Reg spent just under five years at Chelsea eventually being replaced by the emerging Peter Bonetti. Derby County signed Reg in October 1961 and he spent seven years at the Baseball Ground including a year or so under manager Brian Clough. In August 1968 he became player-manager of Rugby Town, succeeding Billy Hails. In October 1968 Reg signed former Coventry City team mate Frank Austin, the defender who was then in his mid-thirties and who would have brought valuable experience to the team. Reg would only spend one season at Rugby Town and in in May 1969 he left the club by mutual consent. The club were relegated from the Southern League Premier Division. Reg only played two home matches due to injuries.

In January 1972 Reg was working at Massey Ferguson's and expressed an interest in helping Massey's team. Alf Wood, a former Coventry City goalkeeper, was also working at the factory. Ron Farmer joined Massey-Ferguson as a player-coach, Ron was thirty-four then. He had recently been Coventry City youth team coach. He joined fellow qualified coaches Stan Smith the manager and John Cassidy who was a player.

In August 1974 Reg was appointed assistant to David Kite at Coventry Sporting, after running Massey Ferguson's team. It would prove to be a very good appointment: Coventry Sporting would have their fine FA Cup run in 1975.

On the 6th of May 1976 Reg guested for Bedworth United in testimonial match for striker David Eades. Sky Blues legends Ron Farmer, Lol Harvey, Brian Nicholas, Ernie Hunt and Gerry Baker also guested in the match. Bedworth played a Coventry City team including Mick Coop, Tommy Hutchison, Paul Dyson, Garry Thompson and Gary Plumley who famously played in the 1987 FA Cup semi-final for Watford due to injuries to Steve Sherwood and Tony Coton.

Reg also played cricket for Rootes who were based in Humber Road, Coventry. Graham Smith played with Reg. He told me that he was a very humble man who was quite overwhelmed by his success.

Reg sadly passed away on 7th October 2001. The funeral was held at St John's Church in Kenilworth, 15 October 2001.

International Career

Reg made his England under 23 debut in a 5-1 win over Italy on 19th January 1955. England fielded a strong team which included Duncan Edwards, Ron Flowers, Johnny Haynes, Peter Sillett (John's elder brother) and John Atyeo. Just over a year later on 14th April 1956 he made his full debut in a 1-1 draw v Scotland at Hampden Park. Reg had a good debut but Scotland took the lead on sixty minutes through Graham Leggat. On eighty nine minutes Johnny Haynes got England's equaliser.

Memorable Match

England 4-2 Brazil – 9th May 1956, Empire Stadium, Wembley

England beat Brazil in their first ever meeting. Tommy Taylor and Colin Grainger scored early goals for England to give them a 2-0 half time lead. Brazil fought back through a Roger Byrne own goal and Didi to level at 2-2. Taylor and Grainger scored again both assisted by Stanley Matthews. Byrne and Atyeo also missed penalties for England. England wouldn't beat Brazil again until 1984!

England – Matthews, Hall. Byrne, Clayton, Wright, Edwards, Matthews, Atyeo, Taylor,
Haynes, Grainger

Reg also played against Sweden, West Germany and Northern Ireland. By the time of the 1958 World Cup in Sweden goalkeepers Colin McDonald, Eddie Hopkinson and Alan Hodgkinson were the preferred choices.

Final Thoughts

Reg is a Coventry City and a city of Coventry legend! His journey from making his debut for Coventry City and playing for England in just over three years is amazing. Reg was a Third Division player when he played for his country, one of the greatest Coventry City goalkeepers of all time.

Les Latham

Les was a centre half who was born in Foleshill on 31st December 1917. Les only played one official match for Coventry City, in 1947. He guested for Coventry City, Aston Villa and Exeter City in the war years. Les is better known in Warwickshire for his time as manager of Bedworth and Lockheed Leamington. As a player he won the Birmingham Senior Cup with The Brakes in 1951.

Dennis Simpson

Dennis was an outside right who was born in Coventry on 1st of November 1919. Spotted playing for Salem Baptist, Dennis made 69 appearances for Coventry City in the 1940s. A regular in the 1947/48 season, most of his time at Highfield Road was as second choice behind Les "Plum" Warner. Dennis also played for Reading, Exeter City and Exmouth Town.

Derek Spencer

Derek was born in Coventry on 10th January 1931. A goalkeeper, he began his career with Lockheed Leamington winning the Birmingham Senior Cup in 1951. He moved to Coventry City in December 1951 and played 23 times for The Bantams. Derek's first team chances were limited as the club had many goalkeepers including Reg Matthews and Peter Taylor. Derek later played for Lockheed Leamington and Banbury Spencer. He passed away in February 1989. I got in touch with Derek's niece Kerrie who told me that Derek was the eldest of two sisters and three brothers. Sadly all of them have now passed away. Derek lived in Sutton Stop and St Luke's Road. Kerrie is very proud of her uncle and is keen to collect any programmes or match reports of when Derek played.

Ron Cox

A centre half who was born in Foleshill on 2nd of May 1919, Ron spent seven years at Coventry City from 1945 to 1952 playing 30 matches. His appearances were restricted due to George Mason being first choice. He made his debut on 2nd September 1946 against West Bromwich Albion. Dennis Tooze, Stanley Kelley and George Lowrie also made debuts. In Ron's second match for The Bantams he faced the legendary Jackie Milburn of Newcastle United. Jackie scored for The Magpies in a 1-1 draw and Tommy Crawley scored for Coventry City. Ron signed from Wyken Pippin FC and later played for Atherstone Town. He worked for Rolls Royce at Ansty for many years. Ron passed away in October 2006 aged eighty seven as the oldest surviving Coventry City player.

Richard (Dick) Mason

Born in Arley on the 2nd of April 1918, Dick was a regular choice in defence for Coventry City. Dick made 263 appearances between 1946 and 1954. He was a strong tackler and good at heading. In 955 he became player-manager of Bedworth Town, playing until he was forty years old.

Billy Gray

Billy was born on 3rd December 1931. One source of information says that he was born in Scotland and moved to Coventry as a child. Another source advises that he was born in Binley: he definitely played for Binley Youth Club. In 1944 the young right half joined Morris Motors FC which was a nursery team to Coventry City. Billy joined Coventry City in 1946 staying with the club for six years but only making two first team appearances in 1951. On 13th October 1951 he made his first team debut against Birmingham City covering for Don Dorman. Billy played for the Bantams reserve team. He moved to Kettering Town in 1954 for a year then returned to Morris Motors FC. Billy lived in the North East in later life and became a member of the CCFPA in 2011. He sadly passed away on 18th July 2014.

Peter Wyer

Peter was a forward who was born in Coventry on the 10th of February 1937. In 1951 he played for Coventry Schoolboys and had spells with Coventry Amateurs and Atherstone Town prior to joining Coventry City in October 1955. Peter made his Bantams debut in a 3-0 defeat against Crystal Palace on 22nd of October 1955. He played inside left in that match, team mates including Reg Matthews, Roy Kirk and Lol Harvey. Peter joined Derby County in June 1956 returning to Coventry City in August 1958 playing four more times for the club. Never a first team regular he went on to play for local non-league teams Nuneaton Borough and Rugby Town. In later years Peter was a regular at Sky Blues matches and a member of the CCFPA. He sadly passed away on the 13th of November 2019.

Jack Evans

Jack was a centre forward who was born in Coventry on the 11th of March 1926. He began his career with Modern Machines then joined Coventry City in 1942. Jack only played eight times for Coventry although he did score on his debut against Fulham in April 1949, his only goal for the club. In 1952 he was released by City and played for Nuneaton Borough, Bedworth, Rugby Town and Banbury Spencer. Jack, who was in his thirties, joined Lockheed Leamington in the late 1950s, by then playing in a more defensive wing half position. In 1962 he scored twice in the Birmingham Senior Cup final as Lockheed beat Rugby Town 5-1. This is one the club's most famous matches: older Leamington fans refer to it as the "old five." It was played at Highfield Road. It was also the first match Coventry City historian Jim Brown attended at the ground. Jack sadly passed away on the 15th of April 2012. Jim has written a lovely tribute about Jack in the gone but not forgotten section of the CCFPA website. Please have a read of Jim's tribute. It also mentions that Coventry played Galatasaray in 1950.

Gordon Simms

Gordon was a right winger who played one match for Coventry City in October 1957. He was born in Royal Leamington Spa on 20th of December 1936. Gordon played for Leamington St John's, South Leamington and, Flavells Athletic FC in his home town before joining City. In 1959 he was on Notts County's books but did not play for the first team. He then joined Nuneaton Borough. During national service he was a PT instructor and played for an Army XI. Gordon played briefly for Lockheed Leamington in 1962 and then from 1962 to 1970 he played for Warwick Town. Gordon attended Coventry matches with his son Chris and other former players Ken Brown, Graham Walker and Ian Goodwin. Sadly Gordon passed away on 11th March 2021 aged 84. Gordon was a lovely man who once told me that he played against Duncan Edwards in junior football. He will be very much missed by the CCFPA, Gordon was a keen Sky Blues fan.

Brinley Thomas (Bryn or Barry)

Bryn who was also known as Barry was a centre forward who played twelve matches for Coventry City in the 1950s. He was born in Coventry on 13th of December 1932. Bryn joined Coventry from Longford Rovers aged seventeen in 1950. In September 1952 he scored for Coventry City Reserves in a 2-2 draw with Tottenham Hotspur Reserves. Bryn had to wait until April 1953 to make his debut away against Colchester United which City won 1-0. Eddy Brown scored the only goal. Full back John Quinney from Rugby also made his debut. Bryn's first team chances were limited due to competition from Eddy Brown, George Lowrie and Ted Roberts. Bryn scored his only goal against Bristol City in a 2-2 draw on 25th of April 1953. Jimmy Hill also scored. Jimmy was an outside left not to be confused with Jimmy the future Coventry City manager and TV personality.

Coventry City team against Bristol City – Matthews, Harvey, Dick Mason, Timmins, McDonnell, Simpson, Jimmy Hill, Lowrie, Thomas, Nutt, Peter Hill.

Bryn was mentioned in an article in the Sports Argus in the same month. He was known as "Barry" and had recently completed his Army service. He was based at Chilwell Army depot in

Nottinghamshire. A few other city players were based there too – Austin, Cresswell, Waldock and Martin.

In April 1954 Bryn was placed on the open to transfer list as Coventry City named the retained list of players. Also on the list was Bryn Allen a former Welsh international inside-left. Bryn left Coventry City in 1954 and played for Banbury Spencer, Rugby Town and Bedworth Town. Bryn's form was good for Banbury Spencer and was watched by Northampton Town and Crystal Palace. In January 1955 he got a hat rick as Banbury beat Cradley Heath 6-3. Bryn scored another three goals in March 1955 as Banbury beat Sutton Town 4-3. In September 1955 he was selected for a Birmingham League representative team along with Banbury Spencer team mate Jack Evans.

Bryn's sons all excelled in sport, Wayne and Dean both became professional footballers who will feature later in the book. Paul played Rugby for Coventry RFC and was a fan's favourite at Coundon Road. Wayne is the oldest then Paul, and Dean is the youngest brother. Paul was a forward who played 280 times for Coventry and he also played for Rugby Lions. In the 1980s Paul played with some good players like Steve Thomas (no relation) Steve Brain, Graham Robbins and Marcus Rose.

Ken Chapman

Ken was a forward who was born in Coventry on 25th April 1932. He lived in Uplands, Stoke Heath. He began his career with Coventry Amateurs and Warwick Town playing with his older brother. Ken signed professional forms with Blackpool in July 1949 but never played for the first team. Blackpool were a strong Division One team with star England players Stan Mortensen and

Stanley Matthews so it would have been a difficult task. Ken then played in the Football League for Crewe Alexandra and Bradford City. He became a prominent player in non-league football for Banbury Spencer, Lockheed Leamington and Bedworth. In December 1955 Ken scored five goals for Banbury Spencer Reserves against Saltisford Rovers in a 9-0 win. Ken played for Rootes Athletic in the early 1960s, In April 1962 he helped the win 'The Coventry Evening Telegraph' Challenge Cup beating Courtaulds 3-2 in the final.

Peter Murphy

Peter was born on 7th March 1922 in West Hartlepool. He played football for local team West Hartlepool St Joseph's. In 1943 he was working and playing for Dunlop prior to joining Coventry City as an amateur, so he possibly moved to the area during war time. Peter was then a right half and he played for the Bantams in the second half of the 1943/44 season prior to service with the RAF. He guested for Millwall in the war. In 1946 Dick Bayliss signed him on professional forms for Coventry City in 1946. Harry Storer who was Peter's manager previously became Coventry City manager again in 1948. On 10th May 1948 Coventry City beat Linfield 3-2 during an Irish tour. Peter scored a hat trick over the Irish League champions who included Peter Doherty the former Manchester City forward as a guest. Two days later the Bantams hammered Derry 5-0, Lockhart scoring two goals and one each for Warner, Soden and Mc Intosh. Peter, who was also called "spud", scored another hat trick against Chesterfield on 3rd December 949. From 1946 to 1950 Peter made 120 appearances scoring 37 goals.

In June 1950 Peter joined Tottenham Hotspur and he played 25 times as they won Division One in 1951. Often played out of position, Peter joined Birmingham City in January 1952. For the rest of the decade Peter would become a great player for the Blues scoring 127 goals which makes him third in the club's all-time list only bettered by Trevor Francis and Joe Bradford. His most famous match for Birmingham City is known as "the Trautmann final": it was the 1956 FA Cup final. The match took place on 5th May 1956, Manchester City beat Birmingham City 3-1. However the final is remembered for a collision between Peter and Bert Trautmann which resulted in the German goalkeeper breaking a bone in his neck. Bert was knocked unconscious but continued to play for the last 10 minutes making saves as Manchester City won the match. Peter was joint top scorer in the 1955–58 Inter-Cities Fairs Cup with four goals. The competition took place over three seasons from 1955 to 1958.

In 1959 Peter retired from playing to take up a coaching role but came back to play some more matches. He appeared in the second leg of the 1960 Inter-Cities Fairs Cup Final with Barcelona beating Birmingham City 4-1 at the Camp Nou. In July 1961 Peter joined non-league Rugby Town at the same time as former Nottingham Forest goalkeeper Charlie Thomson. Rugby had a number of former football league players Bernard Jones, Bill Draper and Jimmy Knox. In October 1961 he scored a hat rick for Rugby Town in a 3-1 win over Tunbridge Wells. At the end of the season they were promoted to the Southern League Premier Division.

Peter retired from playing and became a coach at Coventry City. Peter sadly passed away on 7th April 1975 aged fifty three. He had worked for Davenport Breweries and lived in St Paul's Road in Foleshill.

Graham Walker

Graham was born in Coventry on 27th August 1940. He attended Churchfield High School which was in Brays Lane, Stoke, Coventry. He played for Coventry Schools and he first joined Coventry City on amateur forms then signing professional in 1958. Graham made his debut for Coventry City Reserves against Bournemouth in October 1958 at centre half. He played in the Bantams third team with Arthur Cox who would become a famous manager. In May 1961 Graham was given a free transfer by Coventry City. His only senior appearance for Coventry City was in October 1958 against Sunderland in a floodlit friendly. City lost 3-1, Graham was a second half substitute for Frank Austin. Graham was judged to have fouled former England winger Colin Grainger and Stan Anderson converted the penalty. Brian Hill scored Coventry City's goal. recurring dislocations of the shoulder finished his playing career.Graham worked for Alvis for a number of years. Now aged eighty he often attends Coventry City matches with his son.

Chapter Five – 1960s' and 1970s' Greats

In this chapter we are going to look at players from Coventry and Warwickshire who played for Coventry City in the 1960s and 1970s. At the beginning of the 1960s Coventry City were known as the Bantams but by the end of it were known as the Sky Blues. In 1961 Jimmy Hill was appointed manager, his impact on the club staggering. Within six years Coventry City were a top flight club winning the Second Division championship. In the 1970s the club became an established First Division team even qualifying for Europe. During both decades local players played an important role in the clubs rise through the divisions and consolidation in the top flight.

Dietmar Bruck

A Sky Blues legend, I had the pleasure of speaking to Dietmar. He was born in Danzig, Germany which is now Gdansk (Poland) on 19th of April 1944.Dietmar moved to Coventry as a child and attended Christ the King and Bishop Ullathorne schools. The youngster joined on schoolboy forms and, when he left school, on apprentice forms. As a youth Dietmar went to college to learn shorthand and typing whilst training with the club. The young player progressed through the Coventry 'A','B' and reserve teams which were at a good standard. On the 28th of April 1961 Dietmar made his first team debut at half back in a Division Three match against Swindon Town. The seventeen year old lined up with fellow home-grown players Mick Kearns and Colin Holder and a young George Curtis. Swindon included Mike Summerbee, Don Rogers and future Sky Blue Ernie Hunt. Dietmar became a regular for Coventry City in 1962 under new manager Jimmy Hill. Jimmy insisted on being called JH! Dietmar who had a lot of respect for previous manager Billy Frith, felt honoured to be part of the Jimmy Hill revolution. JH used to switch players around and one time John Sillett and Mick Kearns were injured, Dietmar switched from half back (midfield) to an attacking full back.

In October 1970 Dietmar joined Charlton Athletic then went on to play for Northampton Town, Nuneaton Borough and Weymouth, as player-manager. Whilst at Weymouth he signed former West Bromwich Albion and England striker Jeff Astle. Next was a spell as manager of Redditch United then on to Racing Club Warwick circa 1979. Dietmar has fond memories of his time in Warwick. He recalls good players like Roy Slade, Stuart Fisher, Chris Prophet and Steve Cooper. In one match against Solihull, the weather was terrible playing against the wind and they were losing 3-1 at half time. For the second half they changed the system they were playing with no pretty passing, playing it straight up to Big Lol (Alan Bryan). They won 6-3!

The author is friends with Alan and he remembers that match very well. "Diet was the best manager I had the pleasure of playing under without a doubt. The game he's on about was against Solihull Borough. 3-0 down at half time the wind was unbelievably strong blowing towards the clubhouse. At half-time Diet said we were capable of turning the game around. I don't think we were thinking the same but hey ho we did scoring six of which I got a brace. Fabulous game, fabulous memories. I must add to the story of that game. Our Chairman ' Mr. Racing Club' Eddie Haynes was stood behind the goal. Our six goals went in and he was giving the poor old goalkeeper some right stick."

Dietmar got a bit frustrated at the club because of finances: one time the club received a windfall from the brewery but they invested in other aspects of the club rather than the football side.

In 1985 he got a call from John Williams at Leamington and he took charge briefly when John resigned. One of the first things he did was getting rid of players who were not performing including John Sillett's son Neil. John Williams was reluctant to drop him because of who his dad was and was confident that Neil would deliver but he never did. John Sillett spoke to Dietmar years later and said: "I bet you thought I would give you grief about dropping Neil." John Sillett was of course a manager himself and would have had to make difficult choices.

Dietmar is now seventy six and part of the Coventry City Former Players' Association as a players' liaison. He played 215 times for Coventry City in the glorious days of the 1960s. It was great to speak to Dietmar and I thank Alun French for passing on his contact details to me. Some of this information was taken from an interview that Dietmar did with Coventry City historian Jim Brown which is on you tube.

Mick Coop

Third in Coventry City's all time appearances list with 499, Mick is a true Sky Blue legend. Born in Grimsby on 10th July 1948, Mick grew up in Royal Leamington Spa. Mick attended Cashmore and Oken High School (now called Myton School). In the early 1960s Oken had a fine football team. Mick played with a number of talented youngsters at Oken, team mates including Ian Walker and Dennis Farr who both spent time at Coventry City but injuries prevented them from becoming professional. Mick joined Coventry City in 1963, making his first team debut against Brighton and Hove Albion in September 1966. After playing only four league matches in the Second Division Championship season, Mick began to establish himself in the club's first season in the top flight. For the next fourteen years he would become a dependable right back and towards the end of his time at Highfield Road a classy centre half.

Two seasons stand out in Mick's time at the club, firstly the 1969/70 season when they finished sixth to qualify for the Fairs Cup. Often regarded as one of Coventry City's best ever seasons was the 1977/78 season, by when Mick was playing at centre half alongside the late great Jim Holton. Mick was also a very good penalty taker. If it wasn't for losing his place to Graham Oakey in the 1974/75 season he would have surely beaten George Curtis's appearance record. Mick went on loan to York City in November 1974 but testament to his character and ability he got back into Coventry's first team. In May 1979 he spent time on loan with Detroit Express. He joined Derby County in July 1981. Mick didn't enjoy his time at the Baseball Ground and retired professionally in 1982. He went into the antique trade and played briefly for home town team AP Leamington. In 1986 he made a return to Coventry City as youth team coach and the young Sky Blues won the FA Youth Cup in 1987. In his late thirties he played for Coventry City reserves against Middlesbrough in May 1987. Mick still lives local in Wellesbourne and is a member of the CCFPA. He is a magnificent servant for Coventry City and one of the club's best ever defenders. A Leamington kid to be proud of, it was nice that he was able to play for AP Leamington at the end of his career. Cashmore School was very close to the old ground on Tachbrook Road so he probably watched The Brakes as a kid. AP Leamington won the Southern League in the season Mick was at the Old Windmill which was a nice end to his playing days.

Bobby Gould

It almost didn't happen for Coventry kid Bobby at his home town club, but thankfully Jimmy Hill had faith in the young centre-forward. Bobby was born in Coventry on 12th June 1946, grew up in Wyken and attended Caludon Castle School. He was released by Billy Frith who was sacked after the team suffered a shock defeat to King's Lynn in the FA Cup. Jimmy Hill took over from Billy and invited back the players who had been released, the young Bobby impressing JH. At the age of sixteen and still an apprentice he made his Coventry City debut in a 0-0 draw v Shrewsbury Town on 30th October 1963. Bobby began to get a regular run in the team in October 1964 and scored in a League Cup win over Mansfield Town. Jimmy Hill had so much faith in Bobby that fans' favourite George Hudson was allowed to leave. Bobby repaid his boss by firing the Sky Blues to the Second Division title in 1967.

In total Bobby scored forty two goals in eighty nine appearances before moving to Arsenal in February 1968. Bobby then played for Wolverhampton Wanderers (twice), West Bromwich Albion, West Ham United, Bristol City, Bristol Rovers and Hereford United, a regular goal scorer in every team he played in throughout the 1960s and 1970s.

Bobby coached Aalesunds in Norway and Hereford then was appointed Assistant manager to Geoff Hurst at Chelsea then briefly as caretaker manager when Geoff was sacked in April 1981.

In October 1981 Bobby was appointed manager of Division Three team Bristol Rovers. In his time there he had a few well known players in Gary Mabbutt, Keith Curle, Ian Holloway and Mick Channon. Rovers finished seventh in Bobby's second season at the club, a decent finish.

When Dave Sexton was sacked by Coventry City in May 1983 the Sky Blues turned to Bobby. The summer of 1983 was a turbulent time for the club. Many of the young stars of the team were to leave Highfield Road. Danny Thomas, Gary Gillespie and Mark Hatelely were among those who left. Brian"Harry"Roberts was the only player to play in the last game of the 1982/83 season and the first of 1983/84 season. Bobby had to build a new team. He used his knowledge of the lower leagues to sign Trevor Peake, Michael Gynn and Nicky Platnauer. Players with First Division experience also joined – Dave Bennett, Terry Gibson and Sam Allardyce. In October 1983 he signed a young left back from Wealdstone called Stuart Pearce. Coventry City were relegation favourites but they did stay up. In December 1983 the Sky Blues thrashed Liverpool 4-0. Terry Gibson scored a hat trick and Nicky Platnauer also scored in this famous win, Liverpool still went on to win the League Cup, League Championship and European Cup. An inspired loan signing Mick Ferguson kept Coventry up, scoring important goals which ironically relegated parent club Birmingham City. In the summer of 1984 Bobby signed Steve Ogrizovic and Brian Kilcline and in October Peter Barnes and Cyrille Regis arrived. Bobby had signed the foundations of the cup final team but unfortunately for him he was sacked at the end of 1984.

Bobby returned to Bristol Rovers in 1985 for a second spell, but his next appointment in 1987 would be very special. Wimbledon was his destination replacing the popular Dave Bassett. Bobby signed Terry Gibson from Manchester United. Terry had struggled to make an impact at Old Trafford. His first season was a major success they finishing seventh in the league and on the 14th of May The Dons shocked Liverpool to win the FA Cup.

Bobby left Plough Lane in 1990 then had spells at Queens Park Rangers and West Bromwich Albion before a return to Coventry

City in June 1992. Bobby's lower league knowledge was put to good use with signings Phil Babb, John Williams and his goalkeeping son Jonathan. City enjoyed a great start to the Premier League and were leaders early on when he gave home grown players like Terry Fleming and Lee Hurst a chance in the first team. Bobby's most inspired signing was much travelled Mick Quinn on loan from Newcastle United in November 1992. Mick's form was incredible, City found the money to sign him permanently for £250,000, an absolute bargain.

In December 1992 Liverpool were visitors to Highfield Road and like in 1983 they were soundly beaten. Brian Borrows and Mick Quinn scored twice, Kevin Gallagher also scoring. Next up were Aston Villa on Boxing Day and on a foggy day at Highfield Road the Sky Blues ran out 3-0 winners thanks to goals from Quinn and Rosario. Blackburn Rovers were beaten 5-2 in January at Ewood Park, Mighty Quinn with another brace! In the spring of 1993 Rosario, Gallagher and Smith all left and Rennie, Wegerle and Jenkinson all came in. City finished fifteenth in the end and the season would have to be judged as a success. Star players Phil Babb and Peter Ndlovu remained at the club during the summer of 1993. Coventry City enjoyed an excellent start to the 1993/94 season beating Arsenal away courtesy of a Mick Quinn hat trick. Newcastle United and Liverpool were both beaten at Highfield Road in an eight game unbeaten run. In October City travelled to Loftus Road and were thrashed 5-1, Bobby dramatically resigned after the match. The next match at Highfield Road was a Sunday match against Sheffield United on Sky TV. The match against the Blades was a 0-0 draw but it will be remembers for the fans' protests against the board in support of Bobby.

After a break, Bobby was appointed the manager of the Welsh national team in June 1995. Bobby's time as Welsh manager was eventful but he would have been very honoured to manage a national team. In 1999 he resigned after a 4-0 defeat to Italy. His reign as Wales manager showed a 29% win ratio. Bobby had spells as manager of Cardiff City, Cheltenham Town and Weymouth. "The Gouldfather" as he is affectionately known has appeared on various football shows on Talksport.

Bobby is a Coventry City legend as a player and as a manager. It is a shame that he wasn't manager for longer in both spells, His style of football hasn't always been popular but his passion for Coventry is second to none. Bobby signed some important players for Coventry: the core of the Cup final team was his signings.

Memorable Match

Coventry City 5-0 Ipswich Town – 9th of December 1966 – Division Two at Highfield Road

This was the Sky Blues' third win in a row as they thrashesd Ipswich Town. Bobby Gould scored three goals and Key and Gibson also scored. Gibson pulled the strings in midfield, whilst Gould and Rees proved to be a handful for the Ipswich defenders.

Coventry City – Glazier, Kearns, Bruck, Farmer, Curtis, Clements, Key, Machin (Morrissey)
Gould, Gibson, Rees

Ipswich Town – Hancock, McNeil, Houghton, Harper, Baxter, Lea, Spearitt, Hegan, Crawford, Baker, Brogan

Trevor Gould

Trevor was an outside right who was born in Coventry on 5th of March 1950. The younger brother of Bobby he never quite matched his achievements on the pitch. Trevor played nine times for the Sky Blues in the 1969/70 season making his debut against West Bromwich Albion on the 12th of August 1969. Coventry City beat West Brom 3-1 with fellow former youth team player Willie Carr scoring a hat trick. In October 1970 Trevor moved to Northampton Town then played for Bedford Town and Rushden Town. In the summer of 1983 he was appointed manager of Aylesbury United. Trevor would become the club's most successful manager winning the Southern League Championship and gaining promotion to the Conference. Aylesbury also did very well in the FA Cup reaching at least the First Round proper every season. In 1988 his Aylesbury side played in an unusual friendly against England who were preparing for Euro 88. Trevor returned to Coventry City as youth team coach in 1992 then worked for Northampton Town as the academy manager He retired from the role in 2018.

Brian Hill

Brian was born in Bedworth on 31st of July 1941. He attended Nicholas Chamberlain School in Bedworth and whilst there he represented Warwickshire Schools at football and cricket. Brian left school in 1956 and worked for Jaguar for a short time when he was invited to trials and offered an apprentice contact by The Bantams. On the 30th of April 1958 Brian enjoyed a goal scoring debut against Gillingham in a 3-2 defeat, a team that also included Ray Hill and Peter Hill however they were not related to Brian. At sixteen years old he broke the record for being the club's youngest starter and goal scorer. In his early playing days he played as an inside left or outside left and it wasn't until Jimmy Hill arrived at the club did we see the best of Brian. Jimmy converted him to a half back and he became an exceptional man marker. Brian was a fantastic tackler, very much the unsung hero in the team. He went on to play 286 times for Coventry City becoming one of the most reliable and versatile players of the 1960s. Brian also played for Bristol City on loan, Torquay United and Bedworth United. In March 1976 he had a brief spell with Racing Club Warwick. Brian worked at Jaguar and as a driver for HSBC Bank. He retired in 2003. Sadly Brian passed away on 27th October 2016. He is a Coventry City legend who is very much missed. Only Brian, George Curtis, Ron Farmer and Mick Kearns played in all four divisions during City's rise in the 1960s. Brian played for the club in three decades, a Sky Blues' legend.

Frank Kletzenbauer

Frank was a full back who was born in Coventry on 21st of July 1936. He joined Coventry City from Municipal Sports in 1953, making his first team debut in January 1957. Frank was a regular in the 1960/61 and 1961/62 seasons but once Mick Kearns and John Sillett had established themselves Frank's appearances were limited. In total at Coventry City he made 132 appearances scoring 3 goals. Frank won the Southern Professional Floodlight Cup with Coventry City in 1960. Frank joined Walsall in March 1964 but suffered bad injuries which ended his career in 1966. In January 1966 Lockheed Leamington tried to sign Frank but the deal fell through. I contacted Frank's daughter Lesley and asked her a few questions about her dad. The name Kletzenbauer originates from Austria: Frank's great grandparents were Austrian. Frank grew up in Holbrooks and attended Whitemoor Secondary Modern School.

He was a plumber by trade and didn't go into football coaching after he retired from playing. Frank worked for Coventry City as a Marketing Administrator for nine and a half years. Frank sadly passed away on 8th of August 1996 aged sixty.

Memorable Match

Coventry City 2-1 West Ham United - Southern Professional Floodlight Cup Final – 27th April 1960 – Highfield Road

Coventry City beat a West Ham United team who included Bobby Moore and Noel Cantwell. Ron Hewitt scored twice for City, Cartwright for West Ham.

Coventry City - Lightening, Bennett, Kletzenbauer, Kearns, Curtis, Austin, Stephens, Hewitt, Straw, Hill Daley.

Peter Thomas

Peter was a goalkeeper who only played one match for Coventry City, in November 1966. He made his one appearance because Bill Glazier was injured and Bob Wesson had been sold to Walsall. Peter was born in Coventry on 20th of November 1944 He began his career with St Mary's Youth Club and GEC of Coventry. In 1967 he joined League of Ireland side Waterford FC after being on loan. Peter would become a legend at Waterford as the club won the League of Ireland five times in 1968, 1969, 1970, 1972 and 1973. After becoming an Irish citizen he was called up by Republic of Ireland in 1973 for a match against Poland. Peter won his second and final Irish cap against Brazil in 1974. In 1968 he played against Manchester United in the European Cup. Ironically Bobby Charlton briefly played for Waterford in 1976 Peter played in the same team as him. From 1975 to 1978 Peter also played in the

North American Soccer League for Washington Diplomats, Utah Golden Spikers, Las Vegas Quicksilvers and Sacramento Gold.

Johnny Matthews

Son of former Coventry City player Horace Matthews, Johnny was a youth team player for Coventry City in the 1960s. He was born at Keresley Hospital on the outskirts of Coventry on 27th August 1946. The family lived in Nicholls Street which was next door to the old Highfield Road ground in Hillfields. Johnny attended Frederick Bird School in Swan Lane which was close by to where they lived.

Upon leaving school Johnny worked at the GEC in the Stoke area of Coventry He was spotted playing for Coventry City whilst playing for GEC's team. In October 1963 Johnny scored as GEC hammered Coventry Gauge 6-0 in the Works League. Johnny played in the same youth as Mick Coop and Dudley Roberts but he never made it into the first team because of established wingers Ronnie Rees and John Mitten. On March 22nd 1965 Johnny helped Coventry City 'A' beat Aston Villa 'A' 4-0. Johnny scored two goals. There was an own goal and John Docker also scored. David Matthews also played for Coventry City, no relation to Johnny. In January 1966 Johnny had a great game for Coventry City 'A' as they beat Leicester City 'A' 5-1. Johnny scored two goals, with one each for Chambers, Oakes and Peachey.

In March 1966 Mick Lynch, who was manager of Waterford, approached Jimmy Hill enquiring about players available for loan. Johnny had suffered a cartilage injury. His sister Gloria recalls Norman Pilgrim being the club's physiotherapist at the time. Jimmy agreed to send Johnny on an initial six week loan to gain experience. The young winger was an instant success and signed permanently. In March 1966 he scored the winner for Waterford against Sligo. In a newspaper report Johnny's mum and dad hoped to watch Waterford play against Shamrock Rovers in the Irish Cup Semi-Final. The first match was a 2-2 draw but Shamrock Rovers won the replay 4-2. At the same time Coventry City released an Irish player called Rory Linnie. Johnny and Rory both had cartilage operations earlier in the season. I can imagine that nobody could have imagined the impact Johnny would make at Waterford where he would become a club legend and indeed a League of Ireland legend. In 342 League appearances, he would score a club record 147 goals. In Johnny's first season he helped Waterford win the League of Ireland for the first time in 1966. He won the league with Waterford five more times in 1968, 1969, 1970, 1972 and 1973 and once with Limerick in 1980. Johnny scored famous goals in the European Cup against Celtic and Manchester United and a penalty for a League of Ireland XI against an English League XI whose goalkeeper was Gordon Banks. In a Q&A Johnny did in 2008 he said that the biggest influences on his career was his dad, Jimmy Hill, and Pat Saward. Johnny appeared in three FAI Cup finals but lost them all, the last one in 1979 and he left soon afterwards. Ironically Waterford won the 1980 FAI Cup final, Peter Thomas who joined a year after Johnny picked up a winner's medal.

Johnny signed for Limerick United who were managed by Ireland international Eoin Hand. Limerick won the league in Eoin and Johnny's first season at the club and the following season they faced Real Madrid in the European Cup. On the 17th of September Limerick faced a Real Madrid side at Lansdowne Road in Dublin and gave them a fright! Real who included internationals Camacho, Juanito and Cunningham only just beat Limerick 2-1, Johnny had a goal ruled out for offside. Johnny later played for

Cork United, Waterford United, Galway United, Longford Town and Newcastle West (player-manager). In 1990 he won The League of Ireland First Division with Waterford United. Johnny was a good cricketer and played for Munster alongside Waterford FC team mates Dave Kirby and Peter Thomas. After he finished playing and managing in football he stayed in the game via refereeing. Johnny passed away on 25th of December 2019 aged seventy three.

John Docker

A left winger but who preferred to play at inside-left, John was a bright prospect at Coventry City in the 1960s. I had the pleasure of speaking to John He is from Coventry and attended Caludon Castle School. John signed for Coventry City as an apprentice straight from school. He was in the same age group as Martin Clamp, Pat Morrissey and Mick Coop. He signed amateur forms for City aged fifteen in November 1962 beating off competition from Aston Villa, West Bromwich Albion and Birmingham City. Jimmy Hill had been Coventry City manager a year and was keen to sign talented local players. A month previously John was playing at inside-right and scored four goals against Banbury. On 28th October 1963 he made his debut for Coventry City Reserves against Queens Park Rangers. City lined up as follows – Meeson,Tedds,Burckitt,Saward,Roberts,Oakes,Denton,Turner,Gould,Dwight,Docker. Pat Saward was player-coach, Roy Dwight has a famous cousin, Elton John!

In November 1963 John helped Coventry City youth team hammer Cambridge City 5-0! John scored one goal, Bobby Gould three and John Chambers the other. Also in November 1963 John scored in a thrilling 6-4 defeat to West Bromwich Albion in the FA Youth Cup

First Round. John continued to play for the youth team and the reserves in 1964. In July 1965 he was taken on as a full-time professional along with Pat Morrissey. John had attended a course at Lilleshall School of excellence with team mates Martin Clamp, Mick Coop and Don Peachey. In 1966 John was close to breaking into the first team and in April of 1966 he helped Coventry City 'A' beat Leicester City 'A' 3-1. John signed on loan for Torquay United in July 1967 which is considered the first loan in the format we know today. John played eight times for Frank O'Farrell's Torquay team and scored two goals against Exeter City in the League Cup. In the summer of 1968 he was given a free transfer by Coventry City and joined League of Ireland champions Waterford. John joined former Coventry City players Johnny Matthews and Peter Thomas who were both doing well for the Irish team. It didn't really work out for him in Ireland and by December 1968 he had returned to Coventry in search for a new club. Troubled by a cartilage injury, he only played about four times for Waterford.

In January 1969 John signed for Southern League side Rugby Town, teaming up with former Sky Blues' youth team colleague John Burckitt. John also played for Massey Ferguson and Binley Woods. In October 1971 he scored three goals as Masseys beat Harmo 7-3 in the Birmingham Junior Cup. John talked about a youth tournament in the Netherlands in 1967, which Coventry City won. It took place at The Hague. Coventry City beat Ajax Amsterdam 3-0 in the final. John talked about an offer to play in Durban, South Africa but once they found out he was injured it was end of conversation! He remembers being injured the same time as George Curtis in the 1967/68 season. John talked about George Hudson, Hugh Barr, Willie Humphries, John Sillett and Peter Denton whom he liked at Highfield Road. After football he ran his own business supplying maintenance products to industry.

He still lives in Binley Woods. If John hadn't had that injury I'm sure that he would have had a good career in football. I am grateful to John for taking the time to share his football memories with me.

John Burckitt

John was a full back who was born in Coventry on 16th December 1946. He attended Caludon Castle School and played for Coventry Schools. In 1964 John joined Coventry City and made his first team debut aged seventeen against Manchester City in October 1964. John made seven first team appearances before joining Bradford City on loan in 1967. A year later he signed for Walsall then played local non-league football for Rugby Town and Nuneaton Borough. John was an England youth international and was part of the team which got beaten by East Germany in the under 18 final in 1965. Future Coventry City full back Wilf Smith was in the team as was young Chelsea star Peter Osgood who scored.

East Germany 3-2 England 25th of April 1965 UEFA under 18 final

England: Barnett; Wright, Burkitt; Glover, Brindley, Smith; Morgan, Bond, Osgood, Vincent, Allen

John sadly passed away in November 1999 aged fifty two.

Mick Kearns

Mick was a defender and a fantastic servant for Coventry City in the 1950s and 1960s. He was born in Nuneaton on 10th of March 1938 and played local football for Stockingford Villa before joining Coventry City in September 1955. Mick, along with

George Curtis, Ron Farmer and Brian Hill played in all four divisions during City's great era. He played at full back and left half and made a total of 382 appearances for Coventry City. Mick suffered from knee problems and was forced to retire soon after promotion to the First Division. After playing he helped run the family bingo hall in Nuneaton. In 1986 he returned to Coventry City for six years as Chief Scout and Youth Development Officer. His brothers Tony and Martin played local football. Tony was a good friend of Johnny Matthews. Mick is sixth in the all-time appearance list for City, a true club legend.

Bill Tedds

Bill was a right back who made nine appearances for Coventry City in five years at the club. He was born in Bedworth on 27th of July 1943 and attended Nicholas Chamberlain School. Bill worked at Browns Lane Jaguar after leaving school prior to signing professional for Coventry City in September 1960. Growing up in Bedworth he was a good friend of Brian Hill who was a couple of years older than him. Bill made his Coventry City debut on 16th of September 1961 away at Shrewsbury Town. In 1965 he left Highfield Road to join Cambridge United and he then had spells with Lockheed Leamington and Racing Club Warwick. In 1970 Saltisford Rovers became Racing Club Warwick where Bill was part of a good team that included Ian Walker and Dennis Farr who both spent time at Coventry City. Bill returned to work for Jaguar in Radford for twenty eight years until he retired. A keen Sky Blues fan, he is a regular at matches and legends' days.

Bobby Parker

Bobby was a central defender who was born in Coventry on 11th of November 1952. He attended Caludon Castle School. In December 1967 he was part of Coventry Schools' Under 15 squad which also included Bob Stockley, Charlie Sorbie and Peter McInulty who all enjoyed good non-league careers.

He was part of a great youth team at Coventry who narrowly lost to Tottenham Hotspur in the 1970 FA Youth Cup Final.

Coventry City 1970 Youth Team – Icke, Crossley, Holmes, Mortimer, Dugdale, Parker, Cartwright, Green, Randell, McGuire, Stevenson

Tottenham, who included future stars Graeme Souness, Steve Perryman and Ray Clarke, won the second replay 1-0 after 1-1 and 2-2 draws in the previous matches.

Bobby was seventeen when he made his first team debut in March 1970 and also captained England's youth team. In May 1971 Bobby along with Coventry City team mates Alan Dugdale and Mick McGuire were named in England's youth team. It was a match against Yugoslavia in the "little World Cup" in Czechoslovakia. England also included Steve Daley and Trevor Francis who would both become £1 million players. Prior to the Yugoslavia match, Bobby was featured in an article in the Daily Mirror with Bobby Moore with comparisons between both players as Bobby Moore himself had led England's youth team in 1958. He gave Bobby (Parker) some advice and wished him well. England won the tournament beating Portugal 3-0 in the final, Peter Eastoe and Johnny Ayris with the goals.

He played 91 times for Coventry City before a move to Carlisle United in 1974. Bobby would become a legend in Cumbria playing over 400 games in ten years. He had a two year spell with Scottish team Queen of the South after which he became a Health & Safety Officer and settled in Carlisle.

Barry Powell

Barry was born in Kenilworth on 29th January 1954. He lived in Mortimer Road in the town and attended Castle High School. A promising young player he captained his school team and St John's Boys club and also spent time at Stoke City. Barry's father Ivor was a Welsh youth international who was an outside left for Kenilworth Rangers who had a successful team in the 1950s. In January 1972 an eighteen year old Barry signed as a professional for Wolves. He played fairly regularly for Wolves and won the League Cup with them in 1974. In the summer of 1975 Barry moved to Coventry City with Willie Carr going in the other direction. In 1974 he played for England Under 23 and when his career began to take off Wales expressed an interest in his availability. Looking back Barry would have definitely become a full international for Wales. Once Terry Yorath signed for the Sky Blues, Barry excelled alongside him. The 1977/78 season was one of Coventry's best ever, the club finishing seventh just missing out on a UEFA Cup place. Barry and Terry were terrific in midfield. With Hutchison out wide, Ferguson and Wallace up front it was an entertaining time at Highfield Road. Barry signed for Derby County in 1979 then played for Burnley, Swansea City, Wolves and spent time in USA and Hong Kong. He later worked for Coventry City in the football in the community scheme and he managed Hednesford Town and Aberystwyth Town. Barry played

80 times and scored 30 goals for Coventry City, a Coventry City and Warwickshire great.

Andy Blair

I had the pleasure of speaking to Andy about his football career: he was one of Coventry City's best midfield players in the late 1970s/early 1980s. Andy was born in Kirkcaldy in Scotland on 18th December 1959. At a young age his family moved to Bedworth. He lived in Willis Grove in the town and attended Henry Bellairs School and Nicholas Chamberlain School which were both fairly close by. Andy was a part of a fine team at Nicholas Chamberlain and was captain for five years. Bedworth had some good players: Ray Train who is a few years older than Andy had a good professional career; Wayne Thomas who went to Ash Green School was a year older was a very good player.

In November 1972 Andy scored twice for Nuneaton and District Schools under 13s as they beat Bromsgrove 6-1. The match was played in Bedworth and Nicholas Chamberlain team mate Harris scored three goals. In February 1973 Andy was part of a fine Nicholas Chamberlain under 13s' team who won Nuneaton and District League and Cup competitions. A team mate of Andy was Martin Sockett who went on to have a fine career in non-league football as a player and manager. Andy is very grateful to Roger Jacques who was a maths teacher who got him into Warwickshire Schools which led to Coventry City when he was fourteen.

In the summer of 1977 Andy was part of Coventry City's youth team which finished third in the Whitsuntide International Youth Tournament in Southern Germany which took place in June 1977. Andy, Gary Bannister, Garry Thompson and Frank McGrellis scored Coventry's goals. City won two out of four games beating

Hadjuk Split and Borussia Dortmund. In October 1977 Andy helped Coventry City Reserves beat Aston Villa Reserves 1-0. Donal Murphy scored the winning goal. Coventry included Val Thomas the older brother of Danny. Warwickshire Schools had a strong player base back then as Birmingham was also included, Andy played with future Sky Blues team mates Paul Dyson and Garry Thompson.

Andy progressed through the youth team and made his Coventry City debut on 28th of October 1978 against Birmingham City. It was a winning start as Tommy Hutchison scored twice in a 2-1 win. Andy had a good run in the team in midfield alongside Kenilworth man Barry Powell. Terry Yorath left Coventry City for Tottenham Hotspur in 1979, which allowed Andy to become first choice in midfield. Over the next couple of seasons Andy formed good partnerships with Barry Powell, Steve Hunt and Gerry Daly. In the early 1980s City had a talented young team and reached the League Cup semi- finals in 1981. Andy spoke about the great young players like Thomas, Gillespie, Bodak and Hateley. He was also full of praise for older players Daly and McDonald who were a great influence.

In the summer of 1981 Andy was out of contract and Aston Villa (League champions) and Ipswich Town (UEFA Cup winners) came in for him. Andy decided to join Aston Villa and he made his debut in the Charity Shield on 22nd August against Tottenham Hotspur. Aston Villa had a superb midfield trio of Dennis Mortimer, Des Bremner and Gordon Cowans which meant Andy was often a backup and was a substitute in the 1982 European Cup victory over Bayern Munich in May 1982. He did however play in the 2nd leg of the European Super Cup win over Barcelona in January 1983.

Andy went on loan to Wolverhampton Wanderers in the 1983/84 season. Although it was a struggling Wolves team they did achieve fine wins over Everton and West Bromwich Albion during his loan spell. Andy enjoyed playing with Andy Gray, Wayne Clarke and Kenny Hibbitt at Molineux.

In 1984 Andy joined Sheffield Wednesday who had a very good side and finished eighth in the 1984/85 First Division. Andy formed a solid midfield partnership with Gary Shelton. The Owls had quality players like Mel Sterland, Brian Marwood and Imre Varadi. In November 1984 he famously scored a hat rick of penalties against Luton Town in the League Cup. In July 1986 Andy returned to Aston Villa, then had spells with Barnsley (loan) Northampton Town, Kidderminster Harriers and played in Malta. After finishing from playing he had a spell as Racing Club Warwick manager, Andy recalls telling a couple of lads, "You are too good for this standard of football!"

For the last thirty years Andy has worked in retail and owns Andy Blair Schoolwear in Coundon. Andy's son Matty has enjoyed a good career with York City, Doncaster Rovers and now Cheltenham Town. Andy once broke his foot whilst celebrating one of Matty's goals for York City! Andy represented Scotland under 21s five times, making his international debut against England on 12th February 1980 which was played at Highfield Road. I asked Andy if he ever considered playing for England but it was never an option as he was born in Scotland and both parents were Scottish. Andy played with some quality players for Scotland including Gary Gillespie, John Wark, Steve Nicol and Steve Archibald. Andy scored two goals for Scotland under 21s but never won a full cap: competition was strong in the 1980s and in a different era he would have been a regular. Andy was honest about his time at Aston Villa where it didn't really work out for him but said it was a great club and they treated him well. It was really great speaking to Andy, a local great who was part of one of the most exciting teams ever seen at Highfield Road.

Chapter Six – Non-League Greats

In this chapter we are going to look at some of the great players who enjoyed success for local non-league teams. Over the years teams from Warwickshire have played at a high standard of non-league football. Nuneaton Borough have come the closest to making it to the Football League, AP Leamington were founder members of the Alliance Premier (fifth tier in the league pyramid). VS Rugby won the FA Vase at Wembley; other local sides Bedworth, Atherstone and Stratford have all won the Birmingham Senior Cup.

Ken Brown

My friend Ken, I having known him for about three years now, I first got in touch with when I was researching for my first book Windmill Heroes. Ken signed professional forms for Coventry City in 1955. He played for the A, B and Reserve teams. He also played for Nottingham Forest reserves, Bournemouth and Boscombe Athletic, Torquay United and also a few non-league teams including Lockheed Leamington and Bedworth United. Ken could play anywhere across the forward line, he scored his fair share of goals. In the late 1960s he coached Coventry Amateurs, Ken is famous for his time with Standard Triumph Athletic. From 1978 to 1998 Standard Triumph Athletic won the Premier Alliance league, Birmingham Junior Cup, Coventry Charity Cup and Coventry Senior Evening Telegraph Cup. Ken has always been a keen sportsman playing golf, cricket, bowls and walking football. Myself and Ken have met up on several occasions with some of his former Lockheed Leamington team mates Syd Hall and Geoff Coleman. Now at the age of eighty seven Ken still keeps active and often meets up with members of CCFPA and is still a keen Sky Blues' fan.

Dennis Taylor

A fantastic servant for Lockheed and AP Leamington, I spoke to Dennis about his football career. A Coventry kid, he went to Caludon Castle School where he was in the same team as Trevor Gould. Dennis played for Coventry City C, Stockingford AA and Leicester City Reserves playing three or four games on trial. In 1969 he joined Geoff Coleman's Lockheed Leamington who were in the Midlands League. Dennis recalled the great players that he played with, in the early seasons: Syd Hall, Keith Shrimpton and Tom Sweenie. In 1973 the club changed its name to AP Leamington and were competing in the Southern League Division 1 North. In the 1970s under manager Jimmy Knox, AP Leamington reached the Southern League Premier and finished the decade in the Alliance Premier League. The Brakes also enjoyed FA Cup runs facing league clubs Southend United, Torquay United and Tranmere Rovers. Dennis remembers the FA Cup matches and also the Birmingham Senior Cup finals which Lockheed won in the early 1970s. AP Leamington had some great players in the 1970s, Dennis told me Allan Jones and Roger Brown were a solid centre half pairing. Dennis was a versatile player he could play in most positions even goalkeeper. He played mostly at full back or in midfield. In that era a lot of ex professional players played at that level towards the end of their careers. Dennis talked about Jimmy Greaves playing for Barnet and team mates Micky Boot and Harry Redknapp who were both First Division players. In 1981 he joined Bedworth United linking up with former Lockheed team mate John Brady who was the Greenbacks manager. Bedworth had a good team and Dennis remembers Tommy Gorman an ex-AP Leamington team mate. He was a hard tackling midfielder who once broke his neck playing for AP Leamington against Nuneaton Borough. The Greenbacks also had Mick Martin in goal and had good young players in Liam Halton, Gary Bradder and Martin Smith. Dennis was in his early 30s and played about three or four seasons at the Oval. He later played for Folly Lane over 35s and enjoyed playing walking football. Dennis was nicknamed "the Ferret" because he was fast, a dependable player who gave 100%.

He was given a testimonial match against Coventry City for his long service to the Brakes.

Tommy Gorman

Tommy was a combative midfielder, I spoke to him about his football days. He was born in Belfast in 1954. As a teenager he was there at the height of the troubles in Northern Ireland. Tommy moved over to Coventry aged sixteen or seventeen. He worked in sheet metalling, Tommy told me people had trouble understanding his accent. He played local football for Jet Blades, Willenhall Social and Solihull Borough before being spotted by AP Leamington in 1976. Tommy joined the Brakes at the same time as Harry Redknapp under the management of Jimmy Knox and Bob Ward. He became an AP Leamington fans' favourite with his all action displays in midfield. Tommy once broke his neck playing against Nuneaton Borough when he was twenty three. He came back to play but this injury probably prevented him from playing at a higher level. Tommy joined Bedworth United in 1982/83 then reunited with Knoxy at VS Rugby. Tommy then played for Coventry Sporting, Corby Town, Worcester City, Nuneaton Borough and Alvis. He talked about some of the great players he played against like Geoff Hurst, Jimmy Greaves, Willie Carr and Ernie Hunt. Tommy remembers watching Willie and Ernie play for Coventry City. The toughest player he played against was Dave Lewis of Nuneaton Borough. He also mentioned team mates Allan Jones and Gary Brown as hard players. Tommy talked about Brian Rankin who was with AP Leamington in the 1970s. He wasn't with the club long and got sent off a few times. However Tommy rated him as a player, Brian had previously played for Dundee United. Tommy also talked about Danny Conway, Steve Norris, Ian Crawley, Cliff Campbell and Adrian Stewart. He is sixty seven this year and still keeps fit by playing six a side football.

John Setchell

A Coventry kid who enjoyed a good career in local non-league football, John's father Alf was a good player in the 1940s and 1950s. John was part of the VS Rugby team that won the FA Vase in 1983. I asked John a few questions about his football career.

Could you tell me about your junior career? I believe that you are from Coventry.

Yes. I was from Holbrooks, Coventry. I initially played for Holbrooks Junior School, at the age of eight, and was selected for the Foleshill Schools' Area team. I attended President Kennedy school, and again played for the school team, and represented Coventry Schoolboys in each year from 12- 15. I also played for a very successful under12 and under14 junior team, Bedworth Juniors, and we won everything that we entered. I was scouted from a very early age, with Leicester City being particularly keen, and therefore spent most of my school holiday time at Leicester.Whilst I had several offers to attend other clubs, I felt Leicester was a good fit, hence I stayed after leaving school.

What senior teams did you play for?

In terms of senior teams, I left Leicester at the age of seventeen, and played for Bedworth United, before moving to Nuneaton Borough, Bedford, and Coventry Sporting, and VS Rugby. I had some tremendous times at all these clubs, and met some terrific people.

What are your memories of playing for VS Rugby and the FA Vase success in 1983?

1983 was a fantastic season, with the pinnacle being winning the FA Vase at Wembley. I remember all the games of the run to the final, with Great Yarmouth away 2nd leg probably the most memorable, as actually getting to Wembley itself was unbelievable, but making sure we won, was the mission complete. The team spirit we had throughout that season of 1982/83, was special. All the total squad, gelled into one big family, team spirit along with trust in each other's ability, along with a fantastic Manager - Jimmy Knox, who was a hard task master, but also extremely approachable. Nobody wanted to let Jimmy down, or their team members.

Do you keep in touch with any of your team mates from Butlin Road?

The bond even today is very strong thirty-seven years on and we all still see each other, at least once/twice per year This year nine of that squad went to Benidorm in February 2020, and we have already planned 2021 to celebrate in Portugal. This illustrates just how strong the bond is between us all, and we all live all over the country.

Did you also play for Triumph Athletic?

Yes I did, this was my last club before I retired, I was about 35 years old. Local football was very strong This Triumph team won the Alliance League, Telegraph cup and Birmingham Junior cup, a very good team.

John was a talented schoolboy player. In September 1972 he scored seven goals for President Kennedy under 12s against Bluecoat. In September 1976 Bedworth United were hit by a player crisis and they called up seventeen year old John for his Southern

League debut against Banbury. John was also a good Snooker player for Unicorn in the 1970s.

Memorable Match

VS Rugby 1-0 Halesowen Town – 30th April 1983 FA Vase final, Wembley Stadium

VS Rugby – Burton, McGinty, Harrison, Preston, Knox, Evans, Ingram, Setchell,
Owen,Beecham,Crawley

Ian Crawley got the winning goal in a fine result for VS Rugby. Manager Jimmy Knox, who once played for Rugby Town, was an experienced manager from his time at AP Leamington. Halesowen were a force in non-league football in the 1980s spearheaded by star players the Joinson brothers.

Terry Angus

Born in Coventry on the 14th January 1966, Terry enjoyed a fine career in professional and semi-professional football. In 1979 Terry played for Coventry Dynamos under 13 team who were the invincibles! The won the Coventry Minor League by nine points winning all twenty five matches and scored an incredible 196 goals. Terry scored 92 goals in all competitions and lifelong friend Mark Rosegreen scored 69 goals in a team that included future England goalkeeper Tim Flowers. Mark Rosegreen had an excellent career in non-league for AP Leamington, VS Rugby and Nuneaton Borough he was also an England Schoolboy international. On 17th November 1979 Coventry Schools under-14 beat Nuneaton 5-3 Terry scored two goals with one each for Mark Rosegreen, John Matthews and Nyrene Kelly. In a previous match

Coventry lost 4-3 to King's Norton, Terry, Mark and John with the goals. The Birmingham team included Darren Bradley who scored the winning goal, he went onto play for Aston Villa and West Bromwich Albion.

A number of schoolboy players from that era became professionals including John Gayle, Gary Shaw, Keith Thompson and in a younger age group Simon Sturridge. Terry is remembered fondly for his time with Nuneaton Borough from 1998 to 2006. In 1990 he joined Northampton Town before signing for Fulham in 1993; Terry spent four years at Craven Cottage and then had a brief spell with Slough Town. In October 1993 Terry played against Liverpool at Anfield in a League Cup tie: however it wasn't a happy evening for Fulham as Robbie Fowler scored all five goals in a 5-0 win. Terry told me that Robbie, Marcus Stewart and Craig Hignett were the best forwards he played against.

Terry was part of the Nuneaton Borough team that beat Stoke City in the FA Cup in November 2000, Marc McGregor scoring in a 1-0 win.

I asked Terry a few questions about his career.

What junior teams did you play for?

On Sundays I started at Coventry Dynamos at under 10 level then at 16/17 I played for Twenty FC. I never played on a Saturday but was involved with Coventry Schoolboys from under 12 to 16 levels. I signed for Coventry City at 14-16, Coventry Dynamo until 14. Coventry Sporting 14-16yrs. (Ironically I played with Darren Garforth who went on to represent England at Rugby).

You probably got asked this a lot but how come you reverted to a defender after being so prolific as a striker as a youngster?

When I got to sixteen I lost that edge to my game and remained very small and as other players got bigger I never had the same impact. I joined Coventry Sporting and dropped in at left back for a reserve game then had a growth spurt and stayed left back because I was quick. I adjusted and grew again at around twenty. I was then playing in central defence and left back.

Do you think that you could name a Terry Angus dream team of players that you played with?

GK - Chris McKenzie (just edges Mick Martin) RB - Anthony Riley LB -
Robbie Herreira CB - Neil Moore CB - Liam Holton RMF - Shaun Reay LMF
- Paul Watson CMF - Simon Morgan CMF - Ian Muir CF - Andy Ducros CF - Micky Conroy

Subs - Danny Conway, Mick Martin, Gary Abbott, Barry Williams

Manager - Theo Foley

What were your favourite matches in your career? The Middlesbrough Cup matches were memorable.

Carlisle v Fulham 1997, Nuneaton v Middlesbrough 2005 and Coventry Dynamo v Leamington Ajax under 12s.

You must be so proud of Dior. I really hope that Barrow do get promotion. Have you got a favourite match Dior played in?

Dior has / is still does work so hard to achieve what he has achieved. I sincerely hope he gets the promotion firstly for him then for Barrow. I have many fond memories..... If I am honest just seeing him fulfil his potential is enough for me. If pushed I would say when Kenilworth School beat Woodlands School in the Telegraph Cup U16 at the Ricoh(as it was at the home of Coventry and a lot of family and friends were there to witness it.

Could you tell me a little bit about your role with PFA?

I work as Equalities in Community Executive. I, along with Jason Lee and Head of Equalities Simone Pound, work to ensure players are fully aware of the equalities' agenda and ensure they are fully aware of the reporting process and what to do if they themselves are accused. We support players through any discrimination process to a conclusion. Alongside this we work with other organisations to ensure football and equalities run side by side. I also work with clubs' Community Trusts and Foundations to ensure the programmes they run have an equalities' agenda running through them and work with trusts / foundations to have staff who represent the local demographic,as well as attending community and equality events / programmes linked to player visits and football / sport / social inclusion.

I have been with the PFA for six years after spending fifteen years within Connexions / Youth Justice working with young people and families.

Memorable Match

Nuneaton Borough 1-1 Middlesbrough -7th January 2006, FA Cup Third round

One of the most memorable matches ever seen at Manor Park, 6000 fans packed into the old ground to see Conference North team Boro take on Premiership side Middlesbrough. Terry was the most experienced player in the Boro team although he gave away a free kick for the first goal He marshalled his defence against international strikers Viduka and Yakubu. Mendieta gave Middlesbrough the lead with a free kick, Gez Murphy scored Nuneaton's equaliser in the 90th minute from the penalty spot and it was the least that Boro deserved. Middlesbrough won 4-2 in the replay at the Riverside stadium with Gez Murphy scoring both of Nuneaton's goals. The team did the town of Nuneaton proud.

Nuneaton Borough: Acton, Oddy, Moore, Angus, Love, Collins, Noon, Fitzpatrick (Reeves), Staff (Whittaker), Quailey (Frew), Murphy.

Middlesbrough: Jones, Parnaby, Southgate, Bates, Pogatetz, Morrison, Doriva, Cattermole, Mendieta, Yakubu, Viduka.

Steve Norris

One of the best strikers in non-league football in the 1980s, I had the pleasure of speaking to Steve on the phone. Born in Coventry on 22nd September 1961, Steve grew up in the Toll Bar End/Willenhall area of Coventry. As a youngster Steve played for Folly Lane winning the Coventry Telegraph Cup alongside Ian McConville another good local footballer. A spell at Coventry

Sporting caught the attention of Coventry City and Steve played in a couple of reserves matches against Everton and Wolves alongside Gerry Daly in midfield. Steve recalls Everton had a strong side with the likes of Southall, Stevens, Ratcliffe and Johnson.

Coventry were impressed by him and wanted to sign him but he never got a call! Steve played for Bedworth, Folly Lane and a prolific season with Long Buckby scoring 28 goals in 30 matches. In 1983 Steve signed for Jimmy Knox's VS Rugby to replace Ian Crawley. Steve spent four years at Butlin Road and his form alerted Frank Clark the manager of Leyton Orient. Jimmy told Steve that he wouldn't like London!

Telford came in for Steve in 1987 and his goal scoring at Bucks Head caught the attention of Sheffield Wednesday manager Howard Wilkinson. In the summer of 1988 Steve finally got his deserved break at league football. Scarborough who won promotion to the Fourth Division under Neil Warnock in 1987 signed Steve for £50,000 which was a record at the time for a non-league player. Scarborough enjoyed cup success over Portsmouth and Chelsea, Dundee United came in for Steve but Neil told him that he wouldn't like Scotland! Spells at Carlisle United, Notts County followed and then came a move to Halifax Town in 1990 finishing the 1990/91 season as the Fourth Division's top scorer with 35 goals winning the golden boot. Jimmy Greaves presented Steve with the award, legendary players Nat Lofthouse, Sir Stanley Matthews and George Best were in attendance. Jimmy was full of praise for Steve who scored his goals for a struggling lower league side.

1992 saw a move to Chesterfield which included a memorable night at Anfield. Steve played for Scarborough, VS Rugby for second spells and Worcester City before retiring from football. He now runs Ceiling Pro Chesterfield Ltd at the age of fifty eight he is looking forward to one day retiring and living in Mallorca.

Steve enjoyed playing with Danny Conway and Steve Ross at VS Rugby, Ian Juryeff at Halifax and Andy Morris at Chesterfield. Future Premiership and England striker Kevin Davies was his boot boy at Chesterfield. At Halifax Steve was the first player since Ted McDougall to score more than half his team's league goals, netting 30 of the club's 59. Only Matt Le Tissier and James Beattie, both for Southampton, have done it since.

Memorable Match

Liverpool 4-4 Chesterfield – League Cup 2nd round, 22nd September 1992

A remarkable match at Anfield, Division Three as Chesterfield stunned Premiership giants Liverpool with a three goal lead. An early Steve Norris goal and a brace from Dave Lancaster put The Spireites into dreamland! Rosenthal and Hutchison replied for Liverpool early in the second half. Steve Norris scored a fourth goal for Chesterfield, however Walters and Wright would score to make it 4-4! Liverpool would win the second leg 4-1 at Saltergate to win the tie 8-5, Trevor Hebberd scoring for Chesterfield. The Chesterfield players did the club proud with that performance against The Reds. I am sure Liverpool were mightily relieved to win the tie.

Liverpool – James, Marsh, Burrows, Tanner, Redknapp, Wright, Rosenthal, Charnock (Kozma) Hutchison, Molby, Walters

Chesterfield –Leonard, Lemon, Carr, Williams, Brien, Rogers, Cash, Norris (Turnbull) Morris, Lancaster (Kennedy) Hebberd

Ian McConville (Macca)

Ian was one of the best players in Coventry football in the 1980s and 1990s. He was born in Willenhall, Coventry and attended Whitley Abbey School. Steve Norris played with Macca as youngsters for Folly Lane when they won the Coventry Telegraph Cup. Back then Ian played in defence but later in his career he played up front.

Macca also played for Leamington in the 1985/86 season. Back then a few Coventry lads played for the Brakes. Marie (Ian's wife) kindly sent me some clippings of when Ian was at Leamington in 1986. Brakes manager John Hanna asked Ian to wear a "dustbin bag in training" in order for him to lose some weight. It had the desired effect as Ian had some good games for Leamington including scoring in a 2-0 win over Mile Oak Rovers.

In 1999 Ian was part of the Folly Lane team which beat Alveston to win the Evening Telegraph Challenge Cup. Alveston were fancied to win because they were Endsleigh Combination Premier Champions but Folly Lane of the Coventry Alliance produced a solid display to win 2-1. Steve (Norris) spoke fondly of Macca: "He enjoyed a pint and a fag and a good night out. Macca was a good player at his level and was often picked for pick of the league." In 2002 he won the Birmingham FA Veterans' Cup with Folly Lane as they beat Triplex Star 4-2 after extra time. Macca scored Folly Lane's late equaliser and assisted one of the goals in extra time. He sadly passed away on the 9th of April 2015 aged fifty three.

Josh Blake

A Leamington FC modern day legend, Josh is a cult hero at the New Windmill. Leamington FC reformed in 2000, twelve years after the club went into abeyance in 1988. Josh is the record appearance holder and record goalscorer since 2000. He played local football for Leamington Hibernians and Central Ajax, before being signed by Jason Cadden. From 2000 to 2009 Josh made 405 appearances scoring 187 goals during which time the Brakes won five promotions, four league titles and various cup wins. Josh has also played for Daventry Town, Racing Club Warwick and Coventry United. Josh scored thirty three goals in forty appearances for Coventry United between 2014 and 2016. During his career he formed striking partnerships with Ben Mackay and Joshua O'Grady. He is still playing Sunday League football. He won the Birmingham Sunday Vase with Leamington Hibernian in 2019.

At Daventry, Josh played mostly left back/wing back which is a position he played in his junior days. Josh reached the FA Cup First Round with Leamington and Daventry, enjoyable occasions but not the results. Josh is a modern day Coventry and Warwickshire non-league legend and an "all-round top bloke."

Josh O'Grady

One of the best players in local football, Josh is a talented attacking midfielder very good at taking on players who contributes a lot of goals too. I asked Josh a few questions about his career via email.

Could you tell me what school and junior teams you played for?

I went to King Henry XIII School but they didn't play football there. They played mostly Rugby instead unfortunately! I started playing as a kid with Kenilworth Wardens when I was around nine years old and stayed there for about three or four years before getting picked up by Coventry City. I spent three years at City before being released when I was sixteen.

I believe that you you played with Daniel Sturridge for Coventry Boys?

Yes Sturridge was a year below me at Coventry but regularly played in my age group. He was the stand out player and was head and shoulders above the rest of us. I think I only played for one season with him though before he moved to Man City.

You and Josh Blake formed a fantastic partnership at Coventry United. What do you think made it click?

I played with Blakey for a good number of years and I just think our games complimented each other really well. I liked to play forward passes with balls splitting defences or over the top and he loved to make runs in behind so it worked well. It was just one of those things that clicked almost instantly and we contributed a lot of goals together over the years at Daventry, Coventry United and briefly at Racing club Warwick. He was a top non-league player for a number of years and we remain good friends still now. I'm sure it won't be too long before we are linking up together on Sundays when I get a bit older.

You played in some Coventry derbies between Sphinx and United. Did you play for both teams in those matches and what was the rivalry like?

Yes I think I have played roughly eight or nine Coventry derbies between United and Sphinx playing for both teams. I could be wrong but I think I've had a pretty good record of only losing one game, in a cup replay. You always look forward to that game though and I've always had friends on the opposite side which always makes it that bit more interesting. There are quite a few players who've played for both teams now and you always want to do well against your old clubs so it's an exciting fixture.

Who are you currently playing for?

I haven't officially signed for anyone yet for next season due to Covid-19 but have been training with Coventry United where I will likely stay. We have unfinished business after the league was voided last year when we were sitting top.

Graham Smith

A full back, Graham was born in Coventry and lived in the Stoke / Wyken area. A good friend of Mick Kearns he went to college with him and they also played golf together at Nuneaton Golf Club. Graham spent time at Aston Villa as a young player, then played local non-league mostly for Bedworth and Hinckley.

In the mid-1960s Graham played against Coventry City at Bedworth's Oval ground. He recalls the likes of Bill Glazier, Ronnie Rees, Brian Hill and George Curtis. He suffered a bad Achilles injury and was at Highfield Road for treatment, the physio being Norman Pilgrim. One time there was a film crew filming the changing rooms and there was some curiosity to who Graham was, some thought he was a new signing!

Graham talked about players that he played with including Ken Brown, George Awde and Eddy Brown. The latter became Bedworth player-manager in March 1965. Graham remembers playing in his first match for Bedworth which was a 3-2 win over Bilston. Ken Brown scored in that match for Bedworth. (He is no relation to Eddy). When he became player-manager at Bedworth Eddy was thirty six. He had a good career playing for a few teams including Coventry City and Birmingham City. Other players who stood out were Bobby Hope and David Burnside. Graham feels that David had amazing skill but lacked the toughness to become one of the greats.

Edwin (Eddie) Greaves

Edwin is very well known in the Coventry football scene, I contacted him by phone and had a chat about his career. Edwin was a centre forward as a player for local teams Meadway and Lennon Athletic in the 1980s and 1990s. He was once selected for Coventry pick of the league XI.

Edwin, who is a driving instructor, first managed a Sunday League team called "Edwin School of Motoring" who are still going. Edwin then managed Coventry Amateurs who had reformed from Coventry Sporting FC nineteen years previously and Coventry Spartans on Sundays. A Sky Blues' fan he once lived near Highfield Road but once he started managing he didn't have too much time to watch City.

Coventry United were formed in 2013 from Coventry Spartans, the same time Coventry City announced they would be playing home matches at Sixfields, Northampton. Edwin was named Coventry United's first manager. The club held trials for players in the summer of 2013. The first season was a success they were Midland Combination Division Two runners up. For the beginning of the 2014/15 season the Midland Alliance and Midland Combination merged. United were Placed in Division Two in new structure. Edwin led the team to the league championship and promotion to Division One. A memorable match was when Coventry United hammered Polesworth 28-0 in April 2014. Edwin recalls Brian Ndlovu and Daniel Stokes both getting hat tricks. "It was one of those games when we had to be ruthless. Polesworth had a depleted team."

Edwin enjoyed his time at Coventry United winning trophies. "It was like a family." Football can be cruel and he was sacked by United in the spring of 2016 despite the team looking certain for promotion. It was Edwin's lowest point in football and took him a little while to get back into the game. Edwin had a brief spell in charge of Brinklow FC, then took over at AFC Binley in the Coventry Alliance leading the team to two promotions. Edwin is assisted by Dave Watkins who played for Leamington FC in the 1980s.

Edwin is very passionate about football and providing affordable football for all. He is a very humble man who was a little surprised when I made contact with him about the book. He is still an important part of Coventry's recent non-league football history and is still very much involved with the game.

Brian Ndlovu

Born in Zimbabwe, Brian played for Highlanders Juniors FC in Bulawayo, Zimbabwe. He moved over to UK aged seventeen.

Brian is the youngest of this famous footballing family. When Brian moved to Coventry he didn't know any local teams. He first played for GNP Sports, Finham and Caludon (Sunday) Kenilworth Town and Stratford Town 'A'.

In 2007/ 2008 he suffered an horrific double leg break playing at Newbold Comyn in Leamington. This was a result of a bad tackle on his blindside, it took nine months to recover. During rehab, Brian volunteered as a coach for Young Warriors FC. Once he was back playing, Brian played for Young Warriors in the Midland Combination League, He scored fifty goals in thirty appearances and was top scorer in the Midlands. In the 2011/12 season they resigned mid-season and their record expunged. Brian also had a spell playing for Long Buckby in Northamptonshire. He actually met Edwin Greaves whilst playing against Coventry Spartans. When Coventry United were formed in 2013, Brian and Stefan McGrath son of Lloyd McGrath were the club's first signings.

Brian talked about the 28-0 win against Polesworth, including one of his fastest hat tricks. At Coventry United he played with some great players – Josh Blake, Patrick Suffo, Joshua O'Grady, Gift Mussa, Jean Dacouri, Chris Cox, Ben Mackey and Daniel Stokes, a friendly rivalry with Daniel in which which one of them would be top goalscorer. Brian stopped playing for United in 2016/17 due to having a young family, He has played occasionally since for Coventrians' Reserves, Coventry Plumbing Reserves and he is currently scoring goals for AFC Binley under former Coventry United boss Edwin Greaves. The Ndlovu football family is still going: Brian's son has spent time with Coventry City and West Bromwich Albion academies.

Brian spoke fondly of his footballing siblings: Adam, his sister and another brother all played football. Peter is obviously the most famous of the family. Brian remembers watching him for Coventry City and Sheffield United post 2001. The author told Brian that Sky Blues' fans adored Peter since he scored that fantastic goal against Aston Villa in 1991. The author's personal favourite Nuddy goal was the winner against West Bromwich Albion in the FA Cup in January 1995.

Ian Crawley

The third generation of a very good footballing family, Ian's grandfather was Tommy Crawley Senior who played for Coventry City, Preston North End and Motherwell. During the war time seasons Tommy was one of Coventry City's best players and he scored plenty of goals. Tommy Crawley Junior was Ian's father. He was a striker who played for Nuneaton Borough in the 1960s.

Ian went to Bishop Ullathorne School and played for junior teams Mount Nod and Europa. In 1977 he signed for Nuneaton Borough from Coventry Sphinx. With a successful career in non-league football with VS Rugby, Kettering Town, Solihull Borough, Nuneaton Borough and Telford United. Ian is famous for scoring the winning goal in two Wembley finals in the 1980s.

A Tribute by John Setchell

Ian was obviously a very close friend of mine, and a tragic loss. Ian, was a wholehearted player who provided 100% to ever occasion (on and off field). He processed great heading ability, and was most certainly a handful for opposing defenders. I had the unfortunate situation of mostly getting changed with him, as I probably got more injuries from Ian's elbows and stamping on my foot before we even entered the pitch. Punctuality was not one of his greatest strengths, guaranteed to be always late. Ian, is very sadly missed by all that he engaged with, a really lovely person, and one of the best forwards I played with, I believe Ian still holds the record of scoring winning goals in both FA Trophy and FA Vase finals - God bless him.

Brenton (Brendan) Phillips

Brendan was a talented midfielder who was one of the best players in local non-league football in the 1970s and 1980s. I had the pleasure of speaking to Brendan about his football career. He was born in Jamaica on the 16th of July 1954, Brendan moved to Coventry as a young child. The young Brendan went to Edgwick, Broad Heath and Longford Park Secondary Modern schools. Brendan played for Coventry Boys and Warwickshire Boys from under 12 to under 16 levels. On 2nd November 1968 Brendan was selected for Warwickshire Schools for a match against Worcestershire in Stourbridge. The other Coventry players chosen were Jones and Phillips (Longford Park) Ambrose and Munday (Woodlands) and Starling (Whitley Abbey).

In April 1969 Coventry and District under-15 team visited the North East. 'Brenton' Phillips, an inside-forward from Longford Park School, impressed scouts from Newcastle United. Brendan however had signed associate schoolboy forms with Coventry City. In December 1969 Brendan signed for Coventry City on schoolboy form sat the same time as Michael Wilson from Durham.

After leaving Coventry City he joined Leicester City. Brendan, growing up in Coventry, obviously wanted to play for the Sky Blues but he enjoyed his time at Leicester. In the early 1970s The Foxes had senior players like Keith Weller, Alan Birchenall, Frank Worthington and Peter Shilton, so it was good experience for Brendan. During his time at Leicester he met good friend Tom

Kilkelly who went on to play for Northampton Town and AP Leamington. In March 1971 he scored twice for Leicester in a thrilling 4-3 defeat to Nottingham Forest. On 22nd December 1971 Brendan helped Leicester City Youth beat Coventry City Youth 3-1. Jimmy Holmes scored Coventry's goal from the penalty spot.The young Sky Blues included Graham Oakey, Mick Ferguson and Alan Green. Brendan assisted Joe Waters for Leicester's third goal.

Peterborough United was his next destination and in 1973 Brendan made his Football League debut for The Posh. Notts County were interested in him but he decided against it as Scottish international Don Masson was their midfield star so his first team chances were limited. In 1974 Brendan joined Burton Albion who had Ian Storey-Moore and Peter Ward in their ranks. The next move was the best of his career: in August 1976 Nuneaton Borough manager Stan Bennett signed Brendan on a free transfer from Burton.

It was a great era at Manor Park where there were talented young players in Trevor Peake and Kirk Stephens. Brendan also talked about Bob Turpie, Bobby Vincent and Gary Fleet as great players. In 1979 Howard Wilkinson selected Brendan and Trevor to play for England C (Semi-Professional) team. In May 1979 Brendan, Trevor and Duncan Gardner of AP Leamington were selected to play for a Southern League XI against a Northern Premier League XI. Brendan played for Nuneaton Borough again in the 1980s after spells with Kettering Town, Mansfield Town and Boston United. In the early 1980s Nuneaton Borough had another good team with players like Richard Hill, Trevor Morley and Paul Culpin with whom Brendan felt honoured to play in two very good Boro teams.

Later in the decade Brendan played for Aylesbury United under Trevor Gould who enjoyed success and won promotion to the

Conference. On the 4th of June 1988 Aylesbury played an unusual friendly match against England! Yes the full national team! Brendan remembers this match very well. England were training at nearby Bisham Abbey. The match was arranged by journalist Frank McGhee who was a friend of Aylesbury chairman Charlie Doherty. The match itself was a comfortable 7-0 win for England with Peter Beardsley scoring four of the goals. Aylesbury record goal scorer Cliff Hercules almost scored with a header. Brendan recalls he was mesmerised by the likes of Hoddle, Lineker, Waddle, Barnes and Beardsley who were on a different level spraying passes about the pitch. On YouTube there is some footage of the match and pre match. England were soon off to West Germany for Euro 1988. We were dire at that tournament losing every group stage match and being knocked out early. Aylesbury would spend one season at Conference level finishing twentieth in the 1988/89 season.

Brendan went into management with Bedworth United, Stafford Rangers, Halesowen Town, Nuneaton Borough and Coalville Town. In particular at Boro, Brendan feels like the club should have gone on to another level with the fan base they had. Manor Park possibly should have been developed or moved to a site in the heartlands of the town. Brendan gave one of own clubs Burton Albion as an example of how a non-league club can progress.

A Tribute by Ian Goodwin

Brendan, "The Bear or Huggy Bear". Pure class! He ran the midfield like a general. He had exceptional vision and, boy, could he pick a pass! He had the skills and ability to control the pace of the game which is a rare attribute. I remember we went down to Wealstone on the Saturday and beat then 4-1. On the Wednesday we went to Weymouth and took on player manager Jeff Astle and beat them 4- 1. Brendan contributed so much to what was a pretty good team.

Gary Bradder

One of the best players in Nuneaton in the late 1970s and early 1980s, Gary has enjoyed a good career in non-league football. I spoke to Gary and asked him a few questions about his football career.

Gary attended Manor Park School in Nuneaton. In his early playing days he was a goalkeeper. Gary's first Saturday team was Bermuda WMC who were a successful team. They won the Birmingham Junior Cup. On Sundays he played with future star Nigel Winterburn for Attleborough Mills under popular local manager Sid Clay.

Gary joined Bedworth United who had a good side in the late 1970s. They narrowly missed out on joining the new Alliance Premier in 1979. The Greenbacks however enjoyed success in the Birmingham Senior Cup. Gary played alongside Danny Conway for them.

Gary then joined Atherstone United for his first spell which was about four or five years. He then joined Gloucester City who were managed by former Aston Villa and Wales international Brian Godfrey. Traveling to Gloucester got a bit much and he moved back to Atherstone although, Burton Albion had shown interest. The Adders were a good side in 1990 and they had a good FA Cup run and reached the final of the Birmingham Senior Cup. Gary remembers the Crewe FA Cup match when they gave their league opponents a good game. Atherstone played West Bromwich Albion in the Birmingham Senior Cup. They lost to a Baggies team who included Brian Talbot and Sam Allardyce. Jimmy Knox then signed Gary for VS Rugby at the same time as Ian Crawley. Jimmy had tried to sign Gary when he was in charge of AP Leamington.

In February 1993, at the age of thirty one, Gary joined Nuneaton Borough. They enjoyed a fine Cup run beating Swansea City which Gary says was one of his favourite matches. In July 1994 Gary joined Hinckley Town for a couple of seasons. Gary became player/manager of Sutton Coldfield where he struggled at first but when he was joined by Dave Grundy they enjoyed success. In the 1998/99 season they won the Dr Martins League Cup beating Cambridge City. Gary played briefly for Nuneaton Griff: by then he was forty eight or forty nine possibly the club's oldest ever player. Outside football he is a massive Beatles fan and ran tours. He lived in Liverpool for a couple of years. Gary is hoping to restart the tours again. He told me that Strawberry Fields has been transformed. The author and his wife did the Magical Mystery tour for his 40th and reports that it is very good.

Matty Fowler(Burt)

Matty is a centre half for Coventry Copeswood, I asked him a few questions via Facebook and email. The author worked with him in 2009/2010. He has gone on to have a good career in local football.

What junior teams did you play for?

Jaguar Daimler, Dunlop, Coventry Schools, West Midlands Schools

What senior teams have you played for?

Coventry University 1st Team, Coventry Copsewood, Coventry Sphinx, Copsewood Coventry

Who would you say was the best striker you played against?

Not sure there is a real stand-out but I remember learning a lot as a defender in my first couple of games at Coventry Sphinx. In that league there are lots of experienced strikers that have been around the professional and non-league game for a number of years and I felt these always posed the biggest challenge compared to younger guys. There was one player called Daniel N'ti that I came up against on a few occasions where I always knew I was in for a tough game. He was clever, quick, strong and had an eye for goal. Playing Worcester City at Aggborough in the FA Cup qualifying was probably one of my toughest games as a defender. They had talent throughout the squad and N'ti was playing as the number nine for them at the time. The night before the game they had loaned a winger from Torquay too, so the two of them were a handful on the day and we were knocked out following a second half red-card for us at 1-0 and a couple of first half chances hitting the post for us. Worcester team made it to the second round proper the following year so they were building a strong team.

What are was it like playing at the Ricoh? Were they your favourite matches?

Every final at the Ricoh is a great occasion and is always set up well for an end of season finale if you made it there. Having played there several times and being on winning and losing sides, it's certainly much better being on the winning side! I think captaining Copsewood and scoring there in the same final in 2018 would be my favourite memory. I also hold a pretty good record in the competition as I managed to win the Junior Telegraph Cup as a Y11 schoolboy with Cardinal Newman in 2005, the Senior Telegraph Cup as a player with Copsewood and also the Junior Telegraph Cup as a teacher with our Y11 North Leamington School students 2017 - that is something that I am also extremely proud of.

Craig Dutton

Craig was an experienced midfielder who had a great spell at Leamington under Jason Cadden (Cadzy)

Could you tell me about your junior career what teams you played for?

My Sunday League Junior career I played all my time with Mount Nod. My dad was the manager and my inspiration He pushed me lots as a kid and did so much to set me up and was my biggest fan. We won many league and cups and I had many great times as a kid and some big battles especially with local rivals Ernesford Dynamos at the time. In the early days when first joined the team it was not all plain sailing we had to build a great side, I remember coming home on some Sundays losing 16-0 / 20-0..they were fun times and memories I'll never forget and I stillhave great friends from that time now.

Are you the same Craig Dutton that played in goal for RCW? When did you convert to a midfielder?

I have been in midfielder all my career The benefit of naturally being fit made it an easy choice to make for me plus not being that technically gifted was probably the best outcome. I started mostly left sided in my younger days but then moved more to a central role as got older and wiser. I wasn't bothered in having the lime light but had more satisfaction being the provider/stopper rather than the deliver.

You were a great signing for Leamington. Did you enjoy your time playing for Cadzy?

Thanks. I hope I was a success in my two and a half / three seasons although it seems such long time ago. You do question whether you were successful, Being captain for the club was a special moment too. I loved it with Cadzy. We had a great changing room and I had a great relationship with him. The lads were brilliant We had a mix of young and old heads but the right attitude to win games. Whilst he was not a 'name' manager at that level as such he had a great knowledge about the game, knew what he wanted and brought his own ways and theories to play. Cadzy was great manager and deserves the accolades for what he achieved at the club, a legend!

Who did you play for after Leamington?

I Played for Barwell after Leamington and had another great three years winning the league twice and got to the semi-final of the FA Vase and lost so devastatingly in extra time to Whitley Bay 4 -3. I retired at thirty seven from non-league after playing seventeen

years at a decent level. I miss it so much but miss the banter and
that changing experience more than anything.

Jack Edwards

Jack is currently captain of Leamington FC, born in Coventry on
31st March 1990. He attended King Henry XIII School and he
played junior football for Balsall Hornets and Stratford Town
Under 16. Jack's dad Mark was a coach at Stratford who played for
Coventry Sporting in the 1970s.

Jack spent some time with Coventry City and then began his non-
league career with Studley. He then played for Coventry Sphinx
under manager Danny McSheffrey and coach Lee Knibbs. A spell
at Jimmy Ginnelly's Barwell then followed. Jack studied at
Nottingham Trent University the football team played at an
excellent standard. On 9th February 2013 Jack was part of the
Barwell team that Hammered Leamington 6-0 at the New
Windmill. Jack was playing in defence back then, it was only a
minor hiccup for Leamington as they won the Southern Football
League Premier Division that season. In 2014 Jack joined
Leamington. His performances earned him a move to Solihull
Moors in 2017 but competition for places meant his stay was quite
short and he returned to Leamington. In his second spell with the
Brakes he has become such an important player, the focal point of
the team. Playing in a number ten attacking midfield role Jack is a
big threat in the air and makes the team tick. Jack has made over
270 appearances in the gold and black. Now captain he is an
important player as Leamington compete in the Nationwide North.
Check out a long range effort he scored against Cinderford a few
years ago on YouTube.

Tom Kilkelly

Tom was born in Galway on 22nd August 1955. A defender or midfielder, he was part of a good AP Leamington team of the late 1970s/ early 1980s. He began his career with Leicester City in the early 70s playing with his good friend Brendan Phillips. Tom played for Republic of Ireland at youth level with Joe Waters (a team mate at Leicester City) David Langan, Liam Brady, Frank Stapleton and Don O'Riordan. Senior players at Filbert Street in the early 1970s included Peter Shilton, Keith Weller, Frank Worthington, David Nish, Alan Birchenall and Graham Cross. Tom also played for Northampton Town, and then had a spell in South Africa and with Dublin side Shamrock Rovers. Jimmy Knox signed Tom for AP Leamington and he had five seasons for the Brakes. Tom was part of the team that played in the first season of the Alliance Premier 1979/80. He played for Bedworth United in 1982 then went onto have a successful career in Australia as a player then a coach. I asked Tom a few questions about his career.

How old were you when you moved from Galway?

I was five years old in 1960 when we moved over to England.

Who were your favourite players growing up?

I'm a Derby County fan always have been. My first Rams' favourite was Alan Durban, Frank Upton then Kevin Hector arrived and of course Roy McFarland and Colin Todd . I did have a soft spot for Chelsea - Bobby Tambling and Charlie Cooke.

It must have been great being part of the AP Leamington team that competed in the Alliance Premier. Would you say that it was one of the best teams that you played in?

AP was a really enjoyable period for me, the players & coaching staff. I have fond memories of my time there and the friends I made I still look out for their results.

Representing Republic of Ireland must have been a great honour. How many times did you play for your country?

Playing for my country was unbelievable: just being out there when the national anthem was played was something I will always remember. I was capped fourteen times and eight 8 times I was captain.

Marcus Hamill

Marcus was one of the most talented players in local football in the 1990s and 2000s. He was a couple of years older than the author at Cardinal Newman School. The midfielder / winger played junior football for Christ the King and was scouted by Stoke City and spent time up there going back and forth for about three years. Marcus also played for Coventry Boys. He was told at Stoke at sixteen that he wouldn't be signed because he was too small. His height didn't improve. That was ridiculous as Marcus had so much ability! He then went into local football with Massey Ferguson, Christ the King, Highway and Coundon Court. Marcus is best remembered for his two spells with Stratford Town which was one of the most exciting times in the club's history. Under manager Len Derby they finished second in the 1999/00 Midland Alliance. In Len's time at the club they attracted ex professionals Dave Bennett, Tony Morley, Ian Muir, Dennis Bailey and Michael Gynn. Len also brought the best out of Marcus who rates Len as his best ever manager. Talented Coventry based players Michael Stephenson, Peter McBean and Gerry Carr also played for Stratford Town. Marcus also played for a good Evesham United side in the 1990s, strikers Jason Percival and Danny Finlay benefitted from playing with Marcus in the 1997/98 season. A side which also included Andy Beechey, Paul O'Brien and Marcus Law. Marcus joined Coventry Marconi in 2001 the same time as Darren Dickson and he also played for Wellesbourne, Peugeot and Jaguar. A lot of players who have played with Marcus have told me that he was quality player and one of the best they have played with.

Richard Landon

Richard was born on 22nd March 1965 in Worthing but grew up in Nuneaton. I spoke to Richard and he told me that he began his football journey playing with friends on Sundays for Alderman Smith. Ron Bradbury, who was Atherstone manager, asked him to come down for a trial. Back then he got paid about £38 a week. It wasn't until he moved to Stratford Town under Ron Mason did his career take off. In two seasons he scored 75 goals. In March 1993 he signed dual registration with Nuneaton Borough but didn't make the breakthrough at Manor Park. Richard moved to Bedworth United and hit some form for the Greenbacks. In December 1993 he scored a hat rick against Stourbridge which prompted Halesowen Town to bid for him.

England's legendary goalkeeper Peter Shilton who was player-manager of Plymouth Argyle invited Richard for a trial. In May 1994 he scored a hat rick for Plymouth as they hammered Hartlepool 8-1! Richard rates Steve McCall, his team mate at Plymouth, as the best player with whom he played. Steve previously played Division One football with Ipswich Town and Sheffield Wednesday. Richard also played league football for Stockport County, Macclesfield Town and Rotherham United. He finished his career in non-league with Altrincham, Droylesden. Hednesford Town and Vauxhall Motors, Richard is now the kit man for Stockport County.

Andy Beechey

Andy was a defender most notably for his time with Stratford Town where he made an impressive 191 appearances. He also had a good career in Coventry football with Triumph Athletic, Alvis and JFK.

What teams did you play for?

Junior/ Minor/Youth Teams Sundays

Windmill Lions – Sunday Coventry Minor League first ever club 1973-1975

Stoke Heath Rangers – Sunday Coventry Minor League 1975-78

Mount Nod Juniors – 1978-80 Sunday Coventry Minor League won league and cup

Folly Lane Youth Team – 1980 -1983 Sunday Coventry & Warwickshire Youth League, won league and cup

Adult Sunday Teams

Rose and Woodbine Circa 1983 , Ajax F.C Circa 1984, Alvis S&S Club from around 1989/90 until around 1997/98 (Premier League winners and several cups). JFK 1998-2000 (League & Colwyn Villa Bowl winners)

Youth Teams Saturday

Coventry Boys' Club Coventry Saturday Youth League (Circa1978/79) won the league and a few cups

Saturday Adult Men's Teams

Massey Ferguson (1981/82/83), Racing Club Warwick about (1981/82/83). I was in the reserves at Racing Club; l Ray Hannam was Manager, Dietmar Bruck was first team manager. I did get some first team matches when one of the regular players were injured.

Triumph Athletic 1983/84 (1987 – Telegraph Cup Winners 1988-1989 Alliance Premier Winners 1989-1990). Stratford Town - 1991-1996/97 - 1998/99-2001/02 (191) Appearances club record only beaten recently. Evesham - 1997/98 Chris Robinson Manager Martin Bewell Assistant (Signed for Evesham start of the season but went back to Stratford on Loan around March 1998 but went back the Evesham in April [I ended up playing for both where possible as I was trying to help stop Stratford getting relegated). One week I played Saturday for Evesham, Sunday for JFK Tuesday for Stratford, Wednesday for JFK Thursday for Stratford and then Saturday for Evesham

I re-signed For Stratford 1998/99. We were runners up in the Interlink Alliance 1999/2000 season. I left Stratford for Alveston at the start of 2000/2001 season, I had left around Oct / Nov of the 2001/2002 Season to go to Brooklands Jaguar's First team. I played for the first team under John Flavell, In the 2004/05 season (I played for the 1st team in the Telegraph cup 2004/05 lost 5-0 to Sphinx) 2005/06 won Alliance 2 with the reserves and played the following season 2006/07. For the 2007/08 season I signed for Woodlands first team then Moved to Woodland reserves around

2008/09 till 2009/10 we won Pete Toogood Cup and got man of the match at forty four.

Who were the favourite players that you played with?

Best Manager / management team played under - Ken Brown & Dave Owen

Best Players played with –

Goal Keepers *Paul Fletcher & Andy Russell*

Defenders *- Triumph Athletic John Flavell, Steve Brophy, and Steve Mead we had a solid Back four one of the best in the league at the time. Stratford Town Carl Bannister Mark Robinson (digger) from the 1993 team good defenders and could play football. Also Norman Batchelor strong defender took no prisoners. Richard Holt from 1999 team strong player, Paul O'Brien good defender, good going forward*

Midfielders *Stratford Town - Gary Hannam good friend whilst at Stratford, unbelievable engine and good footballer. Easton Shaw, holding midfielder not many got past him. Marcus Hamill fast, skilful wide midfielder quality player.*

Triumph Simon Saunders, Steve Guest, Steve Quinn all solid players who could play but get stuck in if needed

Forwards *Triumph Kevin Sloan quick and good finisher, Chris Lacey strong, good in the air good finisher.*

Stratford Town - Richard Landon, good all-round striker golden boot winner in Combination Premier League. Craig Martin sharp, skilful and good finisher, Nick Kirk hard to get the ball off sharp

and good finisher. Peter McBean towards the end of his career when I played with him but still quality, linked up well with Craig.

In November 1993 Andy was excelling in a sweeper role and helped Stratford Town beat Wolverhampton Wanderers 1-0 in the Birmingham Senior Cup. In the next round Stratford Town drew 1-1 against a strong Birmingham City team. The Blues included George Parris, Danny Wallace, Paul Peschisolido, Louie Donowa and David Smith. Birmingham City, under new manager Barry Fry, won the replay 2-1.

Andy was part of the Stratford Town team which finished second in the 1999/00 season. In September 1999 they got a great win in the FA Vase beating Wednesfield who were the league leaders 2-1. After going a goal behind, Peter McBean equalised and John Brant got the winner.

Chris Downes

Chris was a forward who was a regular goal scorer in local football. I spoke to him about his playing days. Chris attended Sidney Stringer School where he was in the same class as Terry Hall of The Specials. As a youngster Chris played rugby then got into football and played for Self-Changing Gears FC. In 1978 he joined Coventry Sporting, top scoring for the reserves then playing briefly for the first team. In 1980 Chris joined Bedworth United managed by John Brady. The Greenbacks had some good players – Dennis Taylor, Danny Conway and Ian Crawley. Chris joined AP Leamington in 1983 after they had controversially been denied promotion the previous season. He had a good season with the Brakes playing up front with Kim Casey and Cliff Campbell. One of his best games for AP was in January 1984 when he scored twice in a 4-1 win over Gloucester City. Graham Allner had built a great side but it broke up in the summer of 1984 with a few players joining Allner at Kidderminster. Chris joined Jimmy Knox's VS

Rugby in 1984 then joined Moor Green in 1986. He spent about four seasons with the Birmingham team and played with former AP Leamington team mates Steve Rigby and Malcolm Kavanagh. Future Premiership players David Busst and Ian Taylor were also Moor Green players. Moors finished second in the Southern League Midland Division in 1988. Chris then had spells with Racing Club Warwick and Leicester United. He played in Ian Crawley's testimonial and in a match for a Leamington XI against an Aston Villa All-stars XI. Villa won 9-0, Chris remembers the game well and told me that Dennis Mortimer and Gordon Cowans played in the match. Now a director at an engineering company, Chris manages Coventry Sunday League team The Brooklands FC.

Danny Finlay

Danny was a striker who played for a few non-league sides. He is from Rugby and attended Ashlawn School. Danny played for Atherstone, Rugby Town, Sutton Coldfield, Rothwell, Daventry, Barwell, Long Buckby, Evesham and two spells with Racing Club Warwick. In 2004/ 05 he had a seven day approach to join Leamington and Long Buckby. He chose Long Buckby because he would have better first team chances. Danny was good in the air and strong on the ball, a forward who scored his fair share of goals but also created opportunities for others. Danny was assistant manager at Rugby Borough and played quite a bit and they enjoyed early success after they were formed in 2017. Now in his forties he is still playing Sunday League football for Coundon Vets over 35s Reserves. Danny previously played for Leamington Vets under Tony Clarke. Danny named his best XI that he played with – Steve Cherry, Tony Clarke, Tom McGinty, Dougie Keast, Paul West, Steve Jackson, Andy Kirkup, Rich Lavery, Liam Dixon, Gary Bradder, Keith Russell subs Nicky Kirk, Kieron Sullivan, Leigh Everett, Steve Campbell, Darren Harmon. Danny has played in a few VS Rugby legends' matches and he is a keen Sky Blues fan.

Scott Darroch

Scott was well known striker in Warwickshire football in the 1990s and 2000s. He grew up in Foleshill and Stoke Heath and attended John Gulson, Stoke Heath and Stoke Park Schools. As a kid he was a keen Chess player. He got into football when the Sky Blues won the FA Cup. Scott played for a few teams in junior football. He went to Coventry School of excellence under Lol Cairns and Phil Nardiello. His name wasn't on the list but they gave him a trial. During his time there he played with John Curtis who would go on to play for Manchester United and Blackburn Rovers. Scott told me that John was the stand out player. He was big for his age. Scott spent time with Birmingham School of Excellence and West Bromwich Albion. Getting a professional contract was hard and Scott played for local teams Chaplefields and Bedworth United. Next was Nuneaton Borough who inherited a fine youth team from Bedworth. In November 1996 Scott was part of the Boro youth team that played against Everton in the FA Youth Cup. Nuneaton's youngsters gave a good account of themselves but lost to Everton. The Toffees included Richard Dunne, Michael Ball, Phil Jeavons, Michael Branch and Danny Cadamarteri who all had good football careers. Scott remembers watching Michael Branch a week later in the Merseyside derby for Everton's first team. It goes to show the calibre of players Everton had. Danny Cadamarteri was the stand out player in the Everton team against Boro. Scott played for Nuneaton Borough's youth team and reserves but got released.

Scott had a good spell at Stratford Town and he finished top scorer during the 1999/2000 season. Scott also played for Bedworth, Halesowen, Redditch and Leamington. He talked about some of the players he played with during his career. Jai Stanley who was in the same Nuneaton Borough youth team was class. Scott talked about Peter McBean, Brian Quailey, Paul White, Kevin Elvin, Marcus Hamill and Michael Stephenson. Scott is well travelled: he spent time in Australia, Thailand and now lives in Sweden. He has lived in Stockholm for about twelve years and has learnt to speak fluently in Swedish. Scott didn't play for Leamington very long but is remembered by fans for a brilliant goal against Barwell.

Gary Hannam

Gary was born in South Africa but moved to Coventry at a young age. He played for Wyken Athletic before joining Racing Club Warwick. He also played for AP Leamington and Stratford Town. In 1984 Gary joined AP Leamington. It was a turbulent time for the club as a lot of the senior players had gone. In 1983 AP Leamington won the Southern League but were cruelly denied promotion because the ground was deemed not up to standard. Most of the star players of that team stayed for the 1983/84 season but by the summer of 1984 the likes of Kim Casey, Cliff Campbell had left the Brakes. A lot of the players ended up at Kidderminster Harriers under former AP boss Graham Allner. Gary, along with a few other players from Coventry like Gary Hardwick, Mick McGinty, Steve Ross and Mick Shearer, were in the Brakes team. I asked Gary about his time at the Old Windmill.

Jim Watson had a thankless task that season as he had a load of young local players and threw them in with one or two ex-league apprentices. I don't even remember a pre-season friendly, a very disjointed start! We just about held our own for a few games but with some long suspensions we were down to the bare bones. I remember going to Dover and a few guys were unavailable and along with suspensions I think we got done by six goals. It was very hard for a very young side! Personally I had a bit of success with a brace in the Farnham win and a couple of assists but I had come from a great family club at Racing and being dropped into such a disjointed and cold environment was not great fun. As you know the whole team had left the season before and there was no experienced spine to the team. Jim had a hotshot striker coming in from a top side and needed to budget so he let me and another go, Even though I was a midfielder/wide man at the time. However the next week the striker never moved and he asked me back to play on the Tuesday (apparently the fans quite liked me) but of course that would not have worked so I guess perhaps I only played 10-12 games for Leamington. However playing for Leamington in the Southern League was an honour.

During the 1987/88 season Gary helped Racing Club Warwick win the Midland Combination Premier League. He played over 40 games as the Racers also enjoyed a good FA Cup run. The team had a good blend of experience and youth with players like Darren Deeley, Malc Hyland, Alan Stacey, Craig Dandridge, Ian Bettles and Ian Gorrie.

Chapter Seven - Coventry Sporting FC

The club was formed in 1936 as the works team of the Coventry Tile Company. In 1946 they changed names to Coventry Amateurs FC .In the club's early days they played at the Butts Stadium before moving to Kirby Corner Road in 1948. In 1967 they joined the West Midlands (Regional) League Division One, finishing runners up in 1970 and 1973. In 1974 they changed names to Coventry Sporting. A year later the club had its finest hour beating Tranmere Rovers in the FA Cup. In 1983 they won promotion to The Southern League Midland Division, playing at that level until the club folded in 1989. In this chapter we are going to look at some of the players who played for Coventry Amateurs and Coventry Sporting.

Kenneth Puffett

Kenneth played for Coventry Amateurs in the late 1960s, mainly at left half. I asked him a few questions about his career.

What teams did you play for?

Saturday teams - Sherbourne juniors, Wyken WMC, Bradby Boy's Club, Warwickshire Youth, Hen lane Social and Coventry Amateurs.

Sunday teams- Coventry Railwaymen FC, Tom Mann Social FC. I moved to Hinckley in 1972 and played for a few clubs including Hinckley Athletic. I trained with the Sky Blues In 1968 with Willie Carr and a few others.

Are you still playing walking football?

I am still playing walking football on Tuesday morning: you can tell who played at a decent level of football. It is really enjoyable and I'm lucky enough to be able to still play the game I've loved football since I first started in 1959.

Bob Abercrombie

I asked Bob a couple of questions about his career. He played for Coventry Amateurs in the 1960s and 1970s.

I believe that you went to school with Roy Deakin and Bobby Gould. You must have had a good school team.

I was at school (Caludon Castle) with Roy Deakin and Bobby Gould and we played together in under 13/14/15 teams and also Coventry City Boys. We were a formidable trio!

What position did you play and what other teams did you play for?

After I left school, I played for the Standard, Folly Lane and GEC (which later became called GPT, Marconi and now Copsewood). I left GEC to join the Amateurs in1968 and stayed there for about four and half years before returning to the GEC. My position was right wing (no 7). I was a very fast runner in those days and a good crosser of the ball! I also scored quite a lot of goals, particularly headers! I enjoyed my time at the Amateurs and it was a good experience playing in a higher league of football.

Mel Davis

Mel was a versatile player who played for Lockheed Leamington and Coventry Sporting. I had the pleasure of speaking to Mel and asked him about his career. Mel attended Whitley Abbey School. His first team was Bedworth Town Reserves aged sixteen and seventeen. He played a few games for Bedworth's first team and also Rootes where he worked. Mel then joined Coventry Amateurs in 1968 whom he captained. In April 1969 Mel made the news: he played for Green Lane in a cup match but was due to play for Coventry Amateurs against Bedworth United Reserves. Mel told me: "It was a big fuss about missed communication. The Green Lane match was a hastily arranged semi-final reply. We usually played Amateurs matches on Tuesdays and Thursdays, Amateurs were always my priority. I got a message on the day that as it was the semi-final and it had been agreed it was ok for me to play. It turned out it wasn't! I Played for Amateurs on the following Saturday."

In February 1971 he joined Lockheed Leamington having had a previous spell with them in the summer of 1969. In April 1972 he helped the Brakes win the Birmingham Senior Cup. Lockheed beat Highgate United 1-0 thanks to an extra time penalty from Billy McDerment. Mel remembers Syd Hall, Chris Lightfoot, Tom Sweenie and Dennis Taylor from his time at the Old Windmill.

In April 1973 Mel was one of seven professionals released by new Lockheed manager Jimmy Knox. Coventry Sporting manager Ron Griffis signed Mel in August 1973. Mel talked about the good players at the club like Tony Dunk, Derek Jones and Bob Mundy. Mel was out of action for about eighteen months due to kidney problems and missed the club's famous FA Cup run. Mel could play full back, midfield and sometimes up front but at Coventry Sporting it was mostly in midfield.

In April 1976 Mel joined VS Rugby under his former Lockheed team mate Syd Hall. Mel represented Birmingham County FA. He was a young captain for Coventry Amateurs. He remembers playing against a Wealdstone team that included former Tottenham Hotspur players Cliff Jones and Terry Dyson. Mel had a good career in Sunday League football for Folly Lane, JFK, Green Lane Wanderers and Folly Lane Veterans. He is still involved with football today and, Mel and his wife Marian are Coventry United club presidents. He enjoys watching Coventry United. The current team are doing well they having a good blend of youth and experience. Mel talked about current players Michael Quirke, Lewis Ison, Kevin Thornton and Josh O'Grady. Outside football Mel has raised charity money for Prostate Cancer UK which is a charity close to his heart.

Derek Jones

I asked Derek a few questions about his football career. He is From Coventry and attended President Kennedy School. Derek played for Kenilworth Rangers before joining Coventry Amateurs FC aged seventeen in 1973. In 1974 Derek and Stewart Gallagher signed contracts with the club. By then they were called Coventry Sporting. They had a young side under Dave Kite but also had a couple more experienced players in Jeavons and Dunk. Derek had four or five years at Sporting then played for Redditch United, Hinckley, Coventry Sporting (Second spell) Shepshed Charterhouse and GEC Coventry. Derek won the Telegraph Cup with GEC. He finished playing in 1987 aged thirty two. Derek talked about the good players at Sporting like Charlie Sorbie, Tom

Starkey, Simon Skelcey and Tony Dunk. Tony had a lot of ability and was the maverick of the team. He spent time on Coventry City's books. Derek was in the same age group as other local players Trevor Peake, Kirk Stephens and Roy Slade.

Memorable match

Coventry Sporting 2-0 Tranmere Rovers – FA Cup First Round Proper, 22nd November 1975 at Highfield Road.

Derek was part of Coventry Sporting's fine FA Cup run in 1975. Sporting beat Bromsgrove Rovers, Oldbury United, Halesowen Town, Brierley Hill Alliance and Spalding United in earlier rounds. Coventry Sporting beat Fourth Division Tranmere Rovers 2-0 with Gallagher scoring both of the goals. Sporting would face Third Division Peterborough United next at Highfield Road. However there would be no upset as Posh won 4-0. The Tranmere match was a fantastic result, Sporting did the city of Coventry proud!

Coventry Sporting - Jeavons, Sorbie, Mundy, Dunk, Jones, Skelcey, Randle, Starkey, Gallagher, Gore, Manning

Roy Slade

Roy was a winger/forward who played for a few teams including Racing Club Warwick and top Sunday team Sweeney Todd. I asked Roy a few questions about his football days.

Could you tell me when you played for Sporting?

I had two spells at Sporting the year after the FA Cup run and when I was twenty eight. George Awde and Tony Heal signed me

up as a young man, but they left before the season started because they were let down on promised funds. I stayed at Sporting for a couple of seasons.

Who were the best players that you played with at the club?

There were some good players there at the time - Steve Gibbs, Derek Jones, Lenny Derby, Bob Mundy, Charlie Sorbie, Tony Dunk., Terry Angus, Geoff Brassington, Kenny Hoyte, Paul Surgrue, Johnny Davies, Gez O'Neill, Tim Harrison, Simon Skelcey and Lincoln Liburd. Sugrue went on to play for Manchester City, Angus Northampton and Fulham: they were the younger lads. Dunky was the schemer with a great touch and awareness. Derby was Mr Cool.at the back as was Derek Jones. Brasso was our Denis Law in every way and you would never get the number ten shirt off him. Gibbo was the smiling Assassin with a sweet left foot. Lincoln had great presence and scored for fun from midfield. Johnny Davies was our ex- foreign legion soldier: what a keepe!. Steve Montgomery was a good player on the ball who came to us after a spell in Australia... Geordie Beacham was a top player for us. He had great energy.

Steve (Gibbo) Gibbs

Steve was born in Birmingham but lived in Tile Hill, Coventry most of his life. Steve went to Woodlands School. He played for Coventry Boys and Birmingham County. As a youth Steve played with Don Nardellio and Clive Whitehead who both went onto become professionals. Steve played for Nuneaton Griff and then spent about four years with Nuneaton Borough in his late teens. Dave Kite was youth team manager at Nuneaton Borough before getting the manager's job at Coventry Sporting. Steve enjoyed playing for Boro and playing with Kirk Stephens, Trevor Peake,

Gordon Ritchie, Adrian Stewart, David Pleat and Ernie Wilkinson. Ernie was a senior player at Manor Park. He previously played for Arsenal and Exeter City. David Pleat was a young player-manager in the early 1970s. Alan Jones was at Nuneaton Borough a hard tackling defender and Bob Turpie a fine goal scorer.

Steve was a centre half although he played up front up to the age of fourteen. He joined Coventry Sporting in 1974, playing in most of the cup games in 1975 but got injured and was a sub in the matches against Tranmere Rovers and Peterborough. Steve was at Coventry Sporting for about eight years and then had a spell at Hinckley. Great players at Sporting were Tony Dunk and Geoff Brassington who were both at Coventry City as youngsters and Howard Jeavons the goalkeeper. Steve also played for local teams Sweeney Todd's. JFK and Massey Ferguson. Derek Owen, Peter Mcinulty, Stuart Fisher and Johnny Davies were other players Steve talked about. Johnny was a goal keeper, hard as nails! One time at Sporting they were out having a few beers and they decided to have a press up challenge. Tony Dunk of slight built did 100 then Johnny did more than 100 but with one arm behind his back!

Peter McInulty

Peter was a winger who played for a few local teams in the 1970s. I asked him a few questions about his career.

Could I ask you what junior teams you played for?

I played for my school team Bishop Ullathorne, along with several other players who represented Coventry school boys. Mick Healy, Denis Lyons, Tommy Joyce and Mick Horwood were in the squad that went on to win the Birmingham County Shield final played at Highfield Road in 1968. The manager of the team was Keith

Newbold, who was well known in schoolboy football. The team had players like Bobby Parker, Bob Stockley and Tommy Howard. They all went on to be apprentice professionals at Coventry City. We also played for a youth team called Hartfield, who played on Saturday afternoons in the Coventry youth League. I started out at fourteen playing for a pub team named the Pilot (Sunday league), then went on to play for JFK juniors. At seventeen I played for Tam O' Shanter in the Sunday Premier league. I moved to Green Lane Wanderers next. In this team were Tony Dunk, Bob Mundy, Johnny Davies and Nigel Bunt (all Coventry Sporting) and Andy Karacinski who also played for Bedworth. At JFK where we won the Birmingham Junior Cup. Finally I played for Sweeney Todd with top players Roy Slade, Derek Owen, Ian Muir and Stu Fisher and Arthur Walsh. We won the Birmingham Senior Sunday Shield in 1979. That was my last year playing in Coventry and I Emigrated to South Africa where I have been living for the last forty years.

What was your preferred playing position?

My preferred position was right hand side of midfield, but I could play on the left side as well, a bit like the old wingers from the days of old.

Have you got any favourite matches?

Favourite matches have to be winning the Birmingham Junior Cup for GEC, and the next day winning the Birmingham Sunday Junior Cup with JFK. Probably my best memory is winning the Campbell ORR Shield with the Coventry Alliance team in 1976.There were some great players from the Coventry and Nuneaton area. The highlights of my playing days in Coventry were from 1974 to 1976. I won two Telegraph winners medals, two Campbell Orr Shield winners' medals and the two Birmingham Junior winners' medals. I also won the Birmingham County Shield under 15 schoolboy winners' medal from 1968. These medals are my pride and joy.

Which players stood out in your career team mates and opponents?

I played at Coventry Sporting for three seasons. The standout player was Dennis Mortimer, who I played against while he was still an apprentice at the City. We played them (Cov Boys) at the Ryton training ground. Dudley Tyler, who played for Hereford Town, I played against in 1971 while at Bedworth. This was in the Camkin Cup Semi- final. He went on to play for West Ham United. Tony Dunk was a team mate, one of the best midfielders I had the privilege to play with. One of the best young players I played with was Denis Lyons who sadly broke his leg at an early age, and never really played again. Johnnie Davis was probably the best keeper in the Midlands area at that time and played for Sporting as well.

Did you enjoy playing for Racing Club Warwick?

I only played at Warwick for two seasons but we had some good players and it was a good atmosphere to play in. There were a few of us from Coventry, myself, Stuart Fisher, Derek Owen, Arthur Walsh, Chris Prophet, and Roy. I finished up there at the end of 78/79 season.

David Hudgell

David started his career in local football and went on to have a good career in the USA. I asked him a few questions about his career.

Could you tell me what junior/ school teams you played for?

The youth teams I remember playing for were Chapelfield Colts, Coventry Sporting and Twenty FC. I didn't get much support or promotion from school soccer but did well on these teams with the likes of Tim Flowers and Terry Angus. I was one day a week at Coventry City and Southampton on school holidays but didn't get an apprenticeship with either. I still trained with Coventry while in the sixth form and played a few games for the reserves and Coventry Sporting first team.

How did the move to USA come about?

I ended up going to PE College in London: lots of players who were released went to this college called Borough Road and we won the British Students' Cup four years in a row. I also got the opportunity to go to the States every summer to coach camps and through that met a lot of people and got some opportunities in The US.

What teams have you played for and coached?

My last year I stayed there and played in a few exhibition games and got asked to play in the indoor league MISL but the league folded. I came back and taught PE for a short while and played for Stevenage. I then got a coaching job in the US in Texas and played in the outdoor league USISL (pre MLS) for the Dallas

Rockets. We won the national cup so qualified to play in CONCAAF and got to play against the likes of Hugo Sanchez and Carlos Valderamma. After three years I then went back into the indoor draft and was expecting to play in Dallas for the Dallas Sidekicks but I got drafted by Arizona Sandsharks in what was then the CISL. Played a year there but the team didn't survive and I was taken by Dallas in the next draft. I played 5 years with Dallas before concentrating on coaching full time. Dallas was a big soccer area so the opportunity to both coach youth teams and play was always there and a major attraction to the area.

Les Ebrey

Les was a centre forward and is from Wyken in Coventry and attended Caludon Castle School. I spoke to Les on the phone and asked him about his playing days for Coventry Sporting and other local teams. Les began his career with Wyken WMC, In October 1972 he scored four goals as they beat Christ the King 14.1. His older brothers played for Wyken WMC, one of them played with Bobby Gould at school. In April and May 1977 he played a few games for Nuneaton Borough then moved to Hinckley Athletic. Les then played for Massey Ferguson of the Coventry Alliance, his form catching the attention of Coventry Sporting manager Terry Smith. In December 1979 Les was in fantastic form and he scored fourteen goals from five or six games. Telford United, AP Leamington and Worcester City were all interested in him. In November 1979, Les along with John McGinty and Alan Brotherton, signed contracts with Coventry Sporting. Les then went onto play for Bedworth United (two spells), Worcester City, Coventry Sporting (2nd spell) and Banbury before signing for Jimmy Knox's VS Rugby. Jimmy had tried to sign Les when he was manager of AP Leamington a few years previously. The 1980s was a great era for VS Rugby: in December 1987 they reached the FA Cup second round having beating Warwickshire rivals Nuneaton Borough and Atherstone United in previous rounds. VS were drawn against Bristol Rovers who were managed by former Coventry City midfielder Gerry Francis. VS gave Bristol Rovers a good match at Butlin Road, Rovers who included well known players like Kenny Hibbitt, Nigel Martyn and Gary Penrice were held to a 1-1 draw. Dave Ingram scored for VS Rugby, Les had a goal disallowed in the second half. In the replay Third Division Rovers won 4-0 at Twerton Park in Bath. Les played for Hinckley under Frank Worthington then Folly Lane finishing when he was forty. He talked about some of the great players he played with like Tommy Gorman, Danny Conway, Steve Ross and Ian Crawley. Les played with some great players at Coventry Sporting including Tony Dunk who he described as the Coventry David Silva! Len Derby, John Setchell, Bob Mundy, Alan Harkus and Derek Owen. The latter Derek played with Les at Sporting, Banbury and Nuneaton Borough. Now aged sixty four, Les is a keen cyclist and is about to do a 180 mile challenge in 60 days.

Len Derby

A Coventry Sporting stalwart of the 1980s, he played in central defence alongside Terry Angus. Earlier in his career he played for his school President Kennedy, Coventry Schools, JF Kennedy Athletic and Coundon Social Club. Len played for AP Leamington in the 1979/80 season playing in the Alliance Premier Division. After Coventry Sporting folded he played for Racing Club Warwick in the early 1990s. Len is remembered for his time as Stratford Town manager assisted by Martin Sockett. Stratford had a number of well-known players like Dennis Bailey, Ian Muir, Tony Morley and Michael Gynn as well as top Coventry players Marcus Hamill and Michael Stephenson.

Mark Edwards

I asked Mark a few questions about his football days. His son Jack is current Leamington FC captain.

How did you get into football and what schools/ junior teams did you play for?

School football Coleshill Grammar School, Warwickshire under 19s managed by Alan Fogarty.

Do you remember your debut for Sporting? It must have been great Playing with players like Tony Dunk, Tom Starkey?

I played for Massey Ferguson first team managed by Reg Mathews ex Coventry and Derby goalkeeper. I Transferred to Coventry Sporting I can't remember the team line up but I know I played left back. There were some great players at Sporting as well as Tony and Tom. Howard Jeavons in goal, Bobby Munday, Jack Manning, Stewart Gallagher, Derek Jones to name just a few.

Do you have a favourite match for Coventry Sporting?

The best game, although I didn't play as I was in the dugout, has got to be FA Cup at Highfield Road against Tranmere Rovers which we won 2-1. We drew Peterborough in next round at Highfield Road again and lost I think 4-2.

What other teams did you play for?

I joined Redditch the next season managed by Dietmar Bruck ex Coventry left back for years. Had a really bad dislocated knee and could not play due to less ability to repair that type of injury, no ACL no cartridges.

Do you know what teams your dad played for?

Dad Cliff Edwards was on Coventry's books, I don't think he played in the first team but again serious knee injury put a stop to a potential move to Derby I believe.

Adrian Metcalf

I asked Adrian a few questions about his football career. He played local football in the 1980s.

What junior and senior teams did you play for?

I played for my school team and Coventry Boys for one season. In approximately 1974 I started playing in Coventry and District men's League at fifteen years old. I played for several clubs including Henley Phildown, mainly on Saturdays and with mates' teams on Sundays. I got asked for a trial with Walsall FC in 1981 and I played in a trial game against Norwich City. They included the likes of Steve Bruce and Chris Woods. We were well beaten 5-1 although I did score. However I heard nothing else from them so got asked to trial at Bedworth. The first real game was in John Brady's (Bedworth Manager) testimonial in August 1983. I played a few games for the first team, but was struggling with an ankle injury for which I was getting treatment from a Coventry Physio with injections. I then moved to Coventry Sporting who were being managed by Terry Smith. I played a few games for them including a Boxing Day game at Butlin road. VS Rugby won the game 3-0 I think. Whilst I was there we signed Derek Owen from VS, and in typical Derek style he turned up to his first game in his VS Wembley suit. Soon after I had to pack in as I couldn't play at that level with my troublesome ankle.

Do you have a favourite match in your career?

FA Cup Qualifier for Bedworth v Irthlingborough Diamonds (who went on to become Rushden and Diamonds).

Which players would you say were the best that you played with?

I played with - Tommy Gorman, Liam Halton and Les Ebrey. Players against, three from VS Rugby - John McGinty, Ian

Crawley and Danny Conway and around the same time from AP Leamington Kim Casey.

In November 1978 Adrian scored five goals for Park Rangers as the beat Pegasus 5-2.

Adrian's grandfather, Walter Metcalf, played for Coventry City. He was a wing half or left back who played for the Bantams between 1937 and 1946 making 76 official appearances plus 130 war time games. Walter played for Scarborough, Brentford and spent time with Sunderland prior to joining Coventry City. In November 1946 Walter played for an Army XI against Coventry City at Highfield Road. The Bantams won the match 3-0, Bobby Davidson scoring twice and the other goal was scored by Fred Gardner. The Army XI included Eddie Wainwright of Everton and Jimmy Mullen of Wolverhampton Wanderers. Walter also guested for Nottingham Forest and Northampton Town during the war years. He sadly passed away in 1981.

Jack Manning

Jack was part of the fine Coventry Sporting side which beat Tranmere Rovers. He also played for Bedworth United and top Sunday team Sweeney Todd. I asked Jack a few questions about his football career.

Coventry Sporting side that you played in, was it the best side that you played in?

It was definitely the best side I played in. It was a mixture of experience and younger players, who blended together perfectly.

A lot of people say that Tony Dunk was the best player to play local football.

In my eyes, yes: he rarely gave the ball away and had nice balance for his size.

Who were your favourite strikers in local football?

Stewart Gallagher and John Gore.

Did you play for Nuneaton Borough at one time?

Yes for the youth team for a short time David Kite was manager. A few of the squad came from or went to Boro at one time. Three of Coventry Sporting cup team came from Keresley Village, myself Stewart Gallagher and Keith Randle.

Stewart Gallagher

Stewart was one of the best strikers in local football in the 1970s and 1980s. I contacted Stewart's son Ryan who kindly passed on some questions for his dad to answer about his career.

What school and junior teams did you play for?

Keresley Newlands School and Ansley, I was spotted by Ron Griffiths playing for Ansley against Coventry Sporting in a cup competition. Ron approached me at work in Rolls Royce and told me to be at the Shepherd and Shepherdess pub with Jack Manning that Tuesday. I didn't bother going and so he collected me the next day and told me to be there on the Thursday, so I went and the rest is history. I was the first professional signed by the club.

How long did you play for AP Leamington?

If I remember correctly I left Sporting to go to AP Leamington managed by Jimmy Knox and was there less than a season as they had well established centre forwards like Adrian Stewart and Mick Keeley. I went on loan to VS Rugby. Jimmy pretty much told me I was going on loan which in retrospect was good of him to sort out a club for me. Jimmy later signed me for VS Rugby a few years later when he started to build their reputation which culminated in that fantastic win at Wembley. At the end of that season I signed for Atherstone with Len Willetts at the helm for what was the last season of the old Southern League (scoring 40 goals in that final season of the old Southern League).

Which players did you enjoy playing with?

I played with so many great players, so I could spend all day but those that stand out for me are: Ian Crawley at Nuneaton and VS Rugby; Trevor Peake at Warwickshire Boys; John McGinty at VS Rugby (in my 2nd spell at the club) and of course Tony Dunk when at Coventry Sporting. Like I said though, there are many many great players that I haven't mentioned who were a pleasure to play with.

What was your favourite match during your career?

Without doubt that match against Tranmere Rovers is one of my favourites: scoring those goals against the runaway leaders of the Fourth Division in a great team performance was special. The other standout match for me and arguably more important (to some) was the Bedworth v Nuneaton match in 1982. It was the first time in a long time the clubs had met in the league and it was a local derby. The winners would go to the top of the league and a record crowd for a non-league match (5172) turned up, I scored the only goal in a 1-0 win. Other stand out matches were friendlies against Manchester United whilst at VS Rugby. I also played against Liverpool for Stafford Rangers: it was an honour to score against Ray Clemence.

Ryan Gallagher

Could you tell me a bit about your playing career?

Nowhere near as good as the old man plus I was a centre half by trade. I played for Caludon Castle in the same team as Rich Lavery and for Coventry School boys with Rich and Iyseden Christie. That side also had another notable member -Sean Cunningham who went on to become a member of the Red Arrows. He sadly passed away a few years back due to a faulty ejector seat. We were the year below Marcus Hall. I then played for both Nuneaton and Bedworth's youth teams. I started adult football at the Sphinx, where I was lucky enough to play in the same team as my old man, Ian Crawley and Mark Pollard all in the same match. I think Andy Mee might have also played but can't be sure. I then went to Marconi and played with John McGinty and Peter Hormanschuk, which was another great honour. Then moved to Halesowen Town under Brendan Phillips but he is a wheeler and dealer and preferred to spend around £10k on a centre half rather than an untested lad like me (he has since told me that he should have signed me because Halesowen were relegated that year!)so he put me in touch with Stratford Town (Lenny Derby was the gaffer with Martin Sockett his assistant - both fantastic guys). I spent a couple of seasons and played my best football there with Gez Carr, Michael Stephenson, John Halford and Ady Fitzhugh plus Andy Gallinhagh who went onto have a good league career with Cheltenham Town. Work commitments and repetitive injuries curtailed my career pretty early at around twenty eight. So not a career of note but I enjoyed it immensely, played at some great non-league and professional grounds and players and won (and lost) a fair few trophies along the way.

Nigel Bunt

Nigel was a striker in the 1970s and 1980s, I asked him a few questions about his career. Nigel attended Castle High School in Kenilworth. In the same year was Barry Powell and Steve Flowers (cousin of Tim). Early football memories were going to Hinckley where his dad Ken was a player and manager of Hinckley Athletic. Nigel remembers getting the bus from Coventry to Hinckley. His mother did refreshments at the ground. Ken was a centre half who went on to manage Hinckley's "A", Reserve and first team in a twenty year spell at the club. Nigel played for Kenilworth Boys' Club, Warwickshire Boys and Coventry Boys. He was introduced to Coventry Amateurs by his dad. They were managed by David Kite and Ron Griffiths.

Nigel played for Sunday League team Avonside who played in the Leamington League. He remembers a cup final played at Victoria Park and the replay at the old Windmill ground. In April 1972 Nigel scored against West German team Kiel in an International youth football tournament. The matches were held at Butts Stadium in Coventry and Nigel remembers these matches well. Nigel played for Bedworth United Reserves then the first team. He scored on his debut against Bromsgrove Rovers. In February 1973 he scored four goals in the first half for Coventry Amateurs against Halesowen Reserves. A month previously he scored four goals for his Sunday League team Green Lane Wanderers against J.F Kennedy. Nigel also played for Tamworth under Gordon Dougall, Redditch under Dietmar Bruck, Worcester City, Coventry Sporting and Sunday teams Tam O'Shanter and JFK. He ended his playing career with Coventry Sporting under Terry Smith sometimes playing in midfield and defence. The club had changed since the Coventry Amateurs days. Nigel recalls Terry Smith got the floodlights from steelworks in Corby. In the summer of 1983 Coventry Sporting played a couple of high profile pre-season friendlies against Manchester United and Coventry City. Nigel scored against Coventry City in a 2-1 defeat, Gerry Daly and Nicky Platnauer scoring for City. Manchester United fielded some famous players Mark Hughes and Paul McGrath, Nigel said that Paul was a tough player to play against. Nigel talked about some of the players that he played with – Tony Dunk, Bob Munday, Alan Harkus and John Mason. The famous players he played against include Jimmy Greaves, Jeff Astle, Kenny Burns, Charlie George and Ron Flowers. Nigel is a lifelong Sky Blues fan who has watched them since the 1960s when he went to the famous Wolves match in 1967 and the 1987 FA Cup final.

Alan Harkus

Alan was a left back for Bedworth and Coventry Sporting. His dad Leslie was a prolific forward in the 1940s and 1950s. I asked Alan a few questions about his and his dad's football career.

Do you know what teams your dad played for?

The teams I know he played for were Coventry Tile, Coventry Amateurs and Coventry Radiator. He had one call up for an England Amateur eleven.

What teams did you play for?

I played for Wickmans, Standard Athletic, Atherstone United, Triumph, Coventry Amateurs, Coventry Sporting, Bedworth United. Massey Ferguson over35s, Coventry Sporting over35s, Folly Lane over35s. Plus two Sunday sides Lime Tree Park and Green Lane Wanderers.

Who would you say was the best player that you played with and against?

The best player I played with was Tony Dunk. The best player I played against was Adrian Stewart .I also played against John Charles when he was 50+ and Jeff Astle.

Do you have a favourite match during your career?

My favourite game was when Sporting knocked out holders Stamford 1-0 in the FA Vase at Kirby Corner Road.

Did you have any trials with any football league clubs?

I had a trial for Peterborough United.

Alan had a trial for Peterborough United in May 1974 when they were managed by former Coventry City manager Noel Cantwell. Alan was playing for Bedworth United whose manager Gerry Baker said he was one of the most improved players at the club.

Alan's father (Leslie Harkus) goal scoring was incredible: in September 1945 he scored 8 goals for Coventry Tile against Whoberley Hostels in an 11-0 win at the Butts Stadium. The newspaper report said he scored 186 goals in 90 games since joining the club. Alf Setchell who played for Coventry City was a team mate at Coventry Tile FC.

Wayne Mumford

Wayne was born in Wales on 3rd November 1964 at a young age he moved to Coventry because his dad went to work for Standard Triumph. I spoke to Wayne and asked him a few questions, Wayne attended Limbrick Wood Primary school in Tile Hill. Wayne remembers one match for Limbrick Wood against Holbrooks Primary school when he played against Robbie Jones. It was a good contest by the young players. Robbie, like Wayne, would go on to become a professional footballer. Both players then became teammates for Woodlands School and Coventry Schoolboys. Robbie and Wayne impressed playing at Butts Stadium and got picked up by Manchester City aged eleven. Coventry Schools had some very good teams in the late 1970s/ early 1980s, Wayne was part of the team which reached the semi-finals of the English Cup in 1979 losing to Middlesbrough. Wayne joined Manchester City when Malcolm Allison was manager and played in the same team as Tommy Caton who sadly has since passed away. A full back or midfielder, Wayne signed apprentice forms at Manchester City aged fifteen. John Bond then became the manager at Maine Road and all the apprentices were released, Wayne joined Birmingham City. He made his Blues senior debut on 16th October 1982 against Nottingham Forest. In total he played 7 times for Birmingham City's first team and represented Wales at under 18 level. Wayne suffered a cruciate ligament injury playing for Birmingham's

Reserves and had three operations. His professional career was over and he then played non-league football for Worcester City, Coventry Sporting, Bedworth United and Leamington. One of Wayne's memories of playing for Blues was getting picked up to go to a match by Jim Blyth outside the Hawthorne pub with all his mates outside! Wayne recalls playing with Keith Whiting, Peter Hormantschuk and Terry Angus at Coventry Sporting. At Leamington Kenny Trickett and Mick Shearer were at the club, John Hanna signed Wayne after he was playing for Bedworth against Leamington. Since finishing playing, Wayne has worked in sales, owned his own business and is now the Commercial director for Charlton Athletic.

Keith Whiting

Keith attended Ernesford Grange School. He was a left sided midfielder. He played junior football for Coundon Cockerills, 56 Dynamoes and Coventry Schools. Keith was spotted by Queens Park Rangers who were coached by George Graham. He was part of the 1981/82 youth team at Loftus Road, team mates including Alan McDonald, Martin Allen, David Kerslake and Alan Comfort. Keith also spent time at Oxford United. However injuries would end his professional career. He also played for Bedworth United and Coventry Sporting. Sadly he passed away at the young age of 36 twenty years ago.

Lincoln Liburd

Lincoln was a midfielder who won quite a few trophies in local football in the 1980s and 1990s. I asked him a few questions about his career.

What Junior teams did you play for?

Youth Football: Potters Green U11s under Manager Mr Charnley snr; played 2 games scored 6 goals. I wasn't allowed to play again because my step mother made me go to church.

What senior teams did you play for?

Saturday Football: I played for Wyken Croft where Billy Hollywood was the manager. I got scouted by Ron Griffiths at Coventry Sporting with Kenny Hoyte.

Coventry Sporting's Manager was Terry Smith, I scored 9 goals in 14 games from midfield. I was too wild and immature so messed that up sadly. Hereford United came to watch me but unfortunately I was suspended.

Massey Ferguson under manager John Clarke and we won the Telegraph Cup. Peugeot Talbot Manager Billy Hollywood League and Telegraph Cup double. Unsure if Masseys came before Peugeot I do know I won the Telegraph Cup back to back with two different teams.

Kenilworth Town, John Clarke was the manager and I captained the team to win the Birmingham Vase.

Sunday Football: I played for Jah Baddis. We had several managers and had some mighty football battles with many Coventry teams. Albany Social under manager Dave Sturman a total switch away from Jah Baddis a really nice bunch of players and competed in Premier 2.
Tile Hill Social. The managers were Frank McDermott and Chris Hutt. We had a great bunch of lads again from all sides of life. We were promoted from Premier 2 to Premier 1 and brought through some well-known players. Coventry Apex under manager Maurice O'Keefe top guy, one of the best people, got us together and somehow managed to generally keep a lid on some fiery characters. Progressed up the leagues through the years.

Lincoln played in the same Coventry Sporting side as Len Derby, Tony Dunk, Steve Norris, Derek Owen, Bob Mundy, Alan Harkus and Andy Russell. He won the Coventry Evening Telegraph Cup and Bedworth Nursing Cup with Massey Ferguson: a team mate was the late, great Peter McBean.

Chapter Eight – 1980s' Greats

In this chapter we are going to look at local players who played for Coventry City in the 1980s.

Peter Hormantschuk Chukkie)

Peter was a full back who was born in Coventry on 11th September 1962. I had the pleasure of speaking to Pete on the phone and asked him a few questions about his playing career. Pete attended Caludon Castle School. In his year was Ian Muir. Both Pete and Ian went to QPR as schoolboys. He didn't feel comfortable and got in touch with Bert Edwards who told Pete that he should secure his release and Coventry City would sign him. Pete signed professional for Coventry City in September 1980 and broke into the first team in January 1982. On 2nd of January he made his first team debut coming on a substitute for Ruud Kaiser in a 3-1win over Sheffield Wednesday in the FA Cup. Danny Thomas had moved into midfield allowing Pete to take up the right back spot. Pete got his first start in the fourth round of the FA Cup in a 3-1 win at Manchester City. In the 1982/83 season he made 14 appearances in all competitions and also scored a goal against Manchester United which Pete described a fluke goal. Pete started the 1983/84 season as first choice right back: fellow Caludon Castle old boy Bobby Gould had taken over as manager. City were relegation favourites because it was basically a brand new team because of the departures and arrivals in the summer. Pete was one of a few number of players who had remained at the club from the previous season. The season got off to a fantastic start with a 3-2 win over Watford. In October 1983 Ipswich Town travelled to Highfield Road and won 2-1, one of their goals due to a mistake by Pete. "I had a stinker," Pete told me. He felt so bad as it was his worst experiences in football. It really knocked his confidence. Looking back he was made a scapegoat and didn't get the support. The Ipswich game was his last for the Sky Blues, It is quite sad because he was a Coventry kid who always gave 100% and everyone makes mistakes. The next couple of years Pete suffered knee problems and became ill with Meningitis. Pete made a return to football with Coventry Sporting and Nuneaton Borough under Kirk Stephens. He played for GEC (Copeswood) too, and by then he would have been thirty five. At the age of fifty he would findout he had type 2 Diabetes. In the last few years he has raised a lot of charity money for Diabetes UK and Air Ambulance. Pete has worked for Tesco distribution. He is a keen golfer and a proud member of the CCFPA. Pete made 29 appearances for Coventry City and he has good memories of Dave Sexton, Colin Dobson and John Sillett. Pete enjoyed being part of the generation of youth players at the time like Perry Suckling, Martin Singleton and John Hendrie. I asked Pete who his toughest opponents were. He said Gary Lineker was quality; the Arsenal combination of Graham Rix and Kenny Sansom were tough opponents. Not many Coventry kids have played in the First Division. Pete can say he did and gave everything for the shirt.

Gareth Evans

Gareth was born in Coventry on 14th January 1987 and attended Woodlands School. The young striker was part of a very good Coventry Schools team in 1982 that got to the Cup final against Sheffield Schools. Gareth joined Coventry City aged fourteen and made his first team debut against Manchester United on 2nd of November 1985. In total he made eight first team appearances scoring once in the League Cup against West Bromwich Albion. In

1986 he moved to Rotherham United in part exchange for Dean Emerson.

Gareth's next move in 1988 would be a turning point in his career: he signed for Scottish Premiership side Hibernian. At Easter Road he became a fans favourite playing over 300 games winning the 1991 Scottish League Cup. For a couple of years Gareth played alongside Sky Blues hero Keith Houchen for Hibernian. In the early 1990s Gareth spent time on loan at Stoke City and Northampton Town. In 1996 he joined Partick Thistle and then played for Airdrieonians and Alloa Athletic. When Gareth finished playing in 2004 he took up a coaching role at Alloa Athletic then had roles with Brechin City,Hibernian and Livingston. In June 2013 he was appointed Scotland Women's under-19 national coach a role which lasted for four years. During this time he worked with the Scotland under 17 boys alongside Scott Gemmil. They got to the semi-final of the European Championships in 2014. In September 2018 Gareth was appointed head of youth at Hibernian. Looking back on his time at Coventry City he didn't get much of a chance in the first team due to competition from the likes of Terry Gibson, Cyrille Regis, Paul Culpin and Keith Houchen. Gareth has become a modern day legend in Edinburgh, a thirty year association as a player and coach, a Coventry kid who has done well.

Trevor Peake

One of the finest central defenders to play for Coventry City, Trevor is a club legend. He was born in Nuneaton on 10th of February 1957. Trevor played for King Edward VI School and progressed to Nuneaton Borough youth team. On 4th of September 1975 he made his first team debut for Nuneaton Borough in a

Birmingham Senior Cup match against Oldbury United. Kirk Stephens was also in the team, Bedworth born Geoff Coleman was manager. In May 1976 Nineteen year old Trevor signed professional forms with Nuneaton Borough. As a young player it must have benefited Trevor playing with Ian Goodwin, Roy Cross and Stan Bennett who all had football league experience. In 1979 Trevor and Boro team mate Brendon Phillips played for England at Semi – professional level.

Aged twenty two in July 1979 Trevor joined Fourth Division Lincoln City. He continued his progress at Sincil Bank and made the PFA team of the year twice. Bobby Gould signed Trevor for Coventry City in the summer of 1983. Now aged twenty six, he had a number of years of first team football behind him. During the 1983/84 season he played alongside Steve Jacobs, Ian Butterworth and Sam Allardyce in central defence. Trevor became first choice central defender in his first season at Highfield Road. The summer of 1984 saw the arrival of central defender Brian Kilcline from Notts County and goalkeeper Steve Ogrizovic from Shrewsbury Town. Trevor, Brian and Steve would form the defensive rock for the rest of the decade. The Sky Blues stayed up just about in May 1985 but better times were around the corner. The 1985/86 season City finished higher, however the next season was amazing! Under the leadership of George Curtis and John Sillett the club had its finest hour in the FA Cup and finished a very good tenth in the league. Coventry City were no longer relegation favourites and finished the 1980s with tenth and seventh place finishes. Peakey and Killer were a solid partnership which continued into the new decade.

In March 1990 City reached the League Cup semi-finals, being narrowly beaten by Nottingham Forest. John Sillett was sacked in November 1990 and replaced by Terry Butcher, City finished the season in sixteenth position. Butcher seemed quick to discard the Cup final team and Kilcline and Regis both left in the summer of 1991. Trevor started the first two matches of the 1991/92 season alongside Andy Pearce but was then transferred to Luton Town for £100,000. Ironically his last match for City was a 5.0 win over Luton. Before the season started Trevor, Kenny Sansom and Lloyd McGrath were caught drinking on a three match tour of Scotland. All three players were fined and transfer listed, Trevor was the only one to be transferred.

Trevor served the Hatters well playing into his late 30s then retiring in 1998. Gordon Strachan brought him back to Highfield Road where he coached the under 19 and reserve teams. Trevor and Steve Ogrizovic were caretaker managers for the last game of the 2001/02 season against Burnley. In 2003 Trevor began a seventeen year association with Leicester City retiring in May 2020. Trevor has recently won the Premier League Eamonn Dolan Award which is for his contribution to academy development. During his time at Leicester he has coached Andy King, Harvey Barnes, Richard Stearman and Ben Chilwell who all progressed to the first team. Bobby Gould did try and sign him in 1992 but for some reason the transfer didn't happen. Trevor should have played for England but he did get called up for the England B team but didn't play because of injury. One of the author's lasting memories of Trevor was on that magical day in 1987 when he picked up Clive Allen by one arm with even referee Neil Midgeley smiling! A Sky Blue and Warwickshire legend, enjoy your retirement, Trevor!

Trevor Peake - A Tribute by Ian Goodwin

When he first came into the Boro side, I like man, had concerns in respect of his early pace. It was only when playing with him you appreciated just how well he covered the ground and his reading of the game was superb. Playing in the Southern League I believe taught Trevor so much, pitting his wits against some of the greats who were finishing their career after years in the Football league was a challenge. There was no doubt that the lad was going to go on to greater things and ultimately lift the FA Cup. My lasting memory of Trevor was just how much the lad could eat! We stayed overnight before a game at Maidstone. At dinner he shifted more Bread Rolls than you could count and then demolished a starter, main and sweet course, I don't think he had eaten for a week. I reminded him of this at Bob Turpie's funeral and his wife immediately told me that nothing had changed.

Tony Dobson

Tony was born in Coventry on 5th of February 1989. He attended Ernesford Grange School. A strong left back, he joined Coventry City on YTS terms in 1985 then signed professional in the summer of 1986. Tony was part of the young Sky Blues team that won the FA Youth Cup in 1987. He made his first team debut on 28th of March 1987 against Aston Villa but had to wait patiently for a run in the first team due to being Greg Downs's understudy. In February 1989 he became a regular in the team also gaining international recognition with England under 21s, gaining four caps. Tony played 63 times for Coventry City scoring once against Everton (a great goal too). He was then sold to Blackburn Rovers in January 1991. Tony moved to Ewood Park with fellow youth cup winner Steve Livingstone. Fans were very disappointed to see them leave. Tony and Steve had come through the youth team and did well in the first team and were the future of the club. In 1993 he joined Portsmouth then played for Oxford, Peterborough, West Bromwich Albion, Gillingham, Northampton and Forest Green

Rovers. After retiring from playing he has managed VS Rugby, Solihull Borough and Rugby Town.

Kirk Stephens

Kirk was a talented full back who began his senior career with Nuneaton Borough. He was born in Coventry on 27th of February 1955. Kirk attended Caludon Castle School and was on Coventry City's books but didn't make the grade and joined David Pleat's Nuneaton Borough. On 16th of October 1972 seventeen year old Kirk made his league debut against Chelmsford City. He became first choice right back at Manor Park before reuniting with David Pleat at Luton Town. In September 1982 he famously went in goal away at Liverpool when future Coventry City goalkeeper Jake Findlay got injured. Luton Town won the Second Division in the 1981/82 season and had very good players in Ricky Hill, Brian Stein and Mal Donaghy. In the summer of 1984 Bobby Gould brought Kirk to Highfield Road with Ashley Grimes moving in the other direction. Kirk made his Sky Blues debut in a 1-0 defeat against Aston Villa in August 1984. Steve Ogrizovic, Brian Kilcline, Martin Jol and Kenny Hibbitt joined Kirk in making their City league debuts. Kirk made thirty seven appearances for Coventry City but, unfortunately knee injuries forced him to retire and he went into non-league with Barnet and Nuneaton Borough. Kirk is now president of the CCFPA and has worked in the construction industry.

Graham Rodger

Graham was born on 1st April 1967 in Glasgow but grew up in Kenilworth. He went to Park Hill and Kenilworth School with Tim Flowers. Graham played junior football for Leamington Ajax and

Bilton Ajax. At fourteen years old he signed schoolboy forms for Wolverhampton Wanderers. At sixteen years old Graham played for AP Leamington in the Midland Floodlit Cup. Graham made one senior appearance for Wolverhampton Wanderers at the end of the 1989/84 season. In the summer of 1985 he moved to Coventry City, the team he supported as a boy. Graham made his Sky Blues debut on 6th November 1985 in the League Cup against West Bromwich Albion. His most famous match was a cameo in the 1987 FA Cup final setting up the winning goal. Graham made 44 first team appearances and scored 2 goals for the Sky Blues before moving on to Luton Town in 1989. He then joined Grimsby Town in 1992 winning the Football League Trophy and Division Two Play offs with them in 1998. Graham still works for Grimsby Town as a chief scout and has previously been Sports in the Community Officer and first team manager.

Chapter Nine – Modern day greats

A look at local players who have played for Coventry City from the 1990s to the present day.

Marcus Hall

Our first modern day great, Marcus was born in Coventry on 24th March 1976. He broke into the first team in the 1994/95 season making his debut on 31st December 1994 against Tottenham Hotspur coming on as a substitute for Paul Cook. Marcus made his first start against Manchester United in April 1995. The next season he became a regular for City at left back. He could also play left midfield. Marcus would gain England recognition in October 1996 making his England under 21 debut against Poland at Molineux. He would play nine times for the under 21 team and once for England B in February 1998. Marcus left Highfield Road in June 2002 and spent time with Nottingham Forest, Southampton and Stoke City. In January 2005 he made a return to Coventry City and would help us secure Championship football as we entered the new era at the Ricoh Arena. Marcus was given a well-deserved testimonial in August 2009 against Everton. The match ended 2-2 against a strong Toffees team, Marcus was substituted in the second half and was applauded by both sets of supporters. In 2010 Marcus joined Northampton Town for one season, retiring from playing in 2011. Marcus and Gary McSheffrey both played in the last ever match at Highfield Road and it was special that two Coventry kids played in this emotional match. He didn't score many goals but when he did they were pretty good. Readers can check out his Sky Blues' goals on YouTube. With over 300 appearances for Coventry City, Marcus is a club legend. One personal memory of mine was a pre-season friendly against

Hinckley. By then he was one of the senior players and I remember him talking to and advising young Ashley Cain throughout the game. Younger players could take inspiration and look up to him as Marcus had come through the ranks and become a great professional. After finishing playing Marcus gained qualifications in financial advice and worked as a football consultant. In 2015 he joined Jaguar Land Rover, Marcus now works as an executive consultant for a recruitment company in the social care sector.

I asked Marcus a few questions via email.

Could you tell me how you got spotted by City and when you signed schoolboy forms?

I first got spotted by Coventry City when I was 13/14 years of age. I would have been playing for Ernesford Grange Dynamos in the Sunday Minor League and also playing for Coventry Schoolboys on a Saturday. Ray Gooding and Lol Cairns worked as scouts for Coventry City and invited me to come to their School of Excellence (which was the equivalent of Coventry's Academy) training sessions held at Sidney Stringer School. I signed up to play Coventry's School of Excellence team where we would play against other Midlands clubs such as Leicester City, Aston Villa, Nottingham Forest etc.... The only downside of signing for Coventry's School of Excellence meant that I couldn't play for Ernesford Grange Dynamos as the games were on a Sunday too.

Do you think that it helped your earlier Career that you weren't rushed into the first team and you were given time to develop in the reserves and youth teams?

Yes, I think it was good to get a proper grounding in the reserves playing against men in a much more physical environment than what I was used to in the youth team. By the second year of my two-year YTS I had been converted from a left winger to a left-sided centre-half / left-back so my reserve appearances were usually in one of these two positions. When I got a chance to play in the reserves you realised straight away the difference in the speed and the physicality. I played half a season of reserve team football, playing alongside the likes of Gary Gillespie whose experience and knowledge had a really good effect on me and I learnt so much. This experience of reserve team football definitely got me more prepared for my eventual debut, even though nothing could fully prepare you for it!

Captaining England at under 21 level must have been such a great experience for you? What do you remember about the match for which you were made captain?

Captaining my country was (alongside my City debut) the proudest moment of my career. We were playing away against Poland in Katowice and the manager at the time Peter Taylor let me know at our evening meal the night before the game that he had been impressed with how I'd been performing and the attitude that I displayed and was going to make me captain for the following night's game. I was so happy and couldn't wait to tell my family and friends. Being captain in a team which included players such as Emile Heskey and Jamie Carragher and leading them out and singing the national anthem was a massive privilege. The game itself was a bit of a boring 1 -1 draw but in the end that didn't matter to me!

Have you got a favourite match for Coventry City? I think one of mine would have to be one from the 97/98 season. What a team that was!

Apart from the obvious choice of my full debut against Manchester United at Highfield Road live on Sky's Monday Night Football which will always be at the forefront of my mind, probably my favourite match was when we beat the then Premier Champions Blackburn Rovers 5-0 at a snowy and icy Highfield Road. I remember the game was touch and go because of the weather and we were given the option of wearing dimpled trainers because of the ground being quite hard in places. We got the feeling that Blackburn didn't really fancy it but we were right up for it and took it to them from the first minute. I remember skying a shot over the bar from a right-wing cross where I should have done a lot better! I did make amends when put in a cross that Peter Ndlovu headed back from David Busst to score from. Blackburn couldn't live with us and as I said we ended up winning 5-0 which came as a huge shock for a team that included Hendry, Sherwood, Shearer and co!

Do you think that you could name a Marcus Hall dream team of players that you played with? Any team.

My dream team of players I have played with would be as follows:

GK - Steve Ogrizovic , LB - David Burrows, CB - Paul Williams, CB - Gary GillespieRB - Brian Borrows, LM - Peter Ndlovu, CM - Gary McAllister, CM - Mustapha Hadji
RW - Gordon Strachan, CF - Dion Dublin, CF - Darren Huckerby

Lee Hurst

A fans' favourite of Coventry City's first season in the Premier League, Lee is a local lad who has done well. He was born in Nuneaton on 21st of September 1970 but grew up in Bedworth attending Nicholas Chamberlain School. Lee made his first team debut as a substitute on 29th January 1991 against Southampton in the FA Cup. He made his first start at left back in the next league game against Wimbledon on 2nd February. Steve Sutton on loan from Nottingham Forest made his debut in goal and former youth team mate Terry Fleming also made his debut. Lee made two more appearances in the 1990/91 season before Coventry City signed former England left back Kenny Sansom. The next season Lee made 14 appearances in all competitions mostly at left back. In the summer of 1992 Bobby Gould took over as manager, City just about survived relegation the season before. Coventry City started the 1992/93 season as members of the new Premier League. Lee started the first game against Middlesbrough in midfield and didn't look back. He partnered Robson, Gynn and McGrath in midfield as City had a decent first season in the Premier League with impressive wins over Liverpool, Aston Villa and Blackburn Rovers, Lee excelled in midfield. He made 35 Premier League appearances as Coventry City finished in 15th. In the summer of 1993, on a pre-season army training camp, tragedy struck as Lee tore knee ligaments on an assault course. He would never play for the first team again and soon after on the first game of the season fellow midfielder Stewart Robson suffered a career ending injury. Lee made a brief comeback with American team Charleston Battery in 1998. In total Lee made 55 appearances for Coventry City in all competitions scoring 2 goals, It would have been considerably more if it wasn't for that cruel injury.

Howard Clark

A midfielder who was born in Coventry on 19th September 1968, Howard spent time as a junior with Wolverhampton Wanderers. He joined Coventry City under YTS scheme before he turned professional in September 1986. Howard was part of the team that won the FA Youth Cup in 1987. He made his senior debut against West Ham United on 5th of November 1988 which was a 1-1 draw with Keith Thompson scoring for City. Howard played twenty four times for Coventry City scoring one goal against Nottingham Forest in May 1989. In 1991 he spent time on loan with Darlington then joined Shrewsbury Town on a free transfer. Howard also played for Hereford United, Nuneaton Borough, Crawley Town and Hinckley Town. In 1996 he joined West Midlands Police playing for their team. When Howard signed for Nuneaton Borough in August 1995 he teamed up with former Sky Blues youth team mate Paul Shepstone. At Hereford he was signed by former team mate Greg Downs.

Gary McSheffrey

One of the most exciting players to play for Coventry City since relegation from the Premiership in 2001, Gary was born in Coventry on 13th of August 1982. He attended Bishop Ullathorne School. At the age of 16 years and 198 days on 27 February 1999 Gary made his Premiership debut coming on as a substitute for Darren Huckerby in a 4-1 win over Aston Villa. Gary made three more Premiership appearances in September 1999 and two in the League Cup. Gary was part of the same Sky Blues youth team as Craig Pead, Callum Davenport and Chris Kirkland. In 1999 they reached the FA Youth Cup final but were comprehensively beaten by a Joe Cole inspired West Ham United. In 2000 Coventry reached the FA Youth Cup final again but lost 5-1 against Arsenal over two legs. Gary scored in the first leg at Highfield Road.

Gary didn't play for the first team again until October 2001, between 2001 and 2004 he went on loan four times to IK Brage in Sweden, Stockport County and Luton Town (twice). Gary scored his first senior goal for Coventry in January 2002 at Crystal Palace. He was prolific in his first loan at Luton Town. At one stage it didn't look like he would make it at his home town club, Gary was transfer listed by Gary McAllister in 2003. He stayed and when Eric Black took over as manager, Gary started to flourish in an attacking team. Eric was sacked in May 2004 and replaced by Peter Reid who was only in the job for eight months. Micky Adams took over in January 2005 and Gary was fantastic alongside Dele Adebola and Stern John. By the summer of 2006, Gary's form had attracted the interest of Birmingham City. Early in to the 2006/07 season Steve Bruce got his man for £4 million and Gary was on his way to St Andrews. Coventry fans were of course disappointed to see him leave. Gary did well in his first season as Blues won promotion to the Premiership.

In 2009 and 2010 he had loans with Nottingham Forest and Leeds United, and he was released by Birmingham City in the summer of 2010 and returned to Coventry City. Gary scored eight goals in thirty five appearances in his first season back, but some fans felt that he wasn't the same player, he having lost his cutting edge. In the 2011/12 season Gary was joint top scorer but it was a poor season as Coventry City were relegated from the Championship. Recruitment wasn't good enough and players like King and Gunnarson were not adequately replaced. City faced third tier football for the first time since the 1960s and thoughts of an easy ride in League One were soon over and Coventry did not win in the league until the end of September! Gary played on a regular basis, and the arrival of David McGoldrick saw hope of a play off push but in the end Coventry finished in the bottom half of the table. Gary didn't feature in Steven Pressley's plans and his contract was cancelled and he was soon to join Chesterfield. Gary has since played for Scunthorpe United, Doncaster Rovers, Grimsby Town, Eastleigh and Frickley Athletic.

In total Gary made 281 Sky Blues appearances and scored 72 goals in two spells at CCFC. Fans often fans say he was fantastic in his first spell and not so much in his second. Gary was still a good player for Coventry when he returned. He set the bar so high between 2004 and 2006. You have to remember the sides under Eric Black and Micky Adams were a lot better than the teams he played in between 2010 and 2013. Gary has obtained UEFA A and B licences and he is now Under 23 coach at Doncaster Rovers. The author's favourite McSheffrey goal was scored against Norwich City at the Ricoh when he scored from an angle, pure class! A fantastic Coventry City player and a modern day great.

I asked Gary a few questions about his junior career and his time in Sweden.

What junior and school teams did you play for?

I played for Ernesford Dynamos under 10-11-12's. I played for my school teams at St Benedict's RC primary and Bishop Ullathorne Secondary. I played for Coventry School boys throughout secondary school. That enabled me to play for West Midlands also.

How did you get spotted by Coventry City?

I got spotted at aged about nine or ten by scouts Ray Gooding and Lol Cairns and started training with Coventry at under 10 level which I think was at Sidney Stringer School. At under 12 level I had to stop grass roots with Ernesford as there was a full games programme with Coventry, playing against all the other professional clubs

Did it help as a young player spending time in Sweden?

Maybe it did. It had its pluses and minuses. It possibly made me grow up a bit and I had to live on my own and look after myself. It made me appreciate how good it was at Coventry also. I was a bit homesick at times and missed friends and family but in terms of development I suppose it was seen as good, it would have been easier if I had family around me though looking back, the people were nice though and the team was a good bunch of lads.

Stuart Giddings

Stuart was born in Coventry on 27th March 1986 He attended Foxford School. He joined Coventry's school of excellence when he was ten and the young left back progressed through the youth team. Stuart made his senior debut on the 9th of May 2004 as a substitute against Crystal Palace. The next season he had a run in the team, but an injury prevented him from being a regular and was released in September 2008. Stuart also played for Oldham Athletic, Darlington, Hinckley United and Ilkeston Town. He also represented England at under 16, 17, 18 and 19 levels.

Callum Wilson

A current Premiership and England striker, Callum is a Coventry kid who done very well. He was born in Coventry on 27th of February 1992 and attended President Kennedy School. Callum grew up in Radford and player junior football for Christ the King

Whilst playing for them he got approached by Coventry City Academy. Callum's mum didn't drive so it was hard for him to get to training which was the other side of the city. He joined the academy again at fourteen, Callum was part of an excellent generation of players – Cyrus Christie, Lee Burge, Nathan Cameron and Josh Ruffels have all had good careers.

Callum made his Sky Blues debut against Hartlepool United as a substitute in the League Cup on 12th of August 2009. He spent time on loan at Kettering and Tamworth to gain experience. In January 2013 he started to break into Coventry's first team scoring his first goal against Colchester in March. The summer of 2013 was a turbulent time for the club: a ground share with Northampton Town was announced. Coventry City were also deducted ten points for going into administration. The fans that did watch the team at Sixfields were treated to some fantastic football, Callum formed a superb partnership with Leon Clarke. Carl Baker, John Fleck and Franck Moussa were excellent too, Callum scored 22 goals. Leon joined Wolves in January 2014. If he had stayed maybe City could have made the play offs. In July 2014 Callum signed for AFC Bournemouth, who were in the Championship, for a fee believed to be £3million. Callum had a dream first season as the Cherries won the Championship and he scored 23 goals in all competitions. In his and Bournemouth's first ever season in the Premiership he scored five goals. Bad injuries restricted his appearances but he was still a regular goal scorer, his best return being fourteen Premiership goals in the 2018/19 season. On 15th of November 2018 Callum made his England debut and scored in a 3-0 win over USA. He has now won four caps. In July 2020 Bournemouth were relegated from the Premiership and Callum signed for Newcastle United for a reported £20 million. The author's favourite goal Callum scored for City was against Bradford City away: it was all about pace and power. He looked a class above in the 2013/14 season and, most fans were probably thinking why he hadn't been given a first team chance sooner. If Coventry City had been a Championship club he might have stayed longer, but he has proved to be Premiership class and no doubt he will continue to score goals at the highest level.

Jordan Willis

One of Coventry City's best defenders of recent years, Jordan was born in Coventry on 24th of August 1994. He came through the youth team and made his Sky Blues' debut on 5th of November 2011 as substitute against Southampton in the Championship. Jordan became a regular in the 2013/14 season under Steven Pressley and then became first choice defender. In total he made 208 appearances scoring eight goals between 2011 and 2019. Jordan had become one of League One's best defenders and was linked to teams in the Championship. Jordan scored some important goals for Coventry City against Stoke City in the FA Cup and the play off final against Exeter City. In the summer of 2019 he joined League One rivals Sunderland. Fans were obviously disappointed to see him leave but he served the club well. Jordan did stay when Coventry City were relegated to League Two. Sunderland will be looking to gain promotion from League One this season. Jordan is definitely good enough for Championship level: he is still only twenty six so he should achieve this.

James Maddison (Madders)

One of the Premiership best young English players, James is a Coventry kid with a great future in the game. He was born in

Coventry on 23rd November 1996 and attended Richard Lee Primary School and Caludon Castle School. James joined Coventry City's academy and the talented attacking midfielder progressed through the youth team into the first team. On 13th August he made his Sky Blues debut as a substitute in the League Cup against Cardiff City. James started to become a regular in the 2014/15 season and he scored a last minute winner against Crawley in the last game of the season. His performances caught the attention of a few Premiership teams, The 2015/16 season got off to a great start. The 4.0 win over Millwall on 15th August was particularly impressive, James linked up well with new signings Adam Armstrong and Ruben Lamieras. Tony Mowbray's team looked the real deal, James continued to flourish.

On transfer deadline day on January 31st 2016, Norwich City signed James and loaned him back to Coventry City for the remainder of the season. The 2015/16 season was a wasted opportunity for City, who finished eighth but with the players available should have gone up. In addition to James, Ruben and Adam there were quality loan players like Joe Cole, Jacob Murphy and Ryan Kent. In total James made forty two appearances and scored five goals for Coventry City. In August 2016 he was loaned to Aberdeen, just before that he played for Norwich City against Coventry City in the League Cup, a night Sky Blues' fans will want to forget as it was a humiliating 6-1 defeat! James didn't make his league debut for Norwich until April 2017. James became one of Norwich's best players and in June 2018 he signed for Premiership Leicester City for about £20 million. He has continued to progress for the Foxes and made his England debut against Montenegro on 14th November 2019. James has signed a contract extension with Leicester City although he was heavily linked to Manchester United. It is a shame that Coventry City fans did not see him play longer for the Sky Blues, I'm sure most fans will wish him all the best for his career and no doubt he will play more matches for England.

Cyrus Christie

Cyrus is a right back with Premiership team Fulham and is a Republic of Ireland international. He was born in Coventry 30th September 1992 and went to Woodlands School. He is the nephew of great Coventry boxer Errol Christie who sadly passed away in 2017. Cyrus made his Sky Blues debut on 10th November 2010 in a League Cup match against Morecambe. In early 2011 he had loan spells with Nuneaton Borough and Hinckley United. Cyrus established himself in Coventry's first team in the 2011/12 season which would see them relegated to League One. Cyrus stayed with Coventry until the summer of 2014 playing 124 games in all competitions before a move to Derby County. Fine performances at Pride Park earned him a call up for Republic of Ireland and he made his international debut against USA. Cyrus was part of the Irish team that earned a famous win over Germany in November 2011. He has now won twenty four caps and scored two goals, Cyrus provides excellent competition for Seamus Coleman at right back. Cyrus joined Middlesbrough in July 2017 then signed for Fulham in January 2018. Fulham won promotion back to the Premiership in July 2020, Cyrus has joined Championship side Nottingham Forest on loan. Outside football he has set up Cyrus Christie Foundation to help young people and draw on his own experiences growing up.

Gary Montgomery

Gary is the third generation from this fine footballing family. He was born in Royal Leamington Spa on 8th October 1982. He attended Warwick School and was a talented cricketer and footballer. Gary chose football and came through the youth ranks at Coventry City for whom he made his senior debut in the League Cup against Chelsea on 9th October 2001. Magnus Hedman was injured and Gary kept a first half clean sheet but the second half Chelsea scored twice to win 2-0. Gary spent time on loan with Crewe Alexandra and Kidderminster Harriers. He got a run in Coventry's team at the end of the 2002/03 season. He also spent time at Charlton Athletic when they were in the Premiership, but he returned to Coventry and was released in the summer of 2003 despite being in the first team at the end of the season. Gary joined Rotherham United and in October 2003 was a hero in a League Cup tie with Arsenal. The game went to penalties which Arsenal won 9-8. Gary saved and scored in the shoot-out as they came so close to causing an upset. He also played for Grimsby Town. In 2009 he swapped sports and joined Lancashire Cricket Club and appeared in their second eleven and in ECB40 matches. Gary's grandfather was Dave Montgomery, a centre forward for Birmingham and Lockheed Leamington. His dad Steve was also a forward for Racing Club Warwick, AP Leamington, Banbury United and also played in Australia.

Conor Thomas

Conor is a current midfielder for League Two team Cheltenham Town. He was born in Coventry on 29th October 1993. He attended Coundon Court School and played junior football for Christ the King. Conor made his senior debut in the FA Cup against Crystal

Palace on 8th January 2011 as a substitute. In the same month he spent time on loan with Premiership Liverpool but returned to Coventry by mutual consent after suffering a hamstring injury. In the 2011/12 season he was a regular in the Championship. Probably his best season was the 2013/14 season where he was first choice alongside John Fleck. Conor joined Swindon Town in 2016 and also played in the Indian Super League for ATK. He has also represented England at Under 17 and 18 level. Conor is still only twenty six and has plenty of time to play at a higher level. He did well for Coventry City making 117 appearances in all competitions.

Jordan Clarke

Jordan is a defender for League Two side Scunthorpe United. He was born in Coventry on 19th November 1991, he attended Hollyfast Primary and Coundon Court Schools. Jordan came through the youth ranks making his first team debut on 9th August 2009 against Ipswich Town in the Championship. He played quite regularly for Coventry in the Championship. His best season was the 2013/14 in League One. It looked at one point that he might have been leaving but Steven Pressley reversed the decision and Jordan became first choice in central defence. During the 2014/15 season he joined Yeovil Town on loan with Aaron Martin moving in the other direction. In the summer of 2015 he joined Scunthorpe United and has been there ever since. An England under 19 and 20 international, Jordan made 144 appearances for Coventry City and served the club well in a difficult spell following relegation to League One.

Jordan Shipley

Jordan is a current Sky Blues midfielder who was born in Royal Leamington Spa on 26th September 1997. He went to Trinity School and played for junior team Leamington Hibernians. Jordan came through the Coventry City youth team and made his senior debut against Walsall on 22nd April 2017 in League One. The following season in League Two he became a regular, playing in a left side midfield role. Jordan became popular with the fans scoring a memorable goal against Luton Town and in the Play off final v Exeter City. Coventry City had a decent season after winning promotion and finished eighth in the 2018/19 campaign. In the summer of 2019 it was announced that the Sky Blues would be playing home matches at St Andrews the home of Birmingham City. No one could have imagined how well City would have performed. Jordan was excelling in a central midfield role, Coventry had a brilliant season only losing three league matches before the pandemic ended the season early. The 2019/20 season was curtailed with City top of the league by five clear points and they were crowned League One champions on a points per game basis. Jordan has also gained international recognition with Republic of Ireland's under 21s' team. Now a Championship player, he will looking to gain a full international call up.

Courtney Baker-Richardson

A current striker for League Two side Barrow, Courtney was born in Coventry on 5th December 1995. He progressed through the Coventry City youth team and made his senior debut in the FA Cup against Hartlepool United on 7th December 2013. It would be Courtney's only appearance for the Sky Blues and he joined Tamworth on a youth loan then played for Romulus, Kettering

Town, Nuneaton Town and Redditch United. Courtney joined Leamington in February 2016. He would be a fantastic player for the Brakes scoring 28 goals in 74 appearances. In August 2017 he signed for Premiership team Swansea City. Prior to his move he spent time with Leicester City on trial. Courtney broke into Swansea's team in August 2018 and scored against QPR in a 3-0 win. After a spell on loan with Accrington Stanley in the 2019/20, Courtney signed for Barrow in October 2020. Still only twenty four Courtney has joined fellow Coventry kid Dior Angus in Cumbria as Barrow look to have a good first season in League Two.

Jordan Ponticelli

Jordan is a striker for National League side Wrexham who was born in Nuneaton on 10th September 1998. A prolific scorer for the youth team he broke into the first team during the 2017/18 season in League Two. Jordan made twenty six appearances and scored six goals in all competitions. In the next few seasons he spent time on loan with Macclesfield Town, Wrexham and Tranmere Rovers. A lot of Coventry fans had hoped that he would made the breakthrough and become the club's number nine! At only twenty two he has plenty of time to make a good career in football and fulfil his early potential.

The Next Generation of Local Talent

It Looks like Will Bapaga, Josh Eccles, Jack Burrows and Tom Bilson are players for the future. They are all part of Coventry City's under 23 squad: Josh Eccles is doing well on loan with Gillingham. All four players have made appearances for the senior team and all have potential to become important players for the Sky Blues.

Alfie Bates is a Coventry born midfielder with Walsall, he is currently a regular for The Saddlers in League Two. The Saddlers will hope to win promotion to the third tier of English football.

Josh Dacres-Cogley is a defender on the books of Birmingham City. He was born in Coventry and attended Myton School in Leamington. In the 2016/17 season he made fourteen appearances in the Championship but since then he has struggled to break into the first team with the Blues. Josh played for Crawley Town on loan during the 2019/20 season. He is under contract with Birmingham City until June 2021. An athletic full back Josh has all the attributes to make it at a good level of football.

Josh Ginnelly is currently on loan with Scottish Championship side Hearts. The midfielder/winger who comes from Coventry came through the youth set up at Aston Villa. Josh is still only twenty three and has played for a number of teams including Walsall, Preston North End and Bristol Rovers. He is doing well for Hearts who look to win the league this season, Josh scored recently as Hearts thrashed Dundee 6-2. Josh is the nephew of Nuneaton Borough manager Jimmy Ginnelly.

George Green

Photo courtesy of Chris Goodwin (England online)

Kenneth Edward "Jackie" Hegan

Photo courtesy of Chris Goodwin (England online)

Coventry Tile FC 1940s

Photo courtesy of Paul Jephcott

Coventry United FC

Photo courtesy of Edwin Greaves

Jack Harvey Pritchard

Photo courtesy of Deborah Pritchard

Edwin School of Motoring FC

Photo courtesy - Edwin Greaves

Coventry Boys 1980s Photo courtesy – Marcus Hamill

Leon James

Photo courtesy – Leon James

Nick Kirk celebrating a goal

Photo courtesy – Boyd Young

J F Kennedy Athletic FC

Photo courtesy – Boyd Young

Bermuda WMC FC

Photo courtesy – Jessica Sephton-Bray

Coventry Dynamoes FC

Photo courtesy – Mark Rosegreen

A view of Highfield Road

Photo courtesy – David Featherstone

Brian Hill

Photo courtesy – Mike Young CCFPA

Kyle King

Photo courtesy – Kyle King

Leamington Hibernians Sunday League team

Photo courtesy – Kyle King and Josh Blake

Coventry City Schools' team 1980.

Photo courtesy – Allan Dolby

Nuneaton Boys including a young Kevin Keegan at the Pingles, Nuneaton. Photo courtesy – Dean Nelson

Bedworth United 1982

Photo courtesy – Natalie Downes

Triumph Athletic

Photo courtesy – Andy Beechey

Chris Downes at work before AP Leamington play Gillingham in the FA Cup in 1983.

Photo courtesy – Chris Downes

Andy Beechey lifts a trophy for Triumph

Photo courtesy – Andy Beechey

Johnny Matthews

Photo courtesy – Gloria Lines

Walter Metcalfe

Photo courtesy – Adrian Metcalfe

Craig Herbert in action for Rugby Town

Photo courtesy – Craig Herbert

Mick Brady

Photo courtesy – Yvonne Pamela Brady

Bobby Parker

Photo courtesy – Frank Pritchard

Ken Brown, Gordon Simms and Mick Kearns

Photo courtesy – Mike Young CCFPA

Chapter Ten – Coventry Schools

In this chapter we are going to look at some players who played who have played for Coventry school boys. Players over the years have progressed through the different age groups into Coventry City's youth team and into senior football.

Paul Luckett

Paul was one of the most exciting prospects in Coventry schools' football in the early 1970s. He was born in Coventry on 12th January 1957 and attended Caludon Castle School. Paul was a versatile player who could play up front, in midfield or full back. In November 1970 Paul was selected for Warwickshire for a match against Worcestershire with Caludon team mate Ian Woodward and Simon Skelcey of Whitley Abbey. A year later, in November 1971, he scored a hat trick as Caludon Castle beat Bishop Ullathorne 5-1. Paul also represented Birmingham and District under 15s and scored in an England Schoolboy international trial match in January 1972. In October 1972 Paul signed apprentice professional forms for Coventry City and was part of a good group of young players at the club. In Paul's group of apprentices were Brian Roberts, Tony Bannister (brother of Gary) and Don Nardiello. In the age group before Paul there were Jim Blyth, Graham Oakey, Donal Murphy and Mick Ferguson. Paul told me he was at Coventry City for two years playing for the youth team and in the reserves. He then went to Halifax and played there a couple of seasons and then went to Hartlepool for a season. Paul then played in Australia for Sydney Olympic for about four years. Paul played against Leeds United in August 1975 which was a West Riding Senior Cup Semi-Final. Leeds included the likes of Lorimer, Clarke, Yorath and Madeley and won 4-2. Paul remembers the game: he played left midfield and recalls that Halifax were winning at half time. Paul later played for GEC, winning the Coventry Evening Telegraph Cup in 1987.

Clive Deslandes

I had the pleasure of speaking to Clive who was part of a very good Coventry Schools' team in the 1970s. Clive attended Whitmore Park School and President Kennedy School in Coventry. A seven year old Clive remembers the 1970 World Cup Final. Pele and the Brazilian team were a great inspiration. A year later he remembers the 1971 FA Cup Final between Arsenal and Liverpool, the famous Charlie George goal! Clive recalls one time at school playing football and doing a commentary as kids do." It's Clive Deslandes with the ball for England." One of the other kids said, "You can't play for England!" That was hard for Clive as back in the early 1970s there were not many black professional footballers in England. Clyde Best of West Ham United and later Regis, Batson and Cunningham were role models. Clive told me one time a coach said to him you are a good footballer but we don't want your sort in the team!

Clive was part of a very good Coventry Schools' team which included Peter Hormantschuk, Ian Muir and Abbey Kelly. As a player Clive was a forward with pace, but he admits he was a little greedy at times and maybe should have passed more to teammates. His coach Roy Evans recently described Clive as his Theo Walcott!

In the 1970s and 1980s racism was really bad in English football. Clive and Abbey were the only black lads in the Coventry Schools' team. Black players suffered horrific abuse in the professional game, which would have been extremely upsetting to watch.

Thankfully it is extremely rare to hear racist abuse in football grounds now. However we hear on the news about players being racially abused on social media. This is totally unacceptable and social media companies need to be made accountable and should have things in place for it not to happen in the first place. Whoever is caught giving racist or any discriminatory abuse should face stiffer prosecution.

In October 1977 Clive scored a great breakaway goal for President Kennedy under 15s against Great Barr. In April 1978 Coventry Schools under 15s hammered Aston 8-1 in the Semi-Final of the West Midlands Trophy. Clive scored and also Muir, Deakin, Meggitt and McCallum were on the scoresheet. Clive remembers playing at Highfield Road. This was in May 1978 when Coventry Schools won the West Midlands under 15 Shield. Scouts were looking at Clive because he was scoring plenty of goals. Team mates Peter Hormantschuk and Ian Muir both went onto become professionals. Abbey Kelly should have too for he was a good player. He had a good career in non-league football. After Coventry Schools, Clive and Abbey played for a team called Jah Baddis who had good players like Peter McBean (R.I.P) Lincoln Liburd and Neville Gordon. In November 1979 Jah Baddis were top of the Coventry and Central Warwickshire Senior League.

Clive finished playing in 1981 and he got into his music and discovered clubs. His parents were from Jamaica and grew up listening to Blue Beat / Ska. Popular Jamaican artists of the 1960s. Laurel Aitken and Prince Buster released records on the Blue Beat label. In the late 1970s and 1980s 2 Tone emerged and Coventry was at the heart of it with bands like The Specials and The Selecter. Clive spent a lot of time at Lower Holyhead Road Youth Centre which was used by many artists, using the basement for Jam sessions and Sound System. Clive found his home in music

He knew a lot of the artists in Coventry. His cousin went out with Lynval Golding (The Specials). Now in his fifties Clive is still into his music and he did some shows for Hillz FM. A keen Arsenal fan, his idol is Ian Wright who come through Non-League football to become one of the country's best strikers. Clive made a good point: "If Wrighty was in the England squad for Euro 96 England would have won the tournament." Shearer and Sheringham were quality but with Wright on the bench then maybe England might have been champions..

Gary Hardwick

I asked Gary a few questions about his career. He was part of the very good Coventry Schools' team in the early 1980s.

Could you tell me how your football days began?

I went to Potters Green and Woodway Park schools and I'm now back at Potters Green as a PE teacher. I played for an outstanding Coventry School boy team that reached the English Schools' Final where we were beaten by Sheffield. I was offered a YTS / apprentice at Coventry City and West Bromwich Albion but I chose Coventry. Aged fifteen and in my O level year at school, Coventry asked if I could train twice a week with the club. I was actually training with the first team. Dave Sexton was manager and everything was looking rosy. Then Bobby Gould took over, and the youth team manager was sacked and I never got a sniff for the rest of my time at Coventry.

Were you at Leamington as a young player?

I joined AP Leamington in the Southern Premier League. It was very physical but enjoyable. I played quite a few times in the first team whilst also playing midweek for the youth team. I used to get the bus to town, walk to the train station, get the train to Leamington and then walk to the ground on Windmill Road from the station. It was the season when Jim Watson and Dietmar Bruck were managers and the first team were in the Southern Premier League.

What senior teams did you play for?

I got selected for Birmingham County and was asked to have trial at Bolton and then Shrewsbury. I played for the Reserves at both and was asked to sign pro at Shrewsbury and then they sacked the manager and new manager had different view and the offer was withdrawn. I went to Nuneaton Borough when they were in the Conference and had a couple of first team games but mainly in the reserves. My old PE teacher David Harvey got me to train with Stratford Town, where we won the Midland Combination and the Cup and I scored something like 72 goals in 110 games. I then moved to Atherstone, where Peterborough were interested in signing both myself and Andy Rammell. We got stitched up a bit as Manchester United gazumped them to sign Rammell for £60,000. I was left at Atherstone and eventually signed for Bedworth for £500 and top scored with over 80 goals for them over 3 seasons. I signed for VS Rugby and was top scorer in their Southern Premier League campaign where we heartbreakingly lost to Marlow in the FA Cup 2nd round replay with the winners drawn away to Premier League Tottenham Hotspur. I moved back to Bedworth where Rich Landon was my partner and helped him to gain a move to Plymouth for £30,000. I then moved to Hinckley Town and scored 19 goals in 41 games. I transferred to Nuneaton Borough and won the Beazer Homes Midland title and the cup. I had a fabulous career and lots of "what could have been" but life deals you what it deals you. I have no complaints and thousands of fantastic memories. *I also played for and managed Potters Green and played for Poplar, all in Premier One an extremely competitive league.*

Who were your favourite players that you played with?

Lee Sullivan was on the same wavelength, but loved playing with Pete McBean, Dave Crowley and John McGinty

Sean Crowley

A former pupil of Cardinal Newman School, Sean was part of the excellent Coventry Schools' team in the early 1980s. I asked him a few questions about his football career.

How did you get spotted by Coventry City?

Originally we all tried out for the schoolboy team at 11 and basically if you made it then you played one year for them and did it again. Our captain that year was Jamie Hill (Son of the great Jimmy Hill!!!). He left Coventry to another city after the first year. I then took over as captain.

What position did you play and what were your strengths as a player?

I played sweeper for this team for all seven years (through six form too). I signed for Coventry City on my fourteenth birthday.

Coventry school boys had some great players back then like Mark Rosegreen and Gareth Evans. Which other players stood out in that era?

Mark Rosegreen (Rosie) was a great player but a year older than me. Gareth Evans played with me and had a long career with Hibernian, Peter Shearer played for Birmingham City. I played professional in New York. Players from other teams that were regarded as the best were Rob Jones and Mick McGinty and a year above me was a great player called John Matthews.

Would you say that the 1982 was the best that you played in?

We were regarded as the best team in the country for a couple of years. Unfortunately, we lost to Sheffield over two legs in the English Cup in 1982. We have always been regarded as the best school boy team in Coventry Boy's history. That team broke up after fifth year and I continued to play during the sixth form. I roughly played 95 games and won 92 and lost 3. I lifted 7 consecutive "West Midlands Champions Trophies. In June 1991 we travelled to Germany and won the European Cup meeting Motherwell.

Who did you play for after Coventry City?

I played for JF Kennedy in Coventry and New Jersey Eagles and New Jersey Imperials in America.

Don Gethfield

Don was a central defender for Coventry Schools' very good Under 15 team in 1982. I had the pleasure of speaking to Don who grew up in Radford and Canley and attended Alderman Callow School. As a youngster he played for a Sunday League team, Don's parents were quite religious and he had to go to Sunday School so it took a little while to be able to start playing. Don had Coventry School boy trials and he got in at the second attempt. He played for Coventry Dynamos and Crown Spartak. Back then junior football was very strong. Don talked about players like Terry Angus, Mark Rosegreen, Gareth Evans and Peter Shearer. In June 1979 Don was part of Coventry Schools' under 12s' team that won the West Midlands Inter-Association competition. Maurice Harnett, Sean Crowley, Jamie Hill, Gareth Evans and Peter Shearer were also in this team. The core of this side would play together for a number of years: indeed in 1982 the team would reach the final of the English Schools' Association Trophy. Don had an apprenticeship at Coventry City and when he was released he went into Non-league football. Don played for Mile Oak Rovers and signed a contract with them. Burton Albion came in for him but they wanted £10.000 for him. He stopped playing for about nine months until he was out of contact. Burton were at a higher level and Don was denied an opportunity.

Don had a long career in non-league football playing for Coventry Sporting, Atherstone, VS Rugby, Tamworth, Bromsgrove Rovers, Banbury, Racing Club Warwick, Nuneaton Borough and Bedworth United. He played up to the age of forty and to this day he is still involved with football. Don has lived in Mansfield for over twenty years. He is an academy coach at Nottingham Forest. He has also worked for Chesterfield FC, Ollerton Town FC and was Head

Coach of Bardon Hill Sports FC. Outside football he was a pub landlord including The Bug and Black Bat in Coventry and The Old Engine in Bedworth. Don has also worked for National Express as a Customer Service Manager. He told me that he has been quite fortunate that his bosses allowed him Saturday afternoons off to play football. He talked about some of the great players that he played with like Steve Ross, Steve Norris, Ian Crawley and Danny Conway. Many thanks for your time, Don: it was great speaking to you.

Boyd Young

Boyd was part of a good Coventry Schools' team in the 1980s. I asked him a few questions about his football career.

Could I ask you about your junior career? What teams did you play for?

I played for - Wolston, JFK, Mount Nod JFC, Woodlands School and Coventry School boys.

What senior teams did you play for?

Senior teams - St Mirren, Tamworth, Hinckley Athletic, VS Rugby, Atherstone, Stratford Town, Bedworth, JFK, Highway, Coundon Court and Coundon Court Old Boys.

What were your strengths as a player?

In my junior year I was a central midfielder with a good passing range and an eye for scoring from long range. In my days as pro and semi-pro I converted to a right back and I would say I was energetic, tough tackling with good passing and crossing skills.

Later in my career I would say I read the game well and became a sweeper who used good communication and leadership to make the game easier for everyone.

You were part of a good VS Rugby team with players like Mark Rosegreen. Which other players stand out in your career?

Yes I played in the VS Rugby team that got relegated from the Premier League to the Midland League as the club went into liquidation. With Only Ron Bradbury and myself still on the books at the start of pre-season he managed to get a team together and we got promoted back up straight away coming second to the then very rich Rushden& Diamonds. In that team were Tim Smithers, Tom McGinty, Kim Green, Ashley Warner, Garry Statham, Paul Batchelor, Lee Harriman, Rob Smith, Danny Martin to name but a few.

Nick Kirk

Nick was a Coventry Schools' and Coventry City Youth team forward. On the 9th of July 2013 Nick sadly passed away at the age of forty. "Kirky" was a great player in local football and in December 2009 he scored a goal after just fourteen seconds for Mount Nod.

A tribute by Boyd Young

"Kirky" was my best friend from Primary school and, we went to the same secondary school, The Woodlands, who won the Coventry Schools' Cup five years on the bounce and were the West Midland champions for years 8,9,10 and 11. We also got to the semi-final of the English Schools' Cup losing in Southampton. After school we both signed for Coventry City FC on YTS forms.

After two years Nick was released and went to play for Massey Ferguson FC. He established himself in the first team and was their top goal scorer every season until he left to sign for Stratford Town FC. He also played on a Sunday for the very talented and successful side John F Kennedy. After a successful spell at Stratford he signed for Sutton United and was a great success for them and then he signed for Bedworth United where he became a hero.. After finishing with Bedworth at the same time as me he joined Highway Sports and he was top goal scorer in the league most seasons and was known as (Dial a Hat Rick). He played for Alvis FC under Damian Cassidy and also Peugeot on a Sunday but finished his career back at Highway Sports FC.

Leigh Burdett

Leigh is an old friend from Cardinal Newman School and it was great to catch up with him. He was one of the best players in his year. Back then Leigh played in midfield, a big strong lad with technical ability. The school team had some very good players and a few of the lads played for Coventry Boys including Leigh. In their last year at school the team got to a cup final at West Bromwich Albion's Hawthorns ground. They gave a good account of themselves in a 4-3 defeat and Leigh scored. I remember the excitement and everyone being proud of what they achieved. Leigh was destined to play at a decent level of football and he played for West Midland Schools and had trials with England School boys. In Leigh's year at Coventry boys were Jamie Cleland, Marcus Law and Marcus Hall. Leigh was top scorer for them. After leaving school he played as a forward, sometimes out wide as he had a bit of pace. When Leigh was released by Coventry City he spent time at Shrewsbury, Oxford then joined Tamworth under Sammy Chung who he rates as his best manager. Sammy is best known for his time as Wolverhampton Wanderers manager in the 1970s. At

Nineteen years old Leigh joined Hinckley United, then Stratford Town under Sky Blues legend Barry Powell. Leigh had spells with Moreton Town, Kings Heath, Coventry Sphinx, Folly Lane and Coventry Copeswood, Cheylesmore, Highway and Coventry Postal.

Leigh talked about some of the good players he played with or against and these include a young Emile Heskey when playing against Leicester schools. Other players include Phil Stamp, Marcus Bignot, Simeon Hodgson, Ian Muir and Ian Crawley. Local players whom Leigh thought highly of were Darren Ward, Rob Stevenson, Marcus Hamill and Mark Hodgkinson. Leigh has also done some coaching. He coached the School of Excellence under 12s and Under 15s. Leigh coached the Under 12s for a year under Jose Ascensao and head coach Trevor Gould. The Under 15s was under Ray Gooding who was Leigh's Coventry Boys' manager and in that age group was future star Gary McSheffrey.

Leigh is also a talented Bowls player: in 2009 he helped Copeswood win the North Midlands County Cup after beating Weddington Social. In the deciding game he beat his opponent in a close game to win the cup for the Coventry team.

Kyle King

I asked Kyle a few questions about his career. A junior player in Coventry, he went on to play professionally in a few countries.

How did you get spotted by Coventry City?

I played schoolboys/juniors for Coventry and also a number of Sunday league teams from the age of eleven. I was spotted locally when playing for local teams in Coventry and at Coventry Connexions in Ryton (Indoor Football). I spent five years at

Hinckley United from the age of fifteen which made up the main part of my youth career and my transition into the first team.

I believe that you played in Australia for a while. That must have been a great experience?

I played in Australia, New Zealand, China, Cambodia, Thailand and Vietnam professionally for around five years and top Semi-Professional level for the other two to three year,
great experiences and playing in some amazing stadiums with some pros who chose to retire over in those countries.

Are you still playing now?

I returned from Australia threeyears ago due to the birth of my first child and played locally for Bedworth United. However due to time restrictions with work I now play locally on a Sunday for Leamington Hibs. I find it is still a competitive league and still gives me that buzz to be playing at my age!

Did you play with any famous players in Australia?

I trained with Perth Glory when I first got to Australia and played with William Gallas. I have also played with Chris Coyne formerly of Luton Town, Jay Bothroyd, Paul Ifil and a guy called Chupè who played for Real Madrid. I have played with many international players for all the countries I played in also and who still turn out regularly for their countries.

Chapter Eleven – Coventry City Youth Team

Coventry City has produced some excellent home grown talent. In this chapter we are going to look at youth team players from the 1970s to the 2000s.

Alan Green

A fine striker for Coventry City in the early 1970s, I had the pleasure of speaking to Alan. He was born in Worcester on 1st of January 1954. Alan had a number of teams watching him as a youngster including Coventry City, Aston Villa, Arsenal and Birmingham City. He chose Coventry because of the great set up: the hostel was near Highfield Road and the players were all living together. Coventry City had a very good youth team in the late 1960s / early 1970s In 1970 they lost in the FA Youth Cup final to Tottenham Hotspur. Team mates included Dennis Mortimer, Alan Dugdale, Jimmy Holmes, Mick McGuire, Bobby Parker and Les Cartwright. Alan and these players would all play for the first team, Les and Jimmy becoming full internationals. Dennis won the league and European Cup with Aston Villa in the early 1980s and some would say that it is a travesty he never played for England. Other team mates were Ivan Crossley, Johnny Stevenson and Colin Randell who all had decent careers. Coventry City's goalkeeper was David Icke who played league football for Hereford United, is better known for his career in sports broadcasting and as a Conspiracy Theorist! Alan remembers being interviewed by him for the BBC. Tottenham Hotspur's team included Steve Perryman, Graeme Souness and Ray Clarke, but the young Sky Blues gave them a good game.

Alan made his Coventry City debut on 22nd of April 1972 against Leicester City as a substitute. He made his first start against Tottenham Hotspur on 12th August 1972. In September 1973 Alan scored his first goals for the Sky Blues in a 2-2 draw against Burnley. In total he played 132 times scoring 34 goals for Coventry City. Alan enjoyed playing with Colin Stein, David Cross, Neil Martin and Mick Ferguson. Towards the end of his time at Highfield Road he often played wide when the Ferguson-Wallace partnership was developing. Alan remembers the Wolves match getting a hat rick but he said that he has played better in other games but it is obviously satisfying to score goals.

When he was no longer a first choice at Highfield Road Alan was all set for a move to Sunderland. However after making an impact in a match against Ipswich Town his value went up from £100,000 to £200,000 which put off Sunderland and a few other teams. Understandably frustrated by this Alan at the age of twenty five decided to move to USA in the summer of 1979 having previously been on loan with Washington Diplomats in 1977. In the late 1970s US soccer was at a good standard and many world class players played in the NASL like Pele, Best, Eusebio and Beckenbauer. Alan played with legendary Dutch players Cruyff and Neeskens. Alan played for Jacksonville Tea Men (managed by Noel Cantwell) New York Cosmos, Golden Bay Earthquakes and Team America. If you look on Alan's Wikipedia page it will say that he played one match for USA in 1984. This is true however it was under Team America who were a professional version of the USA national team which played as a franchise in the North American Soccer League (NASL) during the 1983 season. Alan played one match for Team America against Italy in 1984, after obtaining dual citizenship. Team America only lasted one season, Alan soon after decided to retire from football. He was asked to play for Peterborough United under Noel Cantwell but decided against it. Alan has been back in England since 1997 just outside Worcester. He is a member of the CCFPA and has been to the Ricoh a few times.

Garry Thompson

Garry is one of the best players to come through Coventry City's youth team in the 1970s. I asked him a few questions about his early football career.

How did you get spotted by Coventry City?

I was scoring goals for my school and district teams so much, that I was in the Sports Argus for scoring a few hat tricks. My sports master Mr Williams insisted that a few of team were in the photo with me cleaning my boots. One of my team mates in the photo had already been spotted by Coventry City and been for trials and had been called up for England schools trials. He was Paul Dyson. Coventry had asked him if he knew any other good players around and he'd mentioned me and our best mate Malcolm Percival. Nothing happened until we got to the quarter finals of the English Schools' Trophy. Then the Midlands scout Jack Hastings called at my house to speak to my parents. Conversation took a while as my parents were convinced that he'd come about my older brother Ian. They eventually agreed I could go for trials and I went down with Paul for the Easter holidays and it went well. Because they asked me to sign schoolboy contract they asked if I would come down for the summer holidays. They were six weeks long (incorporating pre-season) and I loved it. I played in the Reserves towards the end of the six weeks holiday at fifteen, so even though I played in youth Teams I had kind of leapfrogged it. Coming back after a broken leg I played in an "A "team game but it was predominantly a youth team. I played the full game after eleven months out, played with socks down for first time and went and got drunk after, which was after not having a drink for the same eleven months!

The mid to late 1970s was a fantastic era for the youth team. Which players really stood in the Coventry youth team?

Coventry scouting network was immense and we got kids from all over country. The standard was very high. Bob Dennison ran it and Bert Edwards ran the youth/ reserves with Colin Dobson.

When I first went there schoolboys/youth was ran by a brilliant bloke called Ritchie I want to say Barker but not sure. He went off to Derby as reserves manager. But to be hones the Bert/Dobbo combination was excellent. In my year was Chris Waddle who was with us for ages then disappeared suddenly. Graham Oakey was in the first team, Harry Roberts and Don Nardiello were getting the odd game. Ray Gooding and Lenny Harvey (a kid from Doncaster) we're the favourites to make it just behind them, followed by Frank McGrellis (a centre forward) who had great ability and Val Thomas (Danny's brother).
In my year the players who stood out were Gary Bannister, Dave Butterworth(both wingers)Paul Dyson, Andy Blair, Alan Carruthers and Paul Smith(both defenders)But we were under pressure because year below us, players like - Hateley, English, D Thomas, Dave Barnes, Steve Murcott, Nicky Phillips, Kevin Cooper , Peter Bodak and Clive Haywood. And then out the blue they bought Gary Gillespie, Paul Thompson and Jim Hagan and just a year below them was Ian Butterworth and Martin Singleton.

Which opposition players were really good?

Ivor Linton, who went to Villa as a kid: he terrorised midlands football and a lad who went to Blues Steve Fox.

Garry went onto become a great striker for Coventry City and had a fantastic career. His brother Keith also played for Coventry City. Garry is remembered for being part of the fine Sky Blues team of the early 1980s. The core of that team had progressed through the excellent youth set up at Coventry City. Garry's autobiography "Don't Believe a Word" is out now, an excellent book.

Tommy English

Tommy was an apprentice with Coventry who signed professional in June 1979 and breaking into the first team in August 1979. Tommy, along with fellow young forwards Garry Thompson and Mark Hateley were exciting prospects. After 76 games and 17 goals he moved to Leicester City in exchange for Jim Melrose. From there he played for a number of teams including Colchester United, Plymouth Argyle and Rochdale. Tommy also spent time in Australia and Hong Kong. Tommy's brother Tony also spent time with Coventry City as a youth player His son Tom played professional football too. I asked Tommy's son Luke a few questions for Tommy.

What was your dad's favourite Coventry City match?

The favourite match has to be the hat trick against rivals Leicester City in the 4-1 win at Highfield Road.

Which players did he enjoy playing up front with during his career?

Garry Thompson, Mark Hateley and Mick Ferguson were the best to play with.

Does he remember the 2tone photos that he took with Garry Thompson? They have become quite iconic

Yes he remembers them very well still has a chuckle now.

How did your dad get spotted by Coventry City?

Whilst playing Sunday football in Colchester.

David Smith

I had the pleasure of speaking to David on the phone. In the late 1980s David was one of my favourite Coventry City players He was an exciting player to watch. David was an old fashioned left winger, with excellent ball control and the ability to beat the full back and deliver a fine cross. David was spotted by Bert Edwards playing for local Gloucestershire Schools. He came up to Coventry during holidays aged 13 / 14 then signing apprentice forms in 1984 aged sixteen. David stayed in the club hostel which was by the ground in Catherine Street at the back of the West Stand. In David's year there was Steve Sedgley, Tony Mahan, Roger Preece and John Hathaway. Sadly John passed away in February 2009 at the age of forty. John was a forward and scored on a regular basis for Coventry City's Youth and Central League teams in the mid-1980s. He also spent time with Wolverhampton Wanderers and Swindon Town. John played for and coached Fairford Town.

When Coventry City won the FA Cup and FA Youth Cup, David was in between both teams because he was in the year above the youth team and not quite in the first team picture. He signed professional in 1986 and didn't have to wait too long for a first team chance. On 6th of February 1988 David made his first team debut as a substitute against Manchester United at Old Trafford. It was the 30th anniversary of the Munich disaster: United won the match 1-0 with a goal from Liam O'Brien. David became a regular in the team and his form was so good they couldn't leave him out. Nick Pickering who the Sky Blues first choice left sided midfielder often played at left back because David was now the preferred left winger. David scored goals against Chelsea and Newcastle United in March 1988. Strikers Cyrille Regis, David Speedie and Gary Bannister were benefiting from the young winger from Gloucester. In the summer of 1988 twenty year old David was called up England under 21 manager Dave Sexton. On the 5th of June 1988 David made his under 21 debut against Mexico in the Toulon tournament. England won 2-1 with Nigel Clough scoring both of the goals with Gunners legend David Rocastle as captain.

England under 21 team against Mexico under 21

Martyn, Cooper, Redmond, Chettle, Dicks.Thomas, Gascoigne, Platt, Rocastle, Clough, Smith

David played two more Toulon tournament matches against USSR and Morocco which were both 1-0 wins, however he didn't play in the final which was a 4.2 defeat to France. On 18th of October 1988 England Under 21s played a European Championship qualifier against Sweden Under 21s at Highfield Road. David and City team mate Steve Sedgley played in this match as did future Sky Blue David Burrows making his Under 21 debut. Manchester City forward David White scored for England who were captained by another Man City player Steve Redmond.

England under 21 team against Sweden under 21

Martyn, Statham (Burrows) Cooper, Sedgley, Redmond, Chettle, White, Ripley, Dozzell,(Oldfield)Samways, Smith

David played ten times for England under 21s and was very proud to make his debut. He played with some fantastic players in particular David Platt and Paul Gascoigne who he spoke highly of both" Platt was a great professional and Gazza was a special talent"

England Under 21 data provided by Copyright Barrie Courtney and RSSSF 2004/18 Many thanks

When fans look back at the 1988/89 season it is often overshadowed by the FA Cup defeat at Sutton United. Apart from that result the club had a great season finishing seventh which has only been bettered once in 1970. David played in the Sutton match and he recalls the team had lots of chances "but it just wasn't our day." In April 1989 Coventry City beat Manchester United 1-0 at Old Trafford to complete the double over the Red Devils. David with some fantastic wing play beating Mike Duxbury and Bryan Robson, set up Gary Bannister for the winner. City made a great start to the 1989/90 season and were top of the league thanks to a late winner by David against Manchester City. Liverpool were also beaten in November 1989 which was Coventry's first ever win at Anfield. David scored a superb right-footer in the 2-0 home win over Aston Villa in March 1990 and the club did brilliantly in the League Cup reaching the semi-finals. The 1990/91 season's most memorable match was a 5-4 win over Nottingham Forest in the League Cup. Kevin Gallagher scored a hat trick in that match; he was a great signing from Dundee United in February 1990.

The next season was a struggle for City and they just about stayed up thanks to Notts County beating Luton Town on the last game of the season. David was still a regular but faced competition from young Zimbabwean Peter Ndlovu. One of the results of the season was a 5-0 win over Luton Town in August 1991, David and Kevin linked up well together in this match. Coventry's last game of the season was at Aston Villa away, losing 2-0 with Cyrille Regis and Dwight Yorke scoring for Villa. With another lucky escape the club could look forward to the new Premier League era and Bobby Gould was brought in as manager. David scored in the opening match of the season against Middlesbrough and played another six games for the club. He had a trial for Dundee United and then moved to Birmingham City in March 1993 in exchange for David Rennie. David spent eleven months at St Andrews before moving to West Bromwich Albion in 1994. David spent four years at The Hawthorns where he particularly enjoyed playing for Ray Harford. David had an unusual sequence of matches in the last games of the season in 1992, 1993 and 1994 as they were all last day relegation escapes for three different clubs.

In the 1997/98 season David Joined Grimsby Town linking up with Former Coventry City team mate Steve Livingstone. The Mariners enjoyed two Wembley wins in 1998 in the Football League Trophy and Football League Second Division play-off Final. David had a brief spell with Swansea City in the 2002/03 season before retiring from playing. Since 2003 he has worked at Grimsby Town as a Press Officer, Assistant Commercial Manager and now Commercial Manager. David is good friends with Graham Rodger who also works at Grimsby Town and Kevin Gallagher. When he was at Coventry City Mick Kearns was very helpful to him, Mick was a coach and a former full back and really helped him in training. As for toughest opponents he played against, David told me Lee Dixon, Paul Parker, Steve Nicol and John Humphrey were good full backs. David can look back with pride on his career: he was a fine left winger and also a dependable left back. It would be interesting to find out how many goals David assisted in his time at Coventry. I am sure Cyrille Regis, David Speedie and Kevin Gallagher enjoyed playing with him. He has been to back to watch Coventry City matches on legends days and is a member of CCFPA.

Alun French

Alun was part of a very good Coventry City youth team in the late 1980s. I asked him a few questions about his career.

What junior teams did you play for and how did you get spotted by Coventry City?

The Junior Teams I played for were- Wolston Juniors (under 11 - under 15) - Sunday Minor League. Folly Lane (under 16), Coventry Schools (All Seniors School Years). West Midlands County – (under 14 - under 16).

Bert Edwards and Lol Cairns (Local Scout) and Manager of Folly Lane invited me to the Coventry City School of Excellence who trained on a Thursday Evening on the Astro - Turf up at Bablake Playing Fields. We were coached by John Peacock who now has a position with the FA. We played the occasional game against other Schools of Excellence. After a short time I was offered Schoolboy forms which tied me to the club and enabled us to go to Ryton (training ground) for coaching and assist with apprentice duties during the school holidays. This continued until we were due to leave school, when the club had to make a decision on whether to offer us a place on the newly introduced YTS Scheme which was formally an apprenticeship. This scheme lasted for two years and involved leaving home and living at the Clubs Youth Hostel along with the other lads offered terms and also lads who had just completed their first year on the scheme.

What were your strengths as a player?

My strengths as a player were my leadership skills, ability to read the game and strength in the air. I wasn't easily intimidated and I was also comfortable using both feet which enabled me to be versatile in any defensive role. I was Captain of the Youth Team and was appointed "Head Boy" during the second year of my apprenticeship. I was responsible for all apprentices and had to allocate duties and roles for all the guys such as Cleaning Boots, working with the Kit Man etc.... This was a special honour as I was Head Boy when the Sky Blue Lodge (current training headquarters) were opened by the then England Manager - Graham Taylor. The Sky Blue Lodge was then our new home and housed all apprentices and anyone who came on trial.

Did the lads in your team feel much pressure because the class of 87?

I don't think our age groups felt pressured due to the success of the Class of 87. The pressure came with having the opportunity of playing for your Boyhood Team. Our particular age group intakes were predominantly made up of local lads who had grown up playing for Coventry Schools and rival teams on a Sunday. We were a talented bunch who definitely underachieved. The older lads already at the club such as the Middleton twins, Lee Hurst, Martyn Booty, Tony Dobson, Steve Livingstone & Howard Clark were all great lads who were always available to offer guidance and advice when required.

Who would you say were the best players that you played with or against?

Best Player played against - Whilst still at school I was selected to be a substitute for the Reserve Team to play Manchester United at Old Trafford. This day sticks in my mind because it kicked off at around noon on FA Cup Final day 1989 (Liverpool v Everton). Manchester United had to win the game to maintain their place in the First Division of the Central League and picked a team full of players who had first Team experience such as Mark Bosnich, Steve Bruce, Mike Duxbury, Clayton Blackmore, Shaun Goater and many more. We put out a Youth Team because the season for the majority of the Senior Players had finished the week before when the season had officially ended. It was 0-0 at Half Time and all our lads excelled. Experience shone through in the end and United finally won the game 4-0. I got on for the final 20 minutes and marked Shaun Goater. The best player I played against was probably Dwight Yorke when he was at Aston Villa. Others included Tony Cottee (Everton) and Nigel Clough at Nottingham Forest. Toughest opponent by far was Cyrille Regis when we regularly played practise matches against the first Team for he had Immense strength. Peter Ndlovu came along with his brother Adam from Zimbabwe on trial. The guy had so much natural talent and made mugs of a number of us. I knew he was going to be a special player.

What senior teams did you play for?

When released at the end of a one year Professional contract I went on unsuccessful trials to teams such as Swansea and Swindon and also had the opportunity of playing in Hong Kong with Warren Bufton (my good friend and roommate). I decided not to go but Warren did. Due to not being able to drive I turned down the opportunity of signing for Telford and instead signed for Atherstone United initially then had spells with both VS Rugby and Hinckley Athletic. Due to this level of football not being full time I found myself a job in the Exhibition Industry to ensure commitments could be met. This meant I wasn't always available to train on a Tuesday and Thursday. I could not then expect to play on a Saturday ahead of players who were attending every training session. With that I gradually drifted away from the game as I had to ensure I was earning enough money to ensure my mortgage and bills were paid. Whilst at Coventry City I met my future wife Jayne - who's Dad Dietmar Bruck played for the club during the successful period in the 60s. I am now a Season Ticket Holder and go to games with my dad, son and daughter.

Darren Dickson

Currently manager of Coventry Copeswood FC, I had a chat with Darren and asked him a few questions about his career. Darren has enjoyed a good career in youth and non-league football. It began with Junior team Chaplefield Colts then Folly Lane when he was spotted by Lol Cairns. Darren joined Coventry City aged sixteen, Terry Paine was youth team manager and John Sillett was first team manager. John was very keen to sign up local talent and he said, "My dream is to have eleven Coventry lads in the team." In the late 1980s there was a big intake of local lads. Darren was a left sided winger. His team mates included Lee Hurst, Martyn Booty, Alun French and Terry Fleming. David Smith was Coventry City's first choice left winger. He came through the youth ranks and was very helpful to Darren. The team was very successful and won the league, FA Youth Cup quarter finals and were League Cup runners up. One match that sticks out was a match at Old Trafford in May 1989 against a strong Manchester United team who included Steve Bruce, Lee Sharpe and Mark Robins.

In 1990 Terry Butcher had replaced John Sillett as manager and Darren was told that the club would not be extending his contract. At eighteen years old it was hard to take and for a while after he lost the love for football. Darren had trials for Scarborough and Halifax before joining Tamworth under Sammy Cheung. He started to enjoy football again and had trials with West Ham United, Birmingham City and Cambridge United. Darren then played for a few local teams often under Ron Bradbury and Bob Stockley which were VS Rugby, Bedworth and Atherstone. Then he had a spell at Stratford Town under Lenny Derby and a few local teams including Coventry Marconi. Darren got into coaching with Coundon Cockerills and Dunlop and then began a long spell at Coventry Copeswood. Initially he had seven years in charge at Copeswood then a year out because of a hip replacement then took over again. Darren has won the Coventry Telegraph Cup and Coventry Charity Cup with Copeswood. At the time of writing Copeswood are looking to have a successful season having recruited a few lads from Nuneaton Borough and Racing Club Warwick.

Warren Bufton

Warren was a promising striker in the late 1980s/early 1990s. I asked him a few questions about his career.

Can I firstly ask you about your junior career? What teams did you play for?

I played for a few junior teams – Allesley Sports, Stoke Heath Rangers, Coventry Continental and Folly Lane (I joined them as the CCFC scout Lol Cairns was their manager). I scored lots of goals for all these teams, I think being taller than most at that age helped me.

When I was elevenish I joined the CCFC School of Excellence which was run by John Peacock, who, according to Wikipedia, currently works for FIFA, UEFA and Man United. This led me onto signing schoolboy forms for CCFC at the age of 14. When I left school I signed a two year apprenticeship (YTS) and afternoon that I was given a one year professional contract.

You were a regular scorer for the reserves. You should have been given a first team chance, was you ever in the first team squad?

During this time I was a regular in the reserves but unfortunately I never got into the first team squad.

As a second year apprentice we were the first group of lads to move into the Sky Blue lodge which had Roy and Marie Fletcher running it, feeding us and cleaning. I shared a room with Alun French who was head boy. We had moved from the hostel which was based on Catherine St (I think) which was next to the Highfield Rd. stadium.

As you can imagine with about eighteen lads living together in one place, there were arguments. But mostly it was non-stop mickey taking. We had a table tennis table at Ryton which most of us used to play but Terry Fleming was the guy that no one could beat.

I was told that I had earned a professional contract after playing a youth team match in Stoke. Colin Dobson took me to one side in the changing room and told me that I had earned a one year contract. He said John Sillett had agreed I could have a two year contract but Terry Butcher had since come in as a manager and would only hand out one year contracts as he didn't know us as players.

I had an average professional year at best and Don Howe gave me encouraging words but told me that he was going to release me. I was gutted to be rejected by the team that I love. From there, I had trials at Doncaster and Swindon, but the bizarre one was a trial in St James Park in London for a team called Sing Tao based in Hong Kong. I successfully did a bit of running, control and passing and was offered triple what I was on at Coventry with free board so I was off to Hong Kong.

After three months there I came back. It didn't work out for me for various reasons. I was a young 18 year old with little life experience, missed my girlfriend at the time, so I requested to come back to England. It was reported in the papers over there though that I was sacked!!!

Who would you say were the best players that you played with?

David Speedie, favourite ever Coventry player, even if he took all the headlines after I scored two against Liverpool (reserves). Regis, phenomenal striker, so strong. So many of the FA Cup winning team, Brian Borrows was the most underrated full back: how he didn't play for England I will never know. I played against many famous players but the one that really sticks out is Steve Bruce. He was coming back from injury for Man Utd Reserves but throughout the game he was talking to me, telling me what I could have done instead of what I had. He was coaching me even though he was marking me. A true gent.

Who did you play for after Coventry City?

I came back and played for VS Rugby and Hinckley for the rest of that season. It was the year when, if VS had beaten Marlow, we would have played Spurs in the 3rd round of the FA Cup but we lost in the replay .After that year, I didn't play at a high level as I lost my love for the game. I played for the Highway after Mick Downing called me to play for them. That was enjoyable.

Adam Willis

Adam was a central defender who did really well at Swindon Town. I asked him a few questions about his career.

How did you get spotted by Coventry City?

I was playing for a local team (Jet Blades) in Bedworth at under 11s. I was asked to go the School of Excellence at The AT7 centre. I began going to other clubs at about under 13s level including Sheffield United, Manchester United, Birmingham and Tottenham, but I think I was always going to sign with Coventry as I was a fan as a boy.

Could you tell me a little bit about your time at Coventry? You were a regular in the reserves and youth team. Did you enjoy your time at the club?

I enjoyed the people there, the friends I made and the experiences I had, but I would say that as soon as I started playing professionally I did not enjoy it as much as I would have liked to. I felt pressure to perform well and to earn another contract. My studies since have allowed me to see that I didn't fulfil my potential through psychological deficiencies and fear to play freely. I enjoyed my football most when I played 'in the moment'; that was mostly with the friends I made and when I did not focus on all the other aspects outside of 'playing'.

When you signed for Swindon did it help having a familiar face at the club in Brian Borrows?

Bugsy was a large influence on my life as he was instrumental in recommending me to Steve McMahon (the Swindon Manager at the time). I travelled to Swindon from the Midlands with Bugsy and Mark Walters (Ex Liverpool, Villa and Rangers) for about six months until I bought a flat in Swindon. I spent the next five years with the club and probably enjoyed my football their most. Bugsy retired after my first two years and I played with many managers and players after that. He was a really good man and an excellent player. My life would have panned our very differently I think, if it wasn't for him.

What was your favourite season at Swindon?

I played under several managers in my time at Swindon, but I think the year I was made captain under Colin Todd probably brings back my best memories playing there. I can remember that we made me captain for the last game of the season against Sheffield United; there was a full house at Bramall Lane and they had been promoted I think. The game was a 3-3 thriller and I can remember playing well and having the respect of a lot of our senior pros at the time. I remember being hopeful for the next year and feeling positive about the way my career was going as I had just signed a new contract that tied me to the club for another two years. The following year I started as captain and played every game until I got injured and then spent some time out of the team. Another manager came in and I had to work at building up my performances and reputation again. I made some good friends in the team and look back fondly at that time. I felt comfortable in the Championship and Division One, and was lucky enough to play at some good grounds with some good team mates.

You played with some great players in your career. Who would you choose as your favourite central defender partners?

When I was at Coventry I played with Gary Gillespie, Gary Breen and Dion Dublin amongst others. At Swindon I played with Alan Reeves, "Razor" Ruddock and Brian Burrows and I have fond memories of playing with all of them. I did enjoy playing with Marcus Hall in the youth team as we knew our roles. If there was a high ball we both knew I was the one going to be going for it, and he'd be on the cover. There was maybe a brief glimpse at each other when a goalkeeper took a kick and we both knew what was going to happen!

How did you find playing non-league after leaving Swindon?

I didn't really enjoy non-league at all, and by the time I decided to retire I was relieved. I saw out my contract at Hinckley, but if I'm being honest I was done by the winter of that year. I found it that the lower the level I played the more difficult it was. I didn't really enjoy the standard of pitches and grounds and just hooking things away and just scrapping rather than playing. Heading dozens of balls relentlessly didn't help my neck either. I was also finding it difficult to combine studying for my degree at Worcester and travelling for mid-week games. I was glad to be out of it.

Jamie Barnwell-Edinboro

Jamie was a striker for Coventry City's youth team in the 1990s. I asked Jamie a few questions about his football career.

I believe that you were recommended to Coventry by Ray Gooding?

Yes, however, it was Dave Wood that recommended Ray to come and watch me play. Dave is the father of Simon Wood (Woody). Wood was also courted by most of the top clubs in the country and had already been on trial at Coventry. As such, Dave had agreed to do some scouting for the club.

Although Woody was a year younger than me, such was his talent, we played together in the same Hull Schools' representative team. As luck would have it, we drew Coventry Schools in the later rounds of the English Schools Cup at Boothferry Park. The Coventry team, if memory serves, included Jamie Cleland and Marcus Hall. So, the game presented an opportunity for Ray to watch me play. Thankfully, we won the game 2-0 and I scored a goal and assisted the other. This was enough for Ray, after the game, to ask if I would like to go on trial at the club. Shortly after, Dave drove me to Coventry for a trail game against Norwich City at Ryton. Lol Kearns ran the team on the day.

Over the next few months, I travelled to Ryton in School holidays, staying at the Sky-Blue Lodge under Roy and Maria Fletcher. Bert Edwards headed up the youth section. After a couple of visits, I was asked to sign associated school-boy forms for the club, which I gladly did. Subsequently, I started training more with the youth team under Colin Dobson. The highlight, despite the score, was appearing in the F.A. Youth Cup as a schoolboy against Spurs at White Hart Lane.

At school I believe that you were a good athlete. Do you think that you would have pursued athletics if you didn't become a footballer?

At school, my P.E. teacher, Mr Wilmot was incredibly supportive and believed in my athletic ability. He encouraged me to apply that ability across lots of different sports. Mr Wilmot ran the school rugby league team and was always keen for me to play wing or centre. Most of my friends played rugby league as did my family (I have five uncles) except for my brother. My Dad had played professionally for Hull F.C. whilst my uncle had played for Bradford Northern. I had also started playing open age rugby at fifteen years old along-side my football commitments.

Mr Wilmot specialised in athletics though and suggested I had potential across the sprints, sprint hurdles and triple jump. By year ten (as it is now) my triple jumps were up around the national level for my age. Similarly, from school testing, Mr Wilmot felt I could compete nationally at decathlon. This appealed to me as one of my sporting heroes was Daley Thompson. Mr Wilmot arranged for the school to buy me some athletic spikes and for me to attend regional track and field events, which I did. Despite the success I enjoyed across the athletic meets I did not enjoy the solitary nature of the sport.

Coventry had a good youth and reserve teams when you were at the club. Which players did you enjoy playing with?

We did, which marked my youth team years and first year as a professional as some of my most enjoyable. It also makes it difficult to pick out individuals. Each player at the club at that time brought something unique that made training and playing enjoyable. Across my two years as an YT, being a striker, I was privileged to partner up with Dave Carmichael and Iysden

Christie. Certainly, from my perspective, I thoroughly enjoyed partnering both. Simon Wood, because we knew each other and had played together a lot, complimented me and his passing range brought out the best in me. I had a good relationship with Gavin O'Toole and Willie Boland during the youth team. And, as young professionals we shared a house(s), in which we had great times.

Reflecting now, two players that come to mind are Tony Sheridan and John Williams. Shero was one of the most gifted and natural footballers I have ever seen. He floated about the pitch and could make the ball do what he wanted. This, a lot of the time, was putting it in the 'stanchion.' Like Shero, Willo seemed to play the game like he did not have a care in the world. There seemed to be a freedom to his play that was infectious. For me personally, he was also a fantastic senior professional. When I went out on loan to Swansea, Willo would call me to make sure I was ok. Similarly, he always encouraged me in training.

Do you remember much about your first team debut?

I did some reflective writing on this a few years ago

THE LION IN THE TRIANGLE

I'M SKY HIGH WITH EXCITMENT as I look out of the window of the private charter plane. There's slight apprehension and the feeling I've gone back 60 years, as I notice the plane has visible propellers. I do a quick re-frame to calm my nerves and pretend I'm Indiana Jones flying across a screen map to our destination. I keep looking down at the crest on my tracksuit top. Over the last couple of years, I've had tops with the same crest on and they've always meant a lot and represented a journey of sacrifice, hard work, good fortune and opportunity coupled with this fine club's history. But today it's different, it's real. The plane lands about forty-five minutes later, for a journey that would have taken us about four hours on the team bus, and it's a short walk to join the coach waiting for us. In transit through the busy North-East city it's easy to pick out the already gathering crowds of red shirts making their pilgrimage. We've flown north early to take in a pre-match meal.

When we arrive at the hotel we're met with the utmost hospitality. There's time for the usual banter and craic of fifteen lads, filled with adrenaline before the pre-match meal. It's a banquet fit for a king, that's if the king was an elite athlete fuelling for a football match. This is a step up from the tea and toast or at a push scrambled egg and beans I'm used to before reserve games. There's an unexpected dessert section that's taken advantage of and it seems there has developed an unspoken agreement among the lads, that these are in fact "simple carbohydrates" and "fast sugars" essential for 90+ minutes performance, and not a plant by the gaffer to see who ends up in a sugar coma in the team briefing.

We leave the hotel and get back on the coach. We dissect the now dense traffic, and enlarged crowds, due to the police escort motorcycles in front of the bus. They guide us through junctions and roundabouts and we are soon at our destination. No need for a hastily filled in team sheet or a mad dash to the officials. This place is keeping with the salubrious tone of the day and is brand spanking new. I pick up my toilet bag, which along with a good performance is the only thing I must take care of today that's not done for me. We leave the coach and as fans are gathering, we go through the players' entrance. Everything is pristine and starting its own journey of collecting memories, history, and success. I walk into the changing rooms and straight away it hits me, BANG. Time slows down but my heart rate speeds up. If I was a Loony Tunes character my eyes would now pop out of my head on stalks across the room. Barnwell 28 is hanging on a Sky-Blue shirt across the room, like a product placement, designed to hook me further into this experience. I'm drawn to it, making my way across the room I'm expecting Jeremy Beadle to jump out. My hand reaches out to touch it, checking it's real, and not trusting the nerve signals traveling from my fingers to my brain, that says it is. I pick up the short sleeve shirt and the proud lion inside the triangle, the emblem of The Carling Premier League, stares at me. In my mind's eye he points a judgmental paw at me, "Don't you fuck this up", and so begins the picture board of stories we tell ourselves, turning our thoughts into an illusion of reality. This storyboard has me picturing everything that could go wrong. Grabbing a sugary brew, I sit down to get myself together. Everything is subconscious, autopilot preparation, in the zone, following superstitions and habits. I'm delighted that I haven't seen any solitary Magpie on the journey. But neither have I seen two magpies. Both in the past have had a big impact on my pre-game mentality. "One for Sorrow two for joy", such a simple rhyme could tip the balance on my delicate psyche. Seeing one magpie would equal a shit game, whilst seeing two could equal the chance of playing well. I know there's nothing in it, logic tells me that. But it's something learned from peers, that at this point in my career it can affect my delicate mental state. It's one of a thousand things, fizzing through my head, that's stopping me getting ready. As is the fact in all my years of playing the game, I've never prepared for a 3 o'clock kick off. To this point it's been morning football with the youth team and evening kick-offs for the reserves. 3 o'clock is proper football.

There's light at the end of the tunnel and I make my way towards it. I step out of the glare into a beautiful August afternoon. The glory of the sun is highlighting the different shades of green in the expertly striped grass. A soft chorus of "Play up Sky Blues, while we sing together, we will never lose" starts to my right as a cluster of City fans gather. A brand-new ball pings across the immaculate surface towards me. The unfamiliarity of the occasion means in the short time it takes the ball to reach me I've pictured a hundred ways this situation could embarrass me. Trampoline touch, trip over the ball, it bounces up and smacks me in the face etc. Years of repetition and subconscious action mean I kill it dead. The ball sits on top of the lush grass. I can see the creases in the leather from where it's been packed in its plastic wrapper before being taken out and pumped up for today's game. It's begging for a knee-high driven pass off my left foot, on to the toe of Willie, who's on his toes ready to receive. But what it gets from me is a nervy, safe side-foot. Firm, on target but lacking the confidence and conviction of being drilled with the laces. The next thing I remember is Gary Gillespie telling me to get sprints done as we warmed up in the corner near the City supporters. I look up to see Big Ron giving me the curly finger beckoning me back to the dugout. I'm standing at the white line. It's so perfect Michelangelo himself could have painted it. My heart is racing, thumping so loudly it seems the Sky-Blue fans have started a new chorus of Play up Sky Blues to its audible beat. This is it... The Premier League. How did I get here?

You did well at Cambridge United. Would you say that was your most successful club?

Like Coventry, I left Cambridge United feeling I had not fulfilled my potential. When I first signed for the club, despite aggravating an existing ankle injury in my first training session, and spending a couple of weeks on crutches, I was in a rich vein of form. Tommy Taylor and his assistant Paul Clark both liked me as a player. Clarky especially understood me as a person and his coaching style got the best out of me. Tommy and Clarky left the club about eight months after my arrival, which essential, started my slow demise at the club. Roy McFarland came in as manger and I played sporadically under him before leaving at the end of my contract for Stevenage Borough.

Iyseden Christie

A fine striker for Coventry City's youth and reserve teams in the 1990s, Iyseden was a great finisher. I had the pleasure of speaking to Iyseden.

I really rated him when he was at Coventry City and I feel that in a different era he would have been a first team regular. Iyseden was born on 14th November 1976 in Coventry and attended Barr's Hill Secondary School. Football was not his first love to begin with whereas he was good at athletics. Iyseden began playing football for his school team and a Sunday League team called Allesley Aces. In his early football days he played in defence and was a ball playing centre half who scored a few goals.

Iyseden was a quick and strong player who played for Coventry Schools on a Saturday and Coventry City on a Sunday. Lol Cairns took him under his wing and by the age of fifteen he was playing men's football for Folly Lane and JFK on a Sunday.

In the mid-1990s Coventry City had a good youth team with players like – Marcus Hall, Adam Willis, Jamie Lenton, Andy Ducros and Jamie Barnwell. Iyseden and Jamie Barnwell played together up front, both left footed players. Back then Coventry City was a Premiership club and it was hard for young players to break into the first team. Iyseden was prolific for the Youth and reserve teams and he finally made a deserved first team debut on the 23th September 1995 away against Blackburn Rovers. It was a very special day Iyseden told me. Although Coventry were beaten 5-1 it was a proud moment. Alan Shearer scored a hat rick that day and

Iyseden rates him as his favourite striker. Iyseden played one more first team match in the League cup against Hull City.

In 1996 and 1997 he spent time on loan at AFC Bournemouth and Mansfield Town then signed permanently for the Stags. Iyseden then played for Leyton Orient, scoring in an FA Cup win over Portsmouth in January 2002, this after an injury lay off. A return to Mansfield Town in 2002 was followed by spells at a number of clubs including Kidderminster Harriers, Rochdale and Kettering Town. Iyseden missed out on playing Everton when he was at Leyton Orient but he got his chance to play at Goodison Park with Tamworth in January 2012. The Lambs were managed by Coventry kid Marcus Law who was in the year above Iyseden at Coventry City. Tamworth gave a good account of themselves in this FA Cup third round match but lost 2-0. Callum Wilson, Ashley Cain and Danny Thomas from Leamington Spa all played with Iyseden at Tamworth. Iyseden was still a very good striker well in to his thirties, when, on 27th September 2014, he scored an incredible six goals in an FA Cup match for Halesowen Town. He went on Talksport afterwards. Iyseden also scored the fastest ever League Cup hat-trick, against Stockport County, when he was at Mansfield Town. He played into his early forties. He has finished now and looking to obtain coaching badges.

Iyseden was one of those players who should have been given more of a chance in Coventry's first team. Back then he had players like Dion Dublin, Peter Ndlovu and Noel Whelan in the first team. I am sure the readers will wish him all the best with his coaching badges.

Tom Bates

Tom was a midfielder who made his senior Coventry City debut at the end of the 2002/03 season. He went on to have a good career in non-league football. I asked him a few questions about his career.

Have you got a favourite match for the Coventry City youth team or reserves?

The game that sticks out the most in memory was the reserve team game against West Ham which I think kick started a good few weeks for me. West Ham was always a tough game as, all the players were all so technically gifted and they could mix it as well, which I found out when Anton Ferdinand clattered into me! But in a way that gave me a wake-up for I raised my game instantly. My Dad was always my biggest critic but that night he thought I had a good game totally to my surprise ha ha!

Who were the best players that you played with or against whilst at Coventry?

The best player I played against was Quincy Owusu-Abeyie, from Arsenal: this lad just had it all, pace, strength, every trick in the book. I couldn't believe how good he was. Every time we played against Arsenal he was untouchable. Played with, there's so many...Ben Mackey I formed a good relationship with, when we played together. We understood each other's game really well, another lad that stood out for me was Stuart Giddings who played behind me at left back and never looked under pressure. He talked so much, every little detail was superb, and I really enjoyed our games together.

Who were your favourite senior players at the club?

There were players I used to sit on the bank of the lodge training ground and watch, Safri, Chippo, they just did not stop practising, how they looked after the ball was what I wanted. I played as a striker growing up at Mount Nod but played deeper at Coventry on the left of a four in midfield which then progressed to playing in

centre mid of three midfielders so watching these senior players was a real learning curve for me.

Could you give me an outline of the coaching?

Finishing playing mentally has been one of the difficult choices I've had to make. Yes I feel I could still play but I have wanted to focus on being the best coach I can be. Just like playing, I take each match and it really is a case of learning on the job. I'm on my 3rd season as a coach now starting at Barwell then at Nuneaton Borough but my current time at Coventry United has been perfect for my coaching! Terry Anderson the gaffer and Luke Morton the assistant manager have been brilliant with me. Everything is shared between the three of us and we all put our opinions in so when Terry makes a decision it's fantastic: it makes you feel a part of it. Qualification wise I'm completing my UEFA B licence now with a plan to getting my A licence done within the next 12-18 months. I love the feeling coaching can give you, You can't beat being out on the grass, working away, trying to make improvements as much as you can.

I have opened up a coaching platform for players of all ages and abilities. During this time of Isolation the Footie Coach TV was born on YouTube and Facebook. Each week I am loading lots of different footie content for players to take a look at, from skills, drills, interviews to then hopefully some stadium and training grounds videos! I want the footie coach to be enjoyable for players and to be there for them as extra training when they need it.

Vijay Sidhu

Vijay was a promising young striker for Coventry City's youth team. I asked him a few questions about his career.

How did you get spotted by Coventry City?

I got spotted for Coventry by Ray Gooding and Lol Cairns who watched me play for my Sunday league team Coventry Sphinx and also Coventry Schoolboys.

Could you tell me a bit about your time with Coventry and which players you enjoyed playing with?

I really enjoyed playing for Coventry and met some of my best friends to this day. Two in particular were Andy Gooding and RIkki Baines both brilliant players.

Have you got a favourite match for the youth or reserves?

My favourite reserve game was beating Portsmouth away 1-0 who fielded an eleven who all had played in the Premier League. We had no first team players at all and also scoring the goal was nice too.

Who did you play for after Coventry? Are you still playing?

After playing for city I had really bad problems with my knees as I ruptured my ACL towards the end of my time at Coventry and have gone on to have ten operations in total. One on my left knee ACL and then nine on my right which stopped me playing at the age of 23/24. I played for a few non-league clubs mainly under Marcus law. I played for Quorn FC, Corby Town, Leamington and Barwell.

Do you remember scoring a couple of goals for Leamington playing up front with another ex-City player Ben Mackey?

Yes I do remember playing up top with Ben (which I did a lot at Cov for various age groups) and scoring a few against Barton I believe. Wasn't really given a chance at Leamington to be honest which is a shame as it is a good club.

Brett Healy

Brett was a midfielder for Coventry City's youth team in the 1990s. I asked him a few questions about his career.

How did you get spotted by Coventry City?

I was playing for Coventry School Boys, Coventry Scouts Bert Edwards and Mick Kearns asked me to sign. I didn't sign until I was fifteen as I also had contract offers from Aston Villa and Man Utd.

Could you tell me a little bit about playing for West Midlands schools? It would have been a really good standard to play at.

I always played a year above myself so I played in the same team as Iyseden Christie, Lee Hendrie, Darren Byfield and Ian Ashbee. We had a decent team it was a good level of football I remember playing against Phil Neville who was playing for Greater

Manchester who were very good.

Coventry had some great Irish players in the 90s. Are you of Irish descent?

I am, yes. My grandparents were Irish and I actually got asked to play for Ireland at u15 level by Joe McGrath. I turned it down as it seemed I would be playing for England at that level until I had my back operation just before the first game at Wembley. I got into Lilleshall too but failed the medical due to my back so it was a tough few years for me before going full time with Coventry.

Back then Coventry had some talented players in midfield. Which senior players helped you as a young player?

The senior players were great at the time I was at Coventry. The Premier League had started and the money was taken over so big names were arriving. Players like Gary McAllister, Stewart Robson and Gary Gillespie were very helpful as were people like Oggy and Brian Borrows.

Who did you play for after Coventry City?

When I had my second back operation I was told by Gordon Strachan and the medical team that my back would not stand up to professional football. I went on to play for Nuneaton Borough for two and half years in which we got promotion to the Conference which was huge for the club. I then dislocated my ankle and ending up paying for David Busst at Solihull where we had a very good team and just missed out on promotion. I then had my ACL done on my knee and ended up retiring at the age of 25.

Reis Ashraf

Reis was a youth team striker who went on to play international football for Pakistan. I asked him a few questions about his career.

Could you tell me how you got spotted by Coventry City?

I was around twelve years old playing for Newport Pagnell Town, near Milton Keynes. I was excelling at that level and due to lack of professional clubs around us at the time, my father wrote off to a few clubs near Milton Keynes. These clubs included and Coventry City along with Aston Villa and West Bromwich Albion who also showed interest, but I decided to choose Coventry City.

Do you have a favourite match for Coventry City youth team?

My favourite game as a youth team player was against Tottenham Hotspur, where I scored a hat trick. Scoring always made me happy being an out and out striker. The following game I scored for the reserves in a 1-0 victory. "Scored 4 goals in 4 days," I think the headline was.

Did you enjoy getting experience at Leamington? Back then the Brakes had quite a few forwards so your chances were limited unfortunately.

Leamington was a great experience with a very good team. I got limited opportunities there but I found it a great experience none the less.

Playing for Pakistan must have been such an honour and scoring against Bhutan must have been amazing. What do you remember about the goal?

Playing for Pakistan was great. I was playing in Spain at the Glenn Hoddle Football Academy. He pulled me to the side and said Pakistan had been in contact asking if I was eligible to play for them in the SAFF Cup. It was an honour to play and score on my first start for them, I played only the three games for them, but it was great experience none the less.

Who did you play for after Leamington?

I found that after lots and lots of setbacks, I fell out of love with the game having had a new manager come to Leamington bringing along with him another couple of strikers. I found it very 'cliquey' lower league and unsettling.

I feel like I gave it a very good shot, however do feel quite hard done by, having been top goal scorer nearer enough everywhere I went yet found myself being drafted out time and time again. I never really understood why thus kept happening despite scoring at every level I played, and in the end made me fall out of love with playing as a career.

Jamie Lenton

Jamie was part of a good Coventry City youth team in the mid-1990s. Born in Bedworth, he went to Ash Green School and played for Bulkington Lions. Jamie got spotted playing on Bulkington Rec by Dave Harvey. He then attended Centre of Excellence at Sidney Stringer School which was run by Steve Ogrizovic, Ray Gooding and Lol Kearns. A few clubs were interested in Jamie one of which was Ipswich Town who took him and Gez Murphy to Portman Road for six months. Ipswich offered the youngsters two year contracts but they turned them down, Gez went to Leicester City and Jamie to Coventry City. Ipswich were a Premiership club at the time and the senior players included Jason Dozzell, Chris Kiwomya and John Wark. Jamie looked back and thought that maybe opportunities might have been better at Ipswich. Tony Vaughan was an example of a youth player who broke into the first team when Jamie was there. Whilst at Ipswich the club got them tickets for an FA Cup match at Anfield v Liverpool which was an enjoyable experience.

Jamie suffered a few injuries at Coventry one of which was a hernia which kept him out for five months. He was at Coventry for three years from 1993 to 1996, team mates included Bedworth and Nuneaton lads Adam Willis and Jamie Williams. In Jamie's age group Marcus Hall, Willie Boland, Iyseden Christie and Tony Sheridan all broke into the first team. Tony was a standout player. Jamie recalls he had so much ability. Jamie had spells with Racing Club Warwick, VS Rugby, Nuneaton and Bedworth but is best remembered for his nine years at Hinckley becoming a club legend. In 2008 Jamie joined Leamington linking up with former Hinckley team mate Morton Titterton. Jamie scored a memorable goal for Leamington at title rivals Nuneaton in January 2009. Then he joined Bedworth in the summer of 2009 captaining his home town club. Jamie since finishing has gained UEFA A coaching qualification and is now at Bedworth. During his career he made over 500 non-league appearances in midfield or wing back. Jamie's form at Hinckley attracted the interest of Sheffield United and Notts County.

Memorable Match

**Brentford 2-1 Hinckley United, FA Cup second round replay –
14th December 2004**

After a 0-0 draw in the first match, Brentford edged Hinckley in
the replay at Griffin Park.

Brentford: Nelson, O'Connor, Sodje, Myers, Salako, Tabb, Talbot
(Hutchinson), Hargreaves, Rhodes, May (Harrold), Burton
(Rankin).
Subs Not Used: Julian, Osborne.

Goals: Rhodes, Talbot

Hinckley Utd: Whittle, Willis, Storer (Goodwin), Piercewright,
Cartwright, Lavery, Dyer, Burns (McMahon), Lenton, Lewis,
Barnes (Marrison).
Sent Off: Piercewright

Goals: Lavery

Connor Gudger

Connor was a youth player for Coventry City, a left back, who
played in the same team as future internationals Cyrus Christie and
Callum Wilson. Now with home town team Atherstone Town,
Connor also played for Leamington and Nuneaton Borough.

How did you get spotted by Coventry City?

*I was spotted by Coventry playing for my local youth side
Atherstone Rangers*

Your year was quite a talented group. Did Callum and Cyrus stand out as great prospects?

Cyrus was always an athlete who was aways bigger stronger and faster than everyone else. Callum wasn't the most talented but was a great finisher and had the confidence and self-belief that I have seen in no-one else..

Luke Bottomer was at Leamington. Big Nathan and Lee Burge broke into Coventry's first team. Good group of players?

Yeah I was good mates with Luke - Nathan looked like one that one going to go far.

Adam Walker

Adam was born in Coventry on 22nd January 1991. I spoke to Adam and asked him about his football career. Adam attended Bishop Ullathorne School. Some websites say he was born in Meriden but this is untrue. He did live there though. A talented young midfielder, he was on Coventry City's books from ages eight to nineteen. A Sky Blues fan growing up, he was given a squad number at sixteen by first team manager Iain Dowie. Adam made his first team debut aged seventeen against Sheffield Wednesday on 28th December 2008 in the Championship. He came on as a late substitute for Michael Mifsud as Coventry City won 2-0. Adam made one more substitute appearance against Charlton Athletic in April 2009 and played the full match against Hartlepool United in August 2009. Coventry City had some talented young players back then. In Adam's age group there was Jordan Clarke, Ashley Cain, Nathan Cameron, Curtis Wynter, Jermaine Grandison, Callum Wilson and Cyrus Christie. Adam roomed with Jack Cork who now plays for Premiership Burnley. In the first team, senior players included Clinton Morrison, Danny Fox, Scott Dann, Patrick van Aanholt and Jordan Henderson. During Adams time at the club the reserves team was scrapped and it was just the youth team and first team.

Adam joined Nuneaton Borough on loan in 2009 then joined them permanently in 2010. He had offers from lower league teams but decided to go to university and play in non-league. At Nuneaton Borough Adam became a fans' favourite as they reached Conference Premier Level. Luton Town came in for Adam but he didn't move to Kenilworth Road. Adam then played for Solihull Borough, Brackley Town and now plays for AFC Telford United. I asked him which players stood out in his time at Nuneaton Borough. Adam talked about Mark Noon, Louis Moult, Cyrus Christie and Kevin Thornton. Adam's favourite matches are his first team debut for Coventry City and winning the FA Trophy with Brackley Town at Wembley in 2018. Adam's dad was also a footballer: Rick Walker was a full back who was on Coventry City and Northampton Town's books. Adam celebrated his 30th birthday in January 2021 and sees himself playing for a few more years yet. He has his UEFA B coaching licence and has experience of coaching. Adam is a really nice guy who I'm sure will succeed in what field he goes into in the future.

Chapter Twelve – Coventry City's Irish Youth Players

Coventry City has produced some fantastic Irish youth players since the 1960s. The city has a strong Irish community and fans have seen many great players wear the Sky Blue of Coventry and the Green of Ireland. We are now going to have a look at some of these great players.

Willie Boland

Willie was a battling midfielder who made his full Coventry City debut aged seventeen in May 1993. He was born in Ennis, County Clare on 6th August 1975. Willie got his chance in the first team when cruel injuries ended the careers of Lee Hurst and Stewart Robson. He didn't look out of place and became a regular in the 1993/94 season as Coventry finished a respectable 11th. Willie didn't play as often under Ron Atkinson and Gordon Strachan but didn't let the team down when called upon. In total he made 71 appearances for the Sky Blues before joining Cardiff City in 1999. Willie became a fans favourite at Cardiff as they reached Division One. He later played for Hartlepool United and made one appearance for Limerick in 2010. I asked Willie a few questions about his career.

What junior teams did you play for and how old were you when you moved to Coventry?

I played for Kennedy Park from under 10 to under13 and Carew Park from under14 to under 16. Both schoolboy teams are based in

Limerick. I moved to Coventry a few weeks before my seventeenth birthday.

Do you have a favourite match for Coventry City?

It was either winning 3-2 at Anfield against Liverpool when Peter Ndlovu scored a hat trick or the 0-0 draw at Old Trafford against Manchester United in the 1993/94 season. That season we finished the season in 11th and went 7 games unbeaten in the run in.

You were quite young when you broke into the first team at Coventry. Did it help playing alongside experienced players like David Rennie?

It is always a help to have experienced players around you. It's how you learn, pick up good habits and it also makes you strive to get to their level. Experienced players also play at a level of consistency and are understanding that young players may have dips from time to time.

When you were a youth team player at Coventry did it help having other Irish lads like Tony Sheridan, Karl Wilson?

It helped a lot as going to a different country in a different environment and away from friends and family is difficult for any young lad. Having familiar faces and from similar backgrounds helped in settling in.

Did you ever get called up for the full Republic of Ireland squad? You were a good player for Coventry and Cardiff and deserved a cap.

I played at every level up to B international but never played in a full senior game. There was a possibility of me going to the USA on a summer friendly tour but circumstances meant that I couldn't go. There was a lot of pull outs from that squad so it wouldn't have been on merit anyway.

Pat Morrissey

Pat was born in Enniscorthy, Ireland on 23rd February 1948. He left Ireland aged five with his parents to live in London. Pat then lived there for seven years then moved to Coventry and attended Priory School. He played at wing half and was part of a good Coventry Schools' team. In October 1962 Coventry Boys impressively beat Wolverhampton Boys 4-1 with Pat scoring, John Docker scored twice and an own goal completed the scoring. On 5th June 1966 Pat played for Republic of Ireland under 23s against France. Pat made his senior Coventry City debut on 9th December 1966 against Ipswich Town. In total he made 12 appearances for the Sky Blues including 9 in Division One. Pat joined Torquay United in 1968 then played for Chester, Crewe Alexandra, Watford, Aldershot and Swansea City. Pat continued to play in non-league until his early 40s. He sadly passed away on 19th February 2005 aged 56.

Rory Linnie

Rory was a midfielder for Coventry City's youth team in the 1960s. Jimmy Hill signed him in 1964 after scouts watched him play for Ireland Schoolboys against England in Cork. He went initially on trial at Highfield Road then signed apprentice forms. Rory played for Coventry City's youth team, A and B teams. I spoke to Rory. He stayed in digs in Bell Green when he was on Coventry's books, and he was very young when he was here. At the time there weren't many Irish players: coach Pat Saward was a former Republic of Ireland International. Rory is from Dublin and began his career with John Bosco's club.

During his time with Coventry City Rory suffered a bad cartilage injury and spent time in Coventry and Warwickshire Hospital. Youngsters John Docker and Johnny Matthews both suffered cartilage injuries at the same sort of time. Rory and Johnny Matthews were released in 1966, Rory played for St Patrick's and later joined CYM in Terenure. It took him a good year to recover from his injury. Rory told me in this day and age there is better treatment for them type of injuries and with today's medical advancements he would have probably continued to play at a higher level. Rory talked about Mick Coop, Mick Cartwright and Pat Morrissey who were in the same age group. He also talked about senior players John Sillett, Bill Glazier, Brian Hill and Allan Harris.

In January 2016 Rory did an article for the Irish Independent, shortly after Jimmy Hill had passed away. Rory told an amusing story of the day he saw the club's bus in the club car park and he decided to drive it. The bus went into reverse and crashed into Jimmy Hill's office. Jimmy was inside his office and there was a lot of damage. Rory thought he would be sacked "Jimmy couldn't believe it." He was very annoyed and he told Rory he was going to stop his salary over three years to pay for the damage. However once Jimmy calmed down he let him off. Rory has been to watch the Sky Blues on a few occasions. His son went to school with Barry Quinn. Rory has worked in the packaging industry with his son for a number of years. He has good memories of his time with City and still follows the team's fortunes.

Noel Finglas

In March 1969 Noel signed apprentice professional forms for Coventry City. This was after a consultation between the FA and FA of Ireland due to a protest from Shamrock Rovers. A skilful midfield player, however a serious illness would end his career early. Noel played in Coventry City "A" team with David Icke, Alan Dugdale, Mick Ferguson, Bob Stockley and Graham Oakey. Noel helped fellow Dubliner Jim Holmes decide to join the Sky Blues by telling him how well the club looked after the younger players. In January 1972 Noel was in hospital in Dublin seriously ill with a bone disease which forced him to give up professional football. In March 1972 he was given a £100 cheque which was raised by Coventry City supporters club. In the late 1970s he was playing for non-league teams.

Jim Holmes

Jim was one of the best Irish players to play for Coventry City. He was born on 11th November 1953 in The Liberties, Dublin. The left back began his career with St John Bosco in Dublin who were founded in 1957. I had the pleasure of speaking to Jim about his football career.

When he was living in Dublin with his family a few clubs were interested in him including Coventry City and Manchester United. Jim and his dad met Matt Busby in Dublin and he looked all set for a move to Old Trafford. A week later Coventry City manager Noel Cantwell (a former Republic of Ireland international) visited the family at their home in Dublin. Coventry City's scout was Bunny

Fulham, a friend of Jim's dad and Jim was convinced about moving to Highfield Road. It would be a good move for Jim and he became part of a fantastic Coventry City Youth team that narrowly lost in the FA Youth Cup final to Tottenham Hotspur. Jim talked about that team and told me many of them made it into Coventry City's first team. Players like Alan Green, Dennis Mortimer, Alan Dugdale, Bobby Parker and Mick McGuire all became First Division regulars. Jim was joined at Coventry City briefly by former John Bosco teammates Davy Stokes and Eugene Ryan on trial. Neither player really impressed so they returned to Dublin after a couple of weeks.

Jim became Republic of Ireland's youngest ever full international at 17 years, 200 days on 30th May 1971 against Austria. He made his international debut before his club debut which was against Leicester City on the 4th December 1971. Jim is still Ireland's youngest player, beating Robbie Keane by sixty days.

I asked Jim what his favourite match for Coventry and he talked about a 4-4 draw against Middlesbrough. This match was on 19th October 1974 at Ayresome Park and Jim played in a midfield role. Jim scored twice and Colin Stein and David Cross were the other Sky Blues scorers. Graeme Souness scored twice for the home team. He had played against Jim in the 1970 FA Youth Cup final. One result which sticks out during Jim's time with the Sky Blues was a 3-2 win over Manchester United at Old Trafford on 15th December 1973. Alderson, Cross and Stein scored for City and George Best for United which would be his last ever goal for them. Jim became a regular for the Sky Blues at the beginning of the 1973/74 season and would go on to make 150 appearances in all competitions. In March 1977 he signed for Tottenham Hotspur. Jim enjoyed playing with great players Hoddle, Villa and Ardiles. Steve Perryman played against Jim in the 1970 FA Youth Cup final and often talked about those matches. Jim also played with Terry Yorath at Coventry City and Tottenham Hotspur and young Irish players Chris Hughton and Tony Galvin were also at the club.

On 19th May 1979 Jim broke his leg and complications arose in the setting of the leg. This was whilst playing for Republic of Ireland against Bulgaria in Sofia. Jim joined Johnny Giles' Vancouver Whitecaps in February 1981 and later played for Leicester City, Brentford, Torquay United and Peterborough United. He then finished his playing career in non-league for Hitchin Town, Bedworth United and Nuneaton Borough. Jim talked about Eddie McGoldrick during his time as player-manager of Nuneaton Borough where he stood out as a player. Eddie would later play for Crystal Palace, Arsenal, Manchester City and Republic of Ireland.

When Jim Faced Jairzinho in the Maracana

Brazil 2 Republic of Ireland 1 – 5th May 1974 Rio

Ireland put in a performance to be proud of against World champions Brazil. After a goalless first half, the home team scored two early second half goals from Leivinha and Rivelino. Terry Mancini scored Ireland's goal, a header from a Giles free kick. Ireland included Peter Thomas in goal, the former Coventry City goalkeeper, the only League of Ireland player in the team.

Ireland – Thomas, Kinnear, Mulligan, Mancini, Holmes (Dunne) Hand, Giles, Martin, Conroy, Treacy (Daly), Givens

Brazil – Leao; Ze Maria, Luis Pereira, Mario Peres, Marinho Chagas; Carbone; Rivelino, Paolo Cezar; Jairzinho, Leivinha, Cesar Augusto.

Jim played 30 times for Republic of Ireland between 1971 and 1981 and no doubt he would have won more caps if it wasn't for the injury he got in Bulgaria. Jim told me that Johnny Giles was a great player and leader who organised the team drawing from his experience playing for Leeds United. Jim also talked about Don Givens, Liam Brady, Steve Heighway, Tony Dunne, Paddy Mulligan all very good players and later on players like David O'Leary, Gerry Daly and Mark Lawrenson. I asked Jim to name his favourite Ireland XI. There are some great players in this team.

Jim's Ireland XI

Alan Kelly Snr (Preston North End)
Joe Kinnear (Tottenham Hotspur)
Tony Dunne (Manchester United)
Dave O'Leary (Arsenal)
Mark Lawrenson (Liverpool)
Johnny Giles (Leeds United)
Liam Brady (Arsenal)
Gerry Daly (Manchester United)
Stevie Heighway (Liverpool)
Don Givens (Q.P.R)
Terry Conroy (Stoke City)

In 1985 Jim had a testimonial match at Dalymount Park in Dublin. A Jimmy Holmes International XI beat a Glenn Hoddle International XI 2-1.

After football, Jim served as a police officer for twenty-three years and has also worked as a chauffeur for the mayor of Nuneaton and Bedworth. Jim told me one time he was on duty at Highfield Road at a testimonial match and played because of a shortage of players. In 1985 Jim had a testimonial himself at Dalymount Park against a

Glenn Hoddle XI. If you do get a chance I would recommend *The Day My Dream Ended: The Autobiography of Jimmy Holmes,* an excellent book which I have started to read. It includes forewords by Glenn Hoddle and Johnny Giles.

Michael Stephenson

Michael was a talented striker and a regular for Coventry City Reserves in the 1990s. I asked him a few questions about his career.

What junior teams did you play for?

I played for Christ the King on a Sunday up until I was fifteen. I then played for Folly Lane (Lol Cairns ran this team for one season) for a year and we won the Birmingham Junior Cup.

How did you get spotted by Coventry City?

I was spotted by Lol Cairns and Bert Edwards and went for a trial. I was offered a Professional contract in Switzerland (BSC Young Boys) when Coventry Boys played in a tournament over there. I stayed in Coventry instead. I also played for the Republic of Ireland Youth team.

Who would you say were the best players that you played with or against (any level)?

In England with - Kevin Gallagher

In England against - Glen Hysen (Sweden and Liverpool) l

In America with - Danny Kelly (Harrisburg Heat) pro indoor football. He had two brilliant feet.

In America against - Hector Marinaro (Cleveland)

You were in the CCFC squad photo 1992 (Do anyone remember that red away top?) It must have been a great experience for you being part of the squad.

Great to be in that CCFC photo and was loving my time at the City. The back operation didn't help. Great memories though!

Who did you play for after Coventry City? I know that you played at Stratford under Len Derby.

I went over to America to do some coaching and had a trial with an indoor professional team called the Harrisburg Heat in Pennsylvania. I got into the team and played for 2 years. 1st year - 31 games, 25 goals and 7 assists (1996-1997) and then broke my Tib and Fib (1997-1998 season) and only played 6 games. I coached a girls' U16 team called the Cumberland Valley Sky Blues and we did play in Sky Blue. Came back and played with Stratford Town for Lenny Derby (close friend) and then Brackley Town.

Do you remember any of the lads who played for Republic of Ireland youth team with you?

Yes, Gerard Carr, a Coventry lad, who also played with me at Folly Lane for that year. He went to Cardinal Wiseman. He then went to Sligo Rovers and scored in the Irish Cup Final. Great story! Karl Wilson also played and he is from Dublin.

Tony Sheridan

A wonderfully talented midfielder, Tony came through the ranks at Coventry City. I asked him a few questions about his football career.

What junior teams did you play for and how did your move to Coventry come about?

I played for Lourdes Celtic here in Ireland aged four till I went to Coventry at fifteen. The Coventry scout here was Maurice Fleming who was part of the Dublin District schoolboy league committee, so he was the one who sent me to Coventry.

Which players did you enjoy playing alongside at Coventry?

Some great lads: Warren Bufton. Gerry Carr. Michael Stephenson. Terry Fleming. Karl Wilson and so many other great players.

Do you have a favourite match for the club? The Arsenal game is quite memorable.

Yes I would have to say the Arsenal game was the best game I ever played for Coventry if I had to pick one, but had some great games even in the reserves.

You played some really good football for Shelbourne and scored some great goals. Would you say that was the best football of your career?

I came back to Shelbourne and it was a very good team. We had three wonderful seasons winning two FAI Cups and a League Cup and playing for the league every season. Unfortunately we missed out on the league in the last game of the season in 1998 and were beaten in the FAI Cup and league Cup finals that year.

It must have been an absolute honour to represent your country. What are your memories of your first call up?

Playing for my country was the best feeling ever. I was lucky enough to be capped for Ireland at all levels u15 up to u21 but I never got a senior cap which would have been brilliant for myself and family but it was never to be.

Do you ever come and visit Coventry?

I have never been back for legends games, but myself and Karl Wilson have gone back in the last couple of years on Paddy's weekend. We try to get a game in but Coventry have always played away so never got a game. I have good memories of my time in Coventry, great city with brilliant fans.

In an article for the Irish Mirror Tony selected the best players he played with and against in Ireland. A name which Coventry City fans may remember is Gary Howlett, the midfielder who was on the Sky Blues books in the early 1980s. Gary played in the 1983 FA Cup final for Brighton and Hove Albion. Tony also mentioned Paddy McCourt and Wes Houlahan who both had good professional careers. Other notable Shelbourne players in the 1990s were Stephen Geoghegan, Mick Neville, Alan Gough and Mark Rutherford an English midfielder once of Birmingham City. Mark was a successful player in Ireland and he played for all of Dublin's big four teams during his career. The big four teams are – Shamrock Rovers, Bohemians, Shelbourne and St Patrick's Athletic.

Gerry Carr

I spoke to Gerry on the phone and asked him a few questions about his playing days. Gerry went to Cardinal Wiseman School and played for junior team Stoke Heath Rangers. He was spotted by Bert Edwards and then taken to the School of Excellence under John Peacock, signing schoolboy forms for Coventry City then YTS/apprenticeship. Gerry was given a professional contract by Don Howe. He was captain of the youth and reserve teams.

Capped by Republic of Ireland at under 16, 18 and 21 levels, Gerry was becoming a fine centre half and was looking to break into the first team. Unfortunately he was never given a first team chance and was given a free transfer in 1993 with Terry Fleming and Michael Gynn. A few teams come in for him, Telford under Gerry Daly and Martin O'Neill's Wycombe Wanderers with whom Gerry played a few friendlies. Nothing came out of it. Derry City and Sligo Rovers then came in for Gerry, Sligo offered a contract. It would be an inspired move, Sligo won an historic treble in the 1993/94 season winning the First Division Championship and First Division Shield. The treble was completed on 15th of May 1994 at Lansdowne Road, Dublin as Sligo Rovers beat the favourites Derry City 1-0. Gerry headed in the winning goal on seventy two minutes, now excelling in a midfield position. Sligo Rovers were managed by former Celtic defender Willie McStay and had very good players in Johnny Kenny, Padraig Moran, Gavin Dykes plus Scottish striker Eddie Annand and English striker Riccardo Gabbiadini.

Sligo Rovers team that won the FAI Cup final in 1994: McLean, McStay, McDonnell, Dykes, Boyle, Kenny, Carr, Hastie, Moran, Annand, Gabbiadini

In March 1994 Sligo Rovers played Celtic in a friendly match. Celtic included Hoops legends Pat Bonner and Paul McStay the younger brother of Willie. Albanian international Rudi Vata scored the only goal of the match.

The Celtic eleven was Pat Bonner, Mark McNally, Mike Galloway, Gary Gillespie, Lee Martin, Paul Byrne, Brian O'Neill, Paul McStay, Wille Falconer, Rudi Vata and Wayne Biggins.

The 1994/95 season saw Lawrie Sanchez as manager, Sligo Rovers competed in the European Cup Winners Cup. Maltese team Floriana were beaten 3-2 over two legs. Then Sligo faced Belgian side Club Brugge putting up spirited performances in both legs but they would lose 5-2 to Club Brugge on aggregate.

Gerry spent three months in USA coaching, then back to UK playing non-league whilst doing a bricklaying course. There followed spells at Nuneaton Borough, VS Rugby (under Stewart Robson) Hinckley United and Shepshed Dynamo. There then came a return to Sligo Rovers in the early 2000s as a player /coach and assistant manager. Gerry assisted former Coventry City midfielder Paul Cook at Sligo Rovers and a player he helped develop was Republic of Ireland Captain Seamus Coleman before he moved to Premiership team Everton. Gerry worked with Paul at Chesterfield as the Academy manager and as a scout at Portsmouth and Wigan Athletic. A UEFA Pro Licence coach, Gerry ran an academy in Ireland.

Gerry has enjoyed his time in football and may return if the right opportunity became available. Whilst representing Ireland he played with Garry Kelly and Graham Kavanagh who both had good professional careers.

Paul O'Brien

Paul was a member of Coventry City's youth team in the 1990s. I asked him a few questions about his career.

Can I firstly ask you how you got spotted by Coventry City?

I was spotted by Coventry City playing for Coventry Schoolboys. I was captain of the under 13 side and was asked to play for the under14s for two seasons. The under 14 team was the same year as Gerrard Carr and Michael Stephenson. I was asked by Scout Lol Cairns and Youth Development Officer Bert Edwards to join the School of Excellence and I subsequently signed Schoolboy forms at the age of fourteen.

Sky Blues had some really good Irish players in the youth team. Are you of Irish descent?

We did have some great Irish players. My Dad is from East Wall in Dublin. I myself was born in Coventry. As a result I had a great rapport with the Irish lads and still see a few of them now when I go over to Dublin each year to celebrate my late Dad's birthday or his anniversary.

Who were the best players that you played with or against, any level?

Your next question is very hard as I was very lucky to play with a lot of good players. I played with Paul Scholes for a Great Britain Catholic Schools' team when I was sixteen and a lad called Tony Grant who played for Everton and Burnley. They were both on a different level. I played at school and for Coventry Schoolboys with James Quinn who was outstanding. Tony Sheridan, Michael

Stephenson, Willie Boland and Gavin O`Toole were the stand-outs for me at Coventry and Brian Borrows from the first team. I can never understand how he didn`t get an England cap. At non-league level, an ex-Leamington player, Jai Stanley was hugely talented.

My toughest opponent was Mark Walters. I played for the reserves at Liverpool and I didn't get near him. I went on trial at Stockport County after Coventry and Kevin Kilbane gave me a torrid time playing for Preston`s 'A' Team.

Do you remember a youth match when Coventry beat Aston Villa 2-1 away with Craig Melrose getting the winner?

I do remember the game at Bodymoor Heath. It was ridiculously windy if memory serves me correctly. I think we beat them at home as well 3-2 that year. Again, if my memory is correct. In my second year I often partnered Craig at centre half.

Who did you play for after Coventry?

After I left Coventry I spent a year at Kidderminster but didn't break into the first team. I then spent eleven years as a player in non-league playing for Stratford Town (two spells), Hinckley Athletic, Bedworth Utd (where I played with Jai Stanley) and VS Rugby. I was then Marcus Laws` assistant at RC Warwick, Quorn, Barwell, Tamworth and Chasetown. I then spent four months with him at Kettering Town from where I decided to leave and that was my last involvement in the game.

Gavin O'Toole

Gavin was a promising midfielder for Coventry City's youth team in the 1990s. I asked him a few questions about his career.

Could you tell me how you got spotted by Coventry City?

I got spotted by Coventry City while playing for my club in Ireland, Bushey Park Rangers as well as for the national team. At the time a lot of the committee members of the schoolboys FAI were scouts for English clubs. You get a lot of exposure when you were with the national team and as captain. I went on a lot of trials to many clubs, and in the end decided that Coventry would be the best place for me to play. The scout who sent me over was a man called Maurice Fleming who sadly is no longer with us.

In the 1990s a lot of talented Irish players were at the club. Would you put it down to excellent scouting in Ireland?

In terms of the good Irish players at the club I think it was down to good scouting. Also once one or two Irish lads were at the club, along with the Coventry born Irish lads, it was a good place to be. We lived at the lodge together, The fact that a lot of us knew each other from the national team helped too. Familiar faces helped us settle and also we all felt that we were at a club where we would get a chance.

Do you have a favourite match for Coventry City?

In all honesty there is no one particular game that stands out. But I had three years in the youth team as I joined at 16 and was playing reserves football from then on as well as youth team. In my last year in the youth team I was head boy (captain) and that was easily my best year at the club. Playing a lot of youth and reserves football and making a few first team squads was when it was beginning to happen for me. I scored 17 or 18 goals that season with about 15 or 16 of them penalties!!

Who would you say were the best players that you played with or against during your career?

There were many great players I played against. In my Ireland days I played against Kluivert and Seedorf (captain of Holland - I was captain of Ireland) at the u 16s' European champion ships. I played against De Le Pena from Barcelona who was playing for Spain in the same tournament.

I also played against a full strength Leeds United side for Coventry City Reserves at Elland Road one year as a 17 year old. They included such players as -John Lukic, Gary Kelly, Tony Dorigo, Gary Speed, Gary McAllister, David Batty and Gordon Strachan.

The best I have played with were definitely Strachan and McAllister, just brilliant players and brilliant to learn from in training.

Who did you play for after Coventry?

When I was 21 and just breaking into the Irish under 21 side I went on loan to Hereford in the Third Division. I played in two League games and then got seriously injured in training which effectively ended my full time career. I did go back to Coventry but after three operations my contract wasn't renewed. I then went to Northampton as a non-contract player but could never get back to the levels I had played at before. It was always difficult when I never really got the opportunity to play. I then played in the

Conference for Leek Town, Nuneaton Borough, Aberystwyth Town and a few other min league teams. I did have the chance to go home and play as a few League of Ireland and Irish League teams who were interested but I stayed here in Coventry.

Who did you play play alongside at International level?

I played with lots of great players among them; Willie Boland, Tony Sheridan, Mark Kennedy, Stevie Carr, Shay Given, Gareth Farrelly, Alan Moore, Steve Finnan and Keith O'Neill. I also played with a lad called Eric Miller at Bushey Park Rangers. He went on to become an Irish rugby international and also a British and Irish Lion. Great player with a big left foot!! Think he played for Leicester for a while.

Barry Quinn

Barry was a defender/midfielder who came through the Coventry City youth team. He was a regular in the first team during the 2000/01 Premier League season. Barry also represented Republic of Ireland at full international level. I asked him a few questions about his career.

How did you get spotted by Coventry City?

I got spotted for Coventry whilst playing for the Republic of Ireland under 15s. We actually played Northern Ireland in a game and drew 1-1. I didn't actually play very well that day but managed to get a call from a Coventry scout named Maurice Fleming about having a trial with Coventry City.

What do you remember about your first team debut against Man Utd? It must have been daunting but a thrill to play against Roy Keane and co!

Yes my debut was daunting but was just buzzing to be named in team. All sorts of emotions in my head. I played in midfield against Roy Keane but before the game my manager Gordon Strachan said to me, "If I see you standing off your country's captain I'll take you off." Thus I knew I just needed to get stuck in and forget about every going on around me.

Do you have a favourite match for Coventry City?

Obviously my debut was a memorable game even though we lost. But probably one of my best and favourite games again was another loss when we played Arsenal at the Old Highbury stadium. This was about my fifth game, it was really tough as Arsenal were full of great players but I actually played really well. I remember Trevor Brooking did a couple of minutes piece on my performance on Match of the Day that night.

Who would you say was the best player that you played against?

I played against some great players- Keane, Scholes, Giggs, Shearer, Henry, Bergkamp but probably Ronaldo Was the best when we played Manchester United in pre-season.

Playing for Republic of Ireland at different levels must have been such an honour, do you have a favourite match for your country?

Yes I played nearly all levels for Ireland, my senior debut was memorable even though I got a bad ankle injury and had to come had to go to hospital for an x ray. The night we beat Germany in the Euro under 18 final was my favourite game for Ireland.

Paul McCrink

I had the pleasure of speaking to Paul He joined Coventry City in 2000 aged thirteen. Paul is from a football mad family. His older brothers both played. The youngster played for a youth team in Newry and was spotted by Coventry City's Northern Ireland Scout Willie McKeown. Paul was prolific for Portadown Boys where he scored forty goals in one season. When Paul moved to Coventry he lived at the Sky Blue lodge and then in digs. He attended Bishop Ullathorne School. Paul progressed through the youth teams. At the time there were quite a few Irish lads like Kevin Thornton and Jon Tuffey. He remembers scoring the winner against Everton after coming on as a substitute in a FA Youth Cup match. Paul recalls Richard Money was academy director and Brian Borrows was youth team coach.

At the age of eighteen Paul was released by Coventry City and returned to Northern Ireland to play for Portadown and Newry City. However he did his cruciate when he returned and therefore got into coaching at a young age. In July 2010 at just twenty- two he was coaching Dundalk Schoolboys. Paul represented Northern Ireland at Under 15 to Under 20 levels playing with Trevor Carson and Kyle Lafferty who both had good careers. Paul's most famous moment was when he scored Northern Ireland Elite's second goal in a 2-0 win over Brazil. This was in the Milk Cup, a famous International youth cup competition in Northern Ireland. Paul had a spell as senior manager of Windmill Stars FC and doing his coaching badges. He has been offered roles in football but at the time being he has a young family and work commitments. Paul is in touch with Jon Tuffey who has had a good career and still playing for Glenavon. Still only thirty two Paul still has plenty of time work in football or Gaelic Football which he played a bit of in his younger days. Paul enjoyed his time in Coventry. The city has strong Irish links and he was always made to feel welcome.

Memorable Match

Coventry City 1-0 Everton – FA Youth Cup 3rd round, 3rd December 2003 Highfield Road

Paul McCrink scored an 84th minute header to win this FA Youth Cup match. It was a good win for the Sky Blues youngsters over a good Everton team who included Anthony Gerrard, cousin of Steven.

Coventry City – Tuffey, Oddy,Giddings, Partridge,Wall (McCrink) Osbourne, Hall, Nicell, Mackey, Thornton (Bains), Goodman (Newbold)

Tim Dalton

Tim was a goalkeeper for Coventry City's youth team, joining in 1982. He was born in Waterford on 14th October 1965. Team mates in the youth team included Gareth Evans, Andy Spring, Tony English and John Matthews(not to be mistaken for Johnny Matthews, Waterford FC). Tim never played for the first team at Highfield Road. He went on to to play for Notts County, Boston United, Bradford City, Cork City, Derry City, Gillingham, Farnborough United, Hong Kong, Coventry City (under Bobby

Gould), Bangor, Portadown and Ballymena United. He had his greatest success with Derry City winning the domestic treble in 1989 and winning the Irish League with Portadown in 1996. Tim never played in the first team in his second spell with Coventry City. He represented Republic of Ireland at Under 19 level and since retiring from playing has become a goal keeping coach.

Other Irish players to play for Coventry City's youth team include Frank McMahon, Kevin Thornton, Colin Hawkins, Lorcan Costello, Gary Howlett, Dean Kiely, Jonathan Tuffey and Karl Wilson.

Chapter Thirteen – Slipped Through the Net

In this chapter we are going to look at players who were born in Coventry and Warwickshire but never played for Coventry City. We are also going to look at players who spent time at Coventry City who had good careers elsewhere but never played for Coventry's first team.

Billy Livingstone

Billy was born in Coventry on 13th August 1964. He lived in Willenhall and attended Binley Park School. He played in the same Coventry under 16s' team as Greg Abbott.

A promising young striker, Billy helped Wolverhampton Wanderers win promotion to Division One in 1983. He made his Division One debut on 3rd September in a 3-0 defeat at Norwich City. On 14th April 1984 he scored against Coventry City in a 2-1 defeat at Highfield Road. through Michelle Livingstone.

I asked Billy, through Michelle Livingstone, a few questions about his career.

How did he get spotted by Scotland?

Andy Roxburgh who was Scotland's youth manager at the time came to see Bill play against West Bromwich Albion at RAF Cosford. After that game he chose Bill to play for Scotland youth where he remembered they were a great side, with Dave McPherson, Bryan Gunn. Paul McStay, Jim McInally, Dave

Beaumont and Pat Nevin. He remembers winning the Euro final beating Czechoslovakia 3-1 and he still has the gold medal.

What are his memories of playing and scoring against Coventry City?

He remembers scoring at Coventry heading the ball in. Apparently the police were going to arrest him at half time as they thought he was antagonising the crowd. It was all his friends from Coventry in the stands with whom he was celebrating. He was spotted for Wolves when he was playing for Massey Ferguson by Wolves scout John Hanna. He made his debut against Blackburn Rovers in 1983.

Did he play for Derby County first team and did he play for anyone else after Derby?

No, not at Derby. He went for a month to six weeks before he broke his leg again then went into non-league. After Derby he played for Tamworth where he broke his leg for the third year running. Bill was in plaster for two years and it ended career. He remembers the wages in top league in 1984 was £125 a week.

Who were the best players that he played with or against?

Best player he played with was Pat Nevin, his hero was Andy Gray. He played against Clive Allen and Gary Lineker.

Graham Parker

Graham was born in Coventry on 23rd May 1946. The talented young midfielder nicknamed "Fezz" attended Woodlands School. He joined Aston Villa as an apprentice in 1961, becoming a professional two years later. Graham also played for Coventry and Warwickshire Schools and England Schools. He made his senior Aston Villa debut on 18th April 1964 against Leicester City. Graham made 21 first team appearances for Aston Villa scoring 1 goal, 15 of those appearances were in Division One. He joined Rotherham United in 1967 then played for Lincoln City, Exeter City, Torquay United and Exmouth Town.

Brian Sharples

Brian was a centre-half who lived in Canley and attended Woodlands School. In May 1960 aged fifteen he joined Birmingham City alongside fellow Coventry Boys' player Malcolm John Clarke. He signed professional in 1961 making his debut in September 1962 against West Bromwich Albion. Brian was a versatile member of the Blues' squad playing at centre half, left back and wing half. Brian made 61 senior appearances for the Blues scoring 1 goal. In 1968 he joined Exeter City before a knee injury forced him to retire in 1971.

David Eades

David is another former Woodlands School pupil, the same age group as Graham Parker and Brian Sharples. In May 1960 he helped Coventry Boys share the Birmingham Schools' Shield. Coventry drew 2-2 with Walsall after extra time and it was decided that both teams would share the Shield. David had an excellent match playing at inside-forward. David spent time with Aston Villa but did not progress into the first team. He became prolific goal scorer for Worcester City, Halesowen, Atherstone and Bedworth. In the early 1970s he formed a superb strike partnership with John Mason at Bedworth. In May 1976 David was rewarded with a benefit match against a strong Coventry City XI. He had been with Bedworth for seven years and scored an impressive 108 goals. Coventry City legends Ron Farmer, Reg Matthews and Ernie Hunt were to guest for Bedworth.

Bernard Jones

Bernard was born in Coventry on 10th April 1934. An inside forward, he began his senior career with Northampton Town. Bernard joined Cardiff City in March 1956 playing alongside future England forward Gerry Hitchens. He was never a regular for the Welsh team and signed for Shrewsbury Town in July 1957. In total he made 95 league appearances and scored 31 goals before signing for Rugby Town in July 1960. Bernard joined Lockheed Leamington in the summer of 1965. In August 1965 he helped his new team beat Stamford 3-0 in the Midland League. The newspaper report said that he fitted well in defence. Bernard was a regular for Lockheed in his two seasons at the Windmill He played at wing half or left half later in his career. On 4th October 1965 Bernard played in the first Floodlit game at the Windmill as a Jimmy Hill All-Star XI beat Lockheed 5-4. Jimmy got a hat trick and Benny Glover and Johnny Dixon also scored. Ray Holmes, Barry Shorthouse, Bert Loxley and Len Swindale scored for Lockheed. When Bernard joined Lockheed they were reigning Midland League champions. Syd Hall was a team mate of Bernard at Lockheed and remembers him well He told me Bernard was a very good player. Bernard was captain at both Rugby Town and Lockheed Leamington. He also played for GEC and Massey Ferguson and managed Alvis, Morris and Sphinx.

I asked his daughter Sharon about his life and football career.

*He grew up in the Stoke area, on the GEC estate. He went to
Sacred Heart School. He was the youngest of 11 children! He
always had a love of football since he was a child He played for
Coventry City Boys/ Youth team He joined the RAF and played in
their team. He played against lots of famous players, always
remembering the brilliance of Stanley Matthews. My mum
mentioned Stan Mortensen too. And there were many others he
played against too, including The Busby Babes.*

Bernard sadly passed away on 12th May 2020 aged 86.

Frank Mitchell

Frank was born in Goulburn, New South Wales, Australia on 3rd
June 1922. He moved to England as a boy and he attended
Windmill Road School in Longford, Coventry. Frank played for
Coventry Boys and Longford St Thomas before joining Coventry
City as an Amateur aged 16. On 16th March 1940 Frank made his
Coventry City debut at left half aged 17 against Northampton
Town in a 6-3 win. Frank joined Birmingham as a professional in
1943. During the war he served in the Royal Navy and guested for
Hearts, Portsmouth and Southampton. On 24th April 1946 Frank
played for England in an unofficial international against Scotland.
It was a match for the Burnden Park disaster in which tragically
thirty-three fans lost their lives. England drew 2-2 with Scotland:
Donald Welsh scored twice for England and William Thornton
twice for Scotland. Legendary players Billy Wright, Stanley
Matthews, Frank Swift and Billy Liddell played in the match.
Frank also played for Chelsea and Watford. He is quite possibly
the first Australian born player to play for England. He played
mostly at wing half and was described as strong in the tackle, and a
neat, quick distributor of the ball. Frank was also a fine cricketer

who played for Courtaulds and he played 17 first class matches for Warwickshire between 1946 and 1948. He also played for Cornwall and Warwickshire's second XI. Frank played club cricket with Knowle and Dorridge, where he became groundsman and club secretary. He passed away on 2nd April 1984 in Lapworth, Warwickshire.

Chris Dangerfield

Chris was a midfielder/forward who spent the 1976/77 season with Coventry City but never played in the first team. He went on to have a successful career in the USA, I asked him a few questions about his career.

How did you first get into football?

I lived in Walmely in Sutton Coldfield. I attended John Willmott Grammar School and so I played Rugby and Cricket at school. When I was aged 14-15 I was playing u18s football on Saturday afternoons (St James Athletic) and men's Football in the Coronation Sunday League on Sunday mornings. A scout saw me playing on a Sunday morning and invited me to play with Birmingham schools. After I played with them I had several offers from Professional teams and eventually chose to join the Wolves at seventeen years old. I trained with their youth team for a year on Tuesday/Thursday evenings for a year whilst finishing school...

What are your memories of playing for England youth team? It must have been a great experience?

We played two games vs Wales and two vs Holland looking to qualify for the Youth World Cup. I missed one game through illness; we did not qualify which was very disappointing. But it was a great experience and I gained some good friendships with players like Dave Swindlehurst from Crystal Palace and Don Nardiello from Coventry City who was on the other wing to me. The selection process seemed strange to me as I remember it at Lilleshall. For example we had Ray "Butch" Wilkins at the try outs, but they couldn't find a place for him because we had another central midfield player from Derby called Steve Powell. He was a very good player....but surely you can find a position for a player like Ray Wilkins, who was in the Chelsea first team at the time!

You spent the 1976/77 season at Coventry City where unfortunately you didn't break into the first team. Do you have any favourite matches for the reserve team?

I joined Coventry through a connection with Ron Wylie who was a wonderful man and coach. There was no particular game that I remember, it was more an overall very positive period. I trained and played with a lot of great older professionals and younger players and we had a good year in the Central League.
I was offered a new contract by the Chairman, but I also had offers from the NASL from Las Vegas and Team Hawaii. It was a very difficult decision, although the base money was better in NASL (I also had free accommodations and a car to use). If I had broken into the Coventry team, I am sure I would have made more money. But the decision was not about money: it was about playing....and in the NASL I was starting and playing in front of big crowds, in big stadia and with and against some of the greatest players ever.

Did you ever play with Coventry teammates Barry Powell at Wolves and Alan Green in USA?

There were five players from Wolves who went to the Portland Timbers in 1975 under coach Vic Crowe: Barry Powell, myself, Jimmy Kelly, Don Gardiner and Peter Withe. It was a wonderful 3-4 months and I was very fortunate to play with Barry in the Midfield. Barry was a terrific player. I played with Alan in the Coventry reserves and against him in the NASL when he played for Washington and Jacksonville. He came to the Earthquakes to play indoor soccer but that the year I injured my knee. Alan was a real goal scorer and a great guy.

You went on to have a fantastic career in US Soccer. Looking back you must have some great memories of playing with legends of the game. Which players stood out in particular?

I was lucky to play with and against the top players of the time. I can honestly tell you that they were all very giving of their time and advice and friendship as teammates. The NASL was a special league and it was a wonderful experience for young English players like myself and another ex-Coventry players like Steve Hunt. He was a very important part of the success of the best team in NASL, the New York Cosmos. I played with Cruyff, Best, Eusebio, Suurbier, Cuellar, Toni, Humbert Coelho, Withe and so many more....and the NASL had other greats in every team. It was fabulous!

Are you still working in soccer today?

Yes. I work on the TV broadcast for my old team the San Jose Earthquakes as the colour analyst in MLS.

Craig Herbert

Craig was a central defender who played in the Football League in the 1990s for West Bromwich Albion and Shrewsbury Town. He was born in Coventry on 9th November 1975. I asked Craig a few questions about his career.

Could you tell me what school and junior teams you played for?

St Patrick's Catholic Junior School in Wood End and Cardinal Wiseman Catholic School in Potters Green.

Did you ever spend any time at Coventry City as a young player?

No not at the club itself but I played in a team made up of all the schools in Coventry. We would play different cities and even had a trip to France to play a team over there.

Who were the best players that you played with or against?

I get asked this all the time and it's so hard to name one or two players I've had the pleasure of playing alongside. I was lucky to play in the same team as Justin Fashanu, Mike Phelan, Darren Moore, Gary Strodder, Bob Taylor, Brian Gayle all great players and learnt so much from all of them. I played against some massive names in the game too - Brian Robson, Neil Webb, Jan Molby, David Beckham, Gordon Strachan and again I learnt a great deal from these guys.

Making your Baggies' debut must have been amazing. What is your favourite match for the club?

I think making my debut will have to be the best: just walking out and hearing the fans was surreal and then chanting my name was amazing and for my parents to be there was a dream come true. My parents supported me from a very young age. My dad was a very good player himself and taught me so much. He was a massive influence for me on and off the pitch. I have to say playing against Middlesbrough was a big game too as they were top at the time and had so many big names and Brian Robson as player manager. We were drawing 1-1 on 90 minutes but I made a late tackle and gave away a penalty in the dying seconds which Craig Hignett scored so this game is up there for the wrong reason.

Are you involved with any football now?

I am involved in my local club at under 15 level. My son Liam plays in the team so it's great for me to coach him and watch his progress at the same time. The club is Coventry Sphinx FC. It's a great set up, a lovely family club with age groups from under 5 up to the adult first team.

Craig's father Paddy Herbert was a prominent player in Coventry football in the 1960s. He played for Radford Social Club, Finbarrs, Four Provinces and Coventry Transport. Paddy once got selected for a Coventry district XI for a match at Highfield Road against a Coventry City team who included George Curtis.

Dean Thomas

Dean was born in Coventry on 19th December 1961. He has enjoyed a solid football career. He is best known for his time with

Notts County who played in the First Division in the 1991/92 season. Dean also played for Wimbledon, Northampton Town and German side Fortuna Dusseldorf. He played in all four divisions of the Football League, won at Wembley and played in three Olympic stadiums. Dean also managed Bedworth United, Hinckley United and Kettering Town enjoying success. I asked Dean a few questions about his career.

Did you spend any time at Coventry City before Nuneaton Borough?

No. Even though I was born in Coventry I never played for them. My dad played for them for three seasons in the early 1950s.

How did your moves to Finland and Germany come about?

While I was at Wimbledon FC, manager Dave Bassett was a great believer in helping get his younger players first team experience so he would send them abroad. New Zealand, Sweden and Finland were the chosen countries. I went to Finland and played for Ives Tampere and loved every minute. During my second season we won the championship, the first time in their history, in 1983. I returned to Wimbledon for one more season helping them get promotion to Division Two but decided to move to Germany with Alemmania Aachen in the Second Division. I had a great four years moving into the First Bundesliga Division for £300.000 in 1985.

Who would you say were the best players that you played with or against in the Bundesliga?

Lothar Matthais and Paul Gascoigne were fantastic players I also played against Jürgen Klinsmann.

Did you or Wayne represent Wales at youth levels?

No. Wayne never represented Wales. I was selected in 1985 by Mike England to play against Norway but due to my grandad coming from Wales and not my dad the FA would not sanction it.

Did you ever play against Wayne in Germany?

Yes Fortuna Dusseldorf vs Hannover 96. Lost 1-0. I got. Sent off!!!

Dean was part of a good Notts County side in the early 1990s. They reached the First Division. Although they were relegated in 1992 they gave it a good go winning ten games and only missing out on safety by four points. Magpies' players Craig Short, Mark Draper and Tommy Johnson would all become Premiership regulars after leaving Meadow Lane. Dean is now a swing singer, a well-known performer in Warwickshire and Leicestershire.

Johnny Schofield

Johnny was a goalkeeper who was born in Atherstone on 8th February 1931. He began his career with local teams for Ansley Hall Colliery, Grendon and Nuneaton Borough. In February 1950 he signed for Birmingham City but would spend a lot of the 1950s as deputy to England international Gil Merrick. Johnny worked as a miner. In November 1957 he was hurt in an accident at Baddesley Colliery. He was taken to Manor Hospital, Nuneaton for treatment. A few years later he fractured his skull in a match against Manchester United and he had to have a metal plate inserted in his head as a result of the injury! The early 1960s was a successful period for Birmingham City. Johnny played in two Inter Cities Fairs Cup finals against Barcelona and Roma. The Blues lost both matches but won the 1963 League Cup Final against neighbours Aston Villa. One notable team mate of Johnny at St Andrews was Bertie Auld who was later one of Celtic's famous Lisbon Lions. In 1966 after 237 games for Birmingham City he joined Wrexham, then played for Cork Hibernians, Atherstone Town (player-manager) Tamworth and Bromsgrove Rovers. Johnny became Atherstone manager again. He sadly passed away on 2nd November 2006.

Ian Muir

A Tranmere Rovers legend, Ian is the Birkenhead club's record goal scorer with 180 goals in all competitions. Ian was born in Coventry on 5th May 1963. He attended Caludon Castle School and was in the same year as Peter Hormantschuk. Ian and Peter went to Queens Park Rangers as youth players. Ian went on to play a couple of games for QPR's first team scoring twice on his debut against Cambridge United. First team opportunities were limited at Loftus Road. In the early 1980s Ian played for Burnley, Birmingham City, Brighton and Hove Albion and Swindon Town. In July 1985 Frank Worthington signed Ian for Fourth Division Tranmere Rovers. In 1987 Tranmere appointed Johnny King as manager and he helped turn the club's fortunes around. Johnny signed Scottish target man Jim Steel as a strike partner for Ian, which would be a great signing.

In April 1988 Tranmere Rovers were the surprise package of the Football League Centenary Tournament at Wembley, they beating Wimbledon and Newcastle United before narrowly getting beaten on penalties by Nottingham Forest in the semi-finals. In 1989 Tranmere Rovers finished second in the Fourth Division and won promotion to the third tier of English football. On 20th May 1990

Ian and Jim both scored as Rovers won the Leyland DAF Cup beating Bristol Rovers 2-1. In 1991 Tranmere Rovers won promotion to the Second Division via the play offs. Ian missed the play off final and a defeat to Birmingham City in the 1991 Leyland DAF Final due to a knee ligament injury. When Ian returned from injury, Tranmere who were now in the second tier had signed John Aldridge. A partnership with Aldridge never quite clicked but Ian remained at Prenton Park until 1995 as Rovers pushed for a place in the Premiership. Ian later played for Birmingham City, Darlington, had a spell in Hong Kong then finished his career with Nuneaton Borough and Stratford Town. Ian has been described as the Kenny Dalglish of the lower leagues and one of the best strikers never to have played in the top flight. He is certainly one of the best Coventry born players never to have played for Coventry City.

Geoff Cox

Geoff was a winger/inside-forward who was born in Arley / Stockingford, Nuneaton on 30th November 1934. He began his career with Birmingham City and made his league debut aged seventeen in August 1952. Geoff's first team chances were limited due to first choice wingers Gordon Astall and Alex Govan but he did play in the Inter Cities-Fairs Cup against Inter Milan in 1956. Geoff signed for Torquay United in 1957 and would play for them for ten years, playing 286 games and scoring 72 goals. His most famous match for Torquay was an FA Cup third round match against Tottenham Hotspur on 9th January 1965. Torquay gave Tottenham a real good game at Plainmoor in a 3-3 draw, but Spurs had too much for them in the replay winning 5-1. Tottenham's team was full of great players like Jimmy Greaves, Alan Gilzean, Maurice Norman, Cliff Jones and Alan Mullery. Geoff didn't score but he contributed to a fine performance by Torquay in the first match. He finished his playing career with Bridgwater Town and Welton Rovers before becoming an estate agent. Geoff's son Maurice was also a footballer for Torquay United and Huddersfield Town. In 1979 Maurice scored the fastest goal at the old Wembley for Cambridge University v Oxford University in the Varsity match. Geoff sadly passed away on 3rd November 2011 aged seventy-nine.

Marc Bridge-Wilkinson

Marc was born in Coventry on 16th March 1979 but grew up in Nuneaton and attended Alderman Smith School. He is currently Liverpool's under 18s' coach, Marc joined the club in 2015 and has coached the under 14 and under 16 teams. Marc began his football career with Derby County, making one appearance in the Premiership against Liverpool in November 1998. Marc was a left-sided creative midfielder who scored quite a few goals. He had a loan spell with Carlisle United before joining Port Vale in 2000, Marc would become a fans' favourite at Vale Park. On 22nd April 2001 he scored a penalty as Port Vale beat Brentford 2-1 to win the Football League Trophy at Cardiff's Millennium Stadium. Marc also played for Bradford City, Stockport County, Carlisle United and Darlington. After finishing playing Marc spent some time as Academy coach at Huddersfield Town. It is surprising that a second tier team never came in for Marc for he was one of the best midfielders in the lower leagues. At forty-one Marc looks to have a great future in coaching having made progress in his time at Liverpool.

Kim Casey

Kim is one of non-league's best ever strikers: he was an absolute goal machine! He was born in Birmingham on 3rd March 1961 and began his career with Sutton Coldfield. At AP Leamington he formed a deadly partnership with Cliff Campbell as the Brakes won the Southern League in 1983. Kim had a spell with Gloucester City then moved to Kidderminster Harriers under former AP Leamington manager Graham Allner. In the 1985/86 season he scored an incredible 73 goals! A year later Harriers won the FA Trophy after a replay. Kim also played for Cheltenham Town, Wycombe Wanderers, Solihull Borough and Moor Green. It is often asked why Coventry City never came in for Kim especially when he was in fine form for AP Leamington. I believe that clubs were interested in him but for some reason he stayed and excelled at non-league level. It could have worked out two ways: Kim could have been prolific at a higher level or struggled. A similar comparison is Paul Culpin who was awesome at Nuneaton Borough but didn't really make his mark with Coventry City. I liked Paul as a player and I think if he had been given a chance he would have come good. Anyway Kim is a non-league legend and one of the greatest players to wear the gold of Leamington.

John Curtis

John was born in Nuneaton on 3rd September 1978. He had a great career as a defender for Manchester United and Blackburn Rovers. I asked him a few questions about his career.

Could you tell me what School team / junior teams you played for?

Chetwynd Squirrels, Bulkington Lions & Grove Farm FC. I went to Bulkington St James & George Elliott Schools.

How did you get spotted by Manchester United?

Geoff Watson the Man Utd scout lived in Hartshill and first started watching me when I started playing for the district team.

Which players would you say were the best players that you played against?

Thierry Henry, Paul Scholes & Ronaldinho

Could you tell me a little bit about your current role and how you got into coaching?

I founded a football program called NCE Soccer. We run training programmes across the North East of America with the aim of helping players fulfil their potential.

John began his career with Manchester United and won the FA Youth Cup in 1995. The youth team was captained by Phil Neville and other team mates included Terry Cooke, Ronnie Wallwork and David Johnson. John turned professional in 1997 and made his Premiership debut in October against Barnsley, which United won 7-0. The same year John won young player of the year at Manchester United. First team chances were fairly limited at Old

Trafford due to Gary Neville being first choice at right back but he made nineteen appearances. John represented England at youth and Under-21 level and played once for England B against Russia in April 1998. A successful loan spell with Barnsley in the 1999/2000 season prompted Blackburn Rovers Manager Graeme Souness to sign him for £1.5 million. During his time at Ewood Park he impressed as Rovers were promoted to the Premiership. John then went onto play for Sheffield United, Leicester City, Portsmouth, Preston North End, Nottingham Forest, Queens Park Rangers, Wrexham, Northampton Town and Gold Coast United in Australia. John has coached in England, Italy, Australia and USA and obtained UEFA A Licence and the USSF A Youth Licences. He has had a fantastic career in football, John told me he remembers going to the 1987 FA Cup final and went to a few Coventry City matches as kid. He is a great local player who Sky Blues missed out on.

Martin Hicks

Martin was a defender who was born in Stratford-upon-Avon on 27th February 1957. He began his career with local team Stratford Town under manager Sid Keenan. Martin had a spell at Charlton Athletic then joined Reading in 1978 becoming a legend for the Royals. He would become the club's record appearance holder making 603 appearances before joining Birmingham City in 1991. Martin's most famous match was the 1988 Simod Cup Final which took place on 27th March 1988, a competition which was created in 1985 after the ban on English clubs in European competition. Teams from top two divisions participated. Reading of the Second Division caused an upset by beating First Division Luton Town 4-1. Martin played in central defence alongside future England international Keith Curle but unfortunately Reading couldn't defend the cup and they were also relegated to the Third Division. Martin spent a couple of years with Birmingham City then became player-manager of Newbury Town. Reading fans hold Martin in high regard: they voted him in a best ever Royals XI in 2005.

Marcus Harness

Marcus is currently starring for League One team Portsmouth. The winger was born in Coventry on 24th February 1996. He comes from Binley and attended Ernsford Grange School. Marcus spent time with Coventry City's youth team as a goalkeeper and at right back but was rejected and would join Burton Albion. On 3rd September 2013 he made his first team debut for the Brewers in an EFL trophy match. Marcus featured for Burton as they won League Two in the 2014/15 season under Jimmy Floyd Hasselbaink. During the next season he spent time on loan at Ilkeston and Aldershot. Burton Albion won promotion again in the 2015/16 season finishing second in League One. Marcus played ten matches in the Championship including a famous 1-0 win over local rivals Derby County in August 2016. In July 2017 he joined League Two Port Vale for a season loan. Marcus was a regular at Vale Park. A return to Burton Albion came for the 2018/19 season in League One and he established himself in the first team. Marcus scored an impressive hat-trick against Rochdale in January 2019. In the summer of 2019 he joined Portsmouth and helped Pompey to achieve a play-off spot. Marcus has started the 2020/21 well, he scoring twice against Colchester United in the EFL Trophy. Pompey are looking to gain promotion this season, Marcus has expressed an interest in playing for Republic of Ireland at international level. At twenty four he has a bright future in the game.

Andy Rammell

Andy was a striker who was born in Nuneaton on 10th February 1967. He attended Queen's Road and George Eliot Schools. He began his career with Atherstone United and began to attract the attention of Coventry City, Birmingham City and Leicester City. It would be Manchester United who would sign Andy in 1989 after he was watched by Geoff Watson and Nobby Stiles. Andy loaned the Red Devils for £40,000 and Atherstone used the cash to build a stand and then named it after Andy. A regular for United's reserves he never made the first team and signed for Barnsley in September 1990. Nicknamed "Rambo" he enjoyed a good career at Barnsley, Southend United, Wycombe Wanderers, Walsall and Bristol Rovers. After retiring from football he has worked as a postman and a company called Wise Ability. Andy is quite a cult hero at the clubs he played for. Walsall fans remember him for scoring the winning goals against local rivals Wolves, West Bromwich Albion and Birmingham City in the 1999/2000 season.

Greg Abbott

Greg was a Right back or midfielder who was born in Coventry on 14th December 1963. He began his career at Coventry City from schoolboy forms to professional but never played for the first team. Greg went on to have a long playing career with Bradford City, Halifax Town, Guiseley and Hull City followed by an equally long time in coaching and managing. Greg worked for Leeds United, Thackley AFC, Carlisle United, Bradford City, Notts County and Mansfield Town. In 2011 Greg was considered for the vacant Coventry City manager's job after Aidy Boothroyd had been sacked. Andy Thorn was appointed Sky Blues manager but maybe

Greg might have been a better option. It is a shame that he never got the chance to play for or manage his home town team.

Trevor Morley

Trevor was a Premiership striker who once starred for Nuneaton Borough. He was born in Nottingham on 20th March 1961. His father Bill Morley played for Nottingham Forest. Trevor spent time at Derby County and Corby Town prior to joining Nuneaton Borough in January 1981. Under manager Graham Carr Boro finished second in the Alliance Premier League in 1984 and 1985. In those days there was no promotion to the Football League and it was the closest a Warwickshire team has got to the fourth tier of English football except for Coventry City. In the summer of 1985, Trevor and Eddie McGoldrick followed Graham Carr to Northampton Town. In January 1988 he moved to Manchester City and scored in the famous 5-1 win over Manchester United on 23rd September 1989. Later that year he joined West Ham United in a deal that saw Ian Bishop move to Upton Park and Mark Ward to Maine Road. Trevor was a favourite with Hammers' fans. He signed for Reading in 1995. He also played for Norwegian sides Brann and Sogndal. Trevor has also scouted and managed in Norway. In June 1985 Coventry City signed team mate and striker Paul Culpin. Whilst Paul failed to make an impact at the highest level Trevor scored goals for every team he played for in League football.

Roger Brown

A central defender who is often regarded as one of AP Leamington's best ever players, Roger was born in Tamworth on 12th December 1952. He was an apprentice at Walsall FC. In the summer of 1974 AP Leamington manager Jimmy Knox signed Roger from Paget Rangers. The Brakes were a decent side and reached the FA Cup First Round several times. Roger scored a hat-trick for AP Leamington in a cup match against Enderby Town in November 1977. In February 1978 he signed for AFC Bournemouth. His form then earned him a move to First Division Norwich City in September 1979. Roger transferred to Fulham in March 1980 becoming a cult hero at Craven Cottage. There is an iconic photo of Roger smoking a cigar and having a cuppa after a match when he scored the winning goal to seal promotion to the Second Division. In December 1983 former AP Leamington team mate Harry Redknapp signed Roger for AFC Bournemouth. Roger captained the Cherries when they beat Manchester United in the FA Cup and when they won the Associate Members' Cup. After a short spell with Weymouth he then became player-manager of Poole Town. Roger also managed Colchester United and Bolehall Swifts. He sadly passed away on 17th August 2011 from cancer. He was fifty eight. Roger played with some great players like Martin Peters, Ray Houghton, Tony Gale and Paul Parker. He was an old fashioned centre half who is remembered fondly in Leamington Spa.

Malcolm Shotton

Malcolm was a central defender who began his career with Leicester City. He was born on 16th February 1957 in Newcastle upon Tyne. Malcolm played for Atherstone Town and Nuneaton Borough before joining Third Division Oxford United in 1980. He would become a legend for Oxford forming a solid defensive partnership with Gary Briggs. Oxford United won promotion to the First Division in 1985 and a year later Malcolm captained them in the Milk Cup Final as they beat Queen's Park Rangers 3-0. Team mates John Aldridge and Ray Houghton would go on to star for Liverpool and Republic of Ireland. Malcolm later played for Portsmouth, Barnsley, Hull City, Huddersfield Town and Ayr United. He managed Oxford United and was assistant manager at Bradford City.

David Woodfield

David was born in Leamington Spa on 11th October 1943. He lived in Cashmore Avenue in the town and attended Shrubland Street and Campion Secondary Modern School. David was a central defender who began his career with Wolverhampton Wanderers and became a regular at Molineux. David made over 250 first team appearances before joining Watford in 1971. He subsequently worked in coaching and education in the Middle East and spent a number of years in Malaysia.

Riccardo Scimeca

A central defender or defensive midfielder, Riccardo was born in Leamington Spa on 13th June 1975. He began his career with Aston Villa and made his first team debut on 19th August 1995 against Manchester United. Riccardo tended to be a back up for first choice central defenders Gareth Southgate and Ugo Ehiogu. Whilst at Aston Villa he played for England under 21 and 'B' teams. In 1999 he joined Division One side Nottingham Forest. Riccardo spent four years at the City Ground before a move to Premiership Leicester City in 2003. He then moved to West Bromwich Albion in 2004 who were also a Premiership team. Riccardo then played for Cardiff City, retiring in 2009. He was a solid and dependable player who played in the top two levels of English football throughout his career.

Matty Fryatt

Matty is a former Premiership striker who was born in Nuneaton on 5th March 1986. He went through Walsall's youth teams from Under 9s all the way through to the first team. Matty made his Saddlers' debut in September 2003 and later that year he spent time on loan with Carlisle United. On 29th January 2005 he scored a hat-trick against Huddersfield Town, Matty's team mate and manager was Paul Merson. In the summer of 2005 he starred for England under 19s in the UEFA Under-19 Championship in Northern Ireland. England finished runners up to France. Matty scored four goals in the tournament including a hat-trick against Serbia & Montenegro in the Semi-Final. England colleagues included Mark Noble, Martin Crainie, Dexter Blackstock and James Morrison. Matty's form attracted interest from a few teams and Leicester City secured his services in January 2006. He was a success with the Foxes. In the 2008/09 season helped Leicester City win the League One championship.

In January 2011 Matty moved to Hull City. He did well for the Tigers in the 2011/12 season scoring sixteen goals in the Championship. Matty played in the 2014 FA Cup final defeat to Arsenal/ Earlier in the season he had a loan spell with Sheffield Wednesday. In June 2014 he signed for Nottingham Forest but Matty would have an unhappy time at the City Ground. In 2018 he was forced to retire because of injury and it was announced he was suing Nottingham Forest because he alleges the club was negligent in treating an Achilles problem. Since retiring Matty has worked as a coach for Walsall's Under 15s and as a scout for Cardiff City. At only thirty four Matty would have still being playing at decent level of football. It is hoped that things work out for him and he is able to build a career in or out of football.

Peter Whittingham

A classy midfielder who became a modern day great with Cardiff City, Peter was born in Nuneaton on 8th September 1984. He attended King Henry VIII School in Coventry. From the ages of seven to sixteen he was with Coventry City. He was spotted after the club took on his brother James. Peter joined Aston Villa and was part of the youth team that beat an Everton team including Wayne Rooney in the 2002 FA Youth Cup final. Aston Villa had a strong youth team with players like Liam Ridgewell, Steven Davis, Stefan and Luke Moore. In April 2003 Peter made his Premiership debut and broke into the first team. Peter could play central or wide midfield and he would go on to make sixty six appearances for Villa. During his time as an Aston Villa player he spent time on loan with Championship teams Burnley and Derby County as well as being capped by England Under 21s.

In January 2007 Peter signed for Cardiff City and for the next ten years he would become a Bluebirds' legend, making 457 appearances and scoring 96 goals. Cardiff City spent the 2013/14 season in the Premiership, but they would be relegated after one season. Peter would remain loyal to Cardiff and played in three more seasons in the Championship. In 2017 he joined League One Blackburn Rovers for one season, which would be his last club. Peter was unlucky not to win a full cap by England, especially with his form with Cardiff City. The world of football was shocked in March 2019 with the news that Peter had tragically passed away at the age of thirty-five. A Warwickshire great, he had a fine career and will always be remembered fondly at the clubs for which he played.

Luke Leahy

A left back for League One team Bristol Rovers, Luke was born in Coventry on 19th November 1992. Luke was released by Coventry City academy at twelve then was part of Gordon Strachan Football Foundation. He began his senior career with Rugby Town and was signed by Falkirk manager Steven Pressley in 2012. Luke did well for Falkirk making 158 appearances scoring twelve goals in five years at the club. In 2015 Falkirk reached the Scottish Cup Final and Luke played in the 2-1 defeat to Inverness Caledonian Thistle. Later in the year he scored a goal of the season against Livingston. In the summer of 2017 Luke signed for League One Walsall. In December 2018 he scored twice for Walsall against Coventry City (the team he supported growing up). For the past two seasons Luke has played for Bristol Rovers. In September 2020 he scored a penalty against Sunderland. Luke has a famous Grandfather Mick Leahy, Mick was born in Cork but lived in Coventry most of his life. He became British Middleweight champion in 1963 and beat the legendary Sugar Ray Robinson in 1964. Luke, at the age of twenty seven, has plenty of time to achieve success in the game and he is an established League One player with the potential to play Championship level.

Jamie Paterson

Jamie is a winger for Championship side Bristol City who was born in Coventry on 20th December 1991 and attended Caludon Castle School. He began his career for Walsall. In April 2013 he scored twice as the Saddlers thrashed Coventry City 4-0. Jamie signed for Championship team Nottingham Forest in 2013 and he scored a superb hat-trick against West Ham United in January 2014. He spent the 2015/16 season on loan with Huddersfield

Town and signed permanently for Bristol City in 2016. Jamie spent time on loan with Derby County in the 2019/20 season but is now back with Bristol City and scored in the first game of the 2020/21 season against Coventry City. He has expressed an interest in representing Scotland at international level, I hope that he does get a call up for he has done really well in the Championship. He is definitely a player who was missed by the Sky Blues radar and who has certainly proved a point to his hometown club on a couple of occasions.

Ian Evatt

Ian is currently head coach of League Two team Bolton Wanderers, assisted by former Sky Blues defender Peter Atherton. Ian was born in Coventry on 19th November 1991 and attended Caludon Castle School. He was scouted by Derby County at the age of eleven and signed professional aged seventeen in 1998. Ian started out as a midfielder then converted to central defence. At 6ft 3 he had all the attributes and became an accomplished defender. He made his Derby County debut on 19th May 2001 against Ipswich Town in the Premiership. In the 2002/03 season he became a regular in Division One for the Rams. He also had a spell on loan with Northampton Town whilst a Derby player.

Ian was released by Derby County in the summer of 2003 and joined League Two Chesterfield. Two seasons later he moved to Championship team Queens Park Rangers though his second season would see him join Blackpool on loan. In January 2012 Ian signed Blackpool who were then in League One. It would be a fairy tale story as The Seasiders would win promotion to the Championship then the Premiership. Ian was ever present in the 2010/11 season as Blackpool competed in the top flight. Under manager Ian Holloway they won many friends and beat Liverpool and Tottenham Hotspur along the way, but would be relegated at the end of the season. Ian left Blackpool in 2013 for a second spell with Chesterfield and he retired from playing in 2018.

In April 2018 Ian was briefly caretaker manager of Chesterfield and in the summer Ian was appointed manager of National League team Barrow. In the 2019/20 season he guided Barrow to promotion to the Football League for the first time in forty eight years. Barrow were crowned champions after the season was curtailed but they were worthy champions and deserved their promotion. Ian was appointed Bolton manager in the summer of 2020, The Trotters have been in free fall in recent seasons so he has a tough job on his hands. Still only thirty-eight, Ian has a bright future in coaching and I hope that he can turn Bolton's fortunes around.

Daniel Crowley

Daniel is a current midfielder for Championship side Birmingham City. He was born in Coventry on 3rd August 1997. Daniel grew up in Coundon and attended Christ the King and Cardinal Newman Schools. His dad, Dave Crowley, played for Coventry City Youth and Nuneaton Borough. Daniel played for Christ the King Juniors then joined Aston Villa academy at eight years old. He drew comparisons to Jack Wilshere with his playing style and impressed Arsenal manager Arsene Wenger. Daniel joined Arsenal in the summer of 2013, then turned professional when he was seventeen. Unhappy loan spells with Barnsley and Oxford United were followed by a loan move to Dutch team Go Ahead Eagles. In July 2017 he moved to another Dutch team Willem II on a permanent basis. Daniel also spent time on loan with SC Cambuur during the

2017/18 season. Daniel established himself in Willem II's first team and appeared as a substitute in the 2019 Dutch Cup Final defeat to Ajax. In 2019 he signed for Championship side Birmingham City. Daniel has represented England at Under 16, 17 and 19 levels and he has also represented Republic of Ireland at Under 16 and 17 levels. He has become a regular for Blues and proven to be a good player at Championship level. At twenty three he still has time to play at Premiership level and win full international caps.

Paul Shepstone

Paul, a midfielder/winger, was born in Coventry on 8th November 1990, but never played for the first team. Paul had a spell with Birmingham City but never made a senior appearance. He moved to Blackburn Rovers in 1990 and broke into the first team, making a decent amount of appearances. Paul also played for York City on loan. In 1992 he moved to Motherwell. After a couple of games in Scotland he dropped into non-league football. Paul played for Atherstone United, Stafford Rangers, Wycombe Wanderers and also one game for England Youth in 1989. Outside football he has run a lingerie business and been a mortgage advisor. When Paul broke into Blackburn's team it looked like he was set for a good career in football but for some reason it never worked out for him. He will always be part of Sky Blues history as he was part of Coventry City's FA Youth Cup winning team in 1987.

Matty Blair

Matty is currently playing for League Two Cheltenham Town, a right midfielder who can also play at right back. I had the pleasure of speaking to Matty who he was born in Sutton Coldfield on 21st

June 1989. On a lot of websites it says he was born in Warwick but this is not the case. Matty told me one time his date of birth on line was two years older which nearly cost him a move to a club. "You're 26? ", said a team's manager. "No I am 24," replied Matty. "I should know how old I am!" Once a website has the wrong info it can get copied over to others incorrectly.

Matty moved to Allesley at a young age and then later the family moved to Balsall Common. He attended St Andrew's, Eastern Green and Heart of England Schools. Matty began his playing career for Racing Club Warwick under Bobby Hancocks. He got into the first team at a young age as there didn't seem to be a natural progression from the youth team to the first team. Matty had a spell with Stratford Town under Micky Moore then onto Bedworth United under Liam O'Neill. Bedworth had a good FA Cup run, reaching the FA Cup Fourth round qualifying. Matty played for Redditch United and AFC Telford in the 2009/10 season. In the summer of 2010 he joined Steve Burr's Kidderminster Harriers who were in the Conference Premier. A year later Matty joined York City which would be the turning point of his career. Often when written about as Andy Blair's son, now Matty was making a name for himself. Matty really enjoyed playing for the Minster men and it was a dream first season in which they won the FA Trophy and promotion to League Two. Gary Mills led York City to a Wembley double and Matty scored in both games. On the 12th May Matty scored the opening goal as York City beat Newport County 2-0 in the FA Trophy Final. Eight days later York City beat Luton Town 2-1 in the Conference Premier Play-off final with Matty scoring the winning goal. Matty was named on the Conference team of the year along with Jamie Vardy of Fleetwood Town who joined Leicester City in the summer of 2012. York City finished 17th in League Two in the 2012/13 season.

In March 2013 Gary Mills was sacked. Nigel Worthington was appointed manager and kept York City in League Two. Matty had a solid season in League Two and hoped to stay with the Minster men however Nigel didn't know about a contract that looked like it was agreed. It looked like Matty would join Portsmouth but he signed for League One Fleetwood Town. Matty made another visit to Wembley on 26th May 2014, Fleetwood beating Burton Albion 1-0 in the League One play-off final. Matty had loan spells with Northampton Town and Cambridge United in 2014 then played for Mansfield Town.

In the summer of 2016 Matty joined Doncaster Rovers of League Two, helping them win promotion in the 2016/17 season. Matty became a regular in League One for Donny. After four years in Yorkshire he joined League Two Cheltenham Town. The Robins have made a decent start to the 2020/21 League Two campaign and look to mount a promotion push. They have a decent side with experienced players like Matty, Chris Hussey, Conor Thomas and Reuben Reid. I asked Matty if he could pick a stand out player that he played with and he said James Coppinger (Doncaster Rovers) is absolute class. Now in his late 30s James is still a brilliant player. Matty also told me a player for the future is Ben Whiteman who he believes will play at a higher level one day. Matty is also proud to have played for England C in 2011 and 2012. At 31 he still has a few years left to achieve more in football and I really hope Cheltenham win promotion to League One: at the time of writing they certainly look good enough. Matty is an advocate for mental health since he and his family have gone through a lot and he is now helping others.

Jon Ashton

Jon was born in Nuneaton on 4th October 1982 and attended St. Thomas More School. The defender began his career with Leicester City's youth academy. He progressed through to the first team making his debut on 23rd March 2002 against Leeds United in the Premier League. Jon made 10 appearances in total for the Foxes, during which time he spent a period on loan with Notts County. He went on to make over 500 senior appearances for Oxford United, Stevenage Borough, Grays Athletic, Crawley Town, Rushden & Diamonds, Braintree Town and Nuneaton Borough. Jon won the Conference Premier with Stevenage Borough in 2010. He also represented England C in 2007 in a Four Nations Tournament in Scotland.

Kelvin Langmead

Kelvin was born in Coventry on 23rd March 1985, an experienced defender who currently plays for Banbury United. He has had a solid career playing for a number of Football League clubs including Shrewsbury Town and Peterborough United. I asked Kelvin a few questions about his career.

What junior teams did you play for?

I was a one team kid. I played for Kenilworth Wardens from about the age of seven or eight until I was aged fifteen. At that point I'd signed for Preston North End and they wouldn't allow me to play Sunday league anymore.

How did you get spotted by Preston?

I started to get scouted aged fourteen. I played for the Mid & South Warwickshire district team. We did really well in the National Cup and I think we reached the quarter finals. I remember getting a call from my district manager, who was also my school team manager and PE teacher (Mr. Leggett). He phoned me to say Bury FC were interested, so I went and did a trial game up there. I also ended up going to Blackburn Rovers, Manchester City and Wolves on trial too. However the guy who scouted me for Bury, moved to PNE. He was The Youth Team manager, Simon Davey, and he came to watch a district game. He must have liked what he'd seen because he offered me a scholarship at fifteen years old. They were the only team to put something on the table so it was an easy decision for me. From then on I was only allowed to carry on playing for my school team but would go up and train with the PNE Youth Team during half terms etc.

Who are your favourite players that you played with or against?

I was lucky enough to play with Joe Hart when he came broke through at Shrewsbury Town. I also played with Gylfi Sigurdsson whilst I was there too. However they were very young and only just starting out in their careers. During my time at Peterborough I was very lucky too with players like George Boyd, Grant McCann, Ryan Bennett, Aaron McClean and Craig Mackail Smith. I should also mention Grant Holt at Shrewsbury was also a top top player and went on to do very well in the Premier League. I played against, Conor Wickham and Jordan Rhodes and they both gave me a torrid time!

Robbie Jones

Robbie was a forward who was born in Coventry on 17th November 1964. He was a pupil at Holbrooks, President Kennedy and Woodlands Schools. Robbie played for Coventry Schools and also England Schools. He began his career with Manchester City as an apprentice then moved to Leicester City in September 1982. Robbie scored on his Foxes' debut on 7th May 1983 against Oldham Athletic in a Division Two match. In total he played 17 matches for Leicester City scoring 3 goals. Robbie scored in Division One matches against Stoke City and Nottingham Forest in the 1983/84 season. Robbie played in the same team as Gary Lineker, Alan Smith and Kevin MacDonald. In 1986 he joined Walsall then played for Kidderminster Harriers, Burton Albion and VS Rugby.

Danny Thomas

Danny was a winger or left back who was born in Leamington Spa on 1st May 1981. As a young player he spent time at Lilleshall, the Football Association's School of Excellence in Shropshire, and Nottingham Forest. Danny joined Leicester City and aged eighteen he broke into the first team making three Premiership appearances. He then went on to play for Bournemouth, Boston, Shrewsbury, Hereford, Macclesfield, Kettering, Tamworth and Icelandic team FH. Danny is now retired from playing. He has an excellent podcast called "Back of the net and Beyond" in which he interviews sportspeople who have pursued careers outside of sport. Danny is passionate about promoting that sportspeople have transferable skills to other industries, drawing on his own experiences when he finished playing football.

Roger Bray

Roger was an amateur midfielder/winger from Weddington in Nuneaton. In November 1972 aged seventeen he was playing for Sandon Rangers and was invited for a trial with Leicester City. Roger played for Leicester City's 'A' and Reserve teams putting in some impressive performances against Oxford United, Shrewsbury Town and Derby County. He then signed professional forms with Fourth Division Northampton Town where teammates included Trevor Gould and Dietmar Bruck. Roger also played for Nuneaton Borough and Bedworth United. In the mid to late 1970s Roger was one of the best players in local football for Griff & Coton and Bermuda W.M.C. In 1981 he won the Birmingham Junior Cup with Bermuda.

Tom Kilkelly played with Roger at Leicester City, I asked him about his memories of playing in the same team as Roger.

My memories of Roger are from the youth and Reserves team at Leicester City. We had a small group of players who were always available. These were not signed on full- time and were classed as amateurs. Roger was one of them. I always wondered why he was never signed full- time. There was another called John Lane. These boys were always apart of the big picture. Roger could play anywhere across the front line and even in the midfield .He had great attitude and commitment to the team , a player I always remember and respect for all his attributes.

Nigel Bridge –Wilkinson played with Roger and I asked him a few questions. Nigel was a centre half who played for Sandon Rangers, Bermuda WMC, Nuneaton Tribune and Arley Rectory. He is also the uncle of ex professional footballer Marc Bridge-Wilkinson.

He was the typical local kid full of energy who could juggle with both feet and head and then deliberately bounce it off the bar, from twenty-five yards out. I, like many others (whose skills were basic) could spot talent in others, but couldn't do myself.

When Dave Tearse started playing for Bermuda. He played the old fashioned frontman and with Roger Bray feeding and supporting him we saw some of the best forward play we have ever had at the club. They had both played for top class professional clubs and with the vision and movement they had everyone else could only watch and admire.

Les Green

Les was a goalkeeper who was born in Atherstone on 17th October 1941. He began his career with Atherstone Boys Club, Mancetter, Baddesley Colliery and Atherstone Town. Les had a trial at Arsenal but failed because he was too small at 5 ft 8 in. He then played for Hull City, Nuneaton Borough, Burton Albion, Hartlepool United, Rochdale. In 1968 he replaced Reg Matthews as Derby County's goalkeeper. The Rams were managed by the legendary Clough and Taylor who had previously been Les's boss at Hartlepool. Les won the Second Division Championship with Derby in 1969, a side that included great players like Dave Mackay, Roy McFarland and John McGovern. He finished his playing career with Durban City in South Africa. Les later managed Nuneaton Borough, Bedford, Hinckley and Tamworth. He was described as being a great shot-stopper, agile and athletic. Les sadly passed away on 30th July 2012 aged seventy.

Ray Train

Ray was a defensive midfielder who was born on 10th February 1971. He grew up in Bedworth and attended Nicholas Chamberlain School. Ray began his career with Bedworth United he failed a trial at Coventry City because of his height. In 1967 he joined Walsall then enjoyed a long career in league football. Ray played for Carlisle United, Sunderland, Bolton Wanderers, Watford, AFC Bournemouth, Oxford United, Northampton Town, Tranmere Rovers before finishing his career with Walsall. In November 1978 he became Watford's record signing at £50.000. Ray helped the Hornets reach Division One in 1982 under Graham Taylor. After retiring from playing he has had different roles with Walsall, Port Vale and Middlesbrough.

Simon Rea

Simon was born in Kenilworth on 20th September 1976. He attended Park Hill and Kenilworth Schools. A talented junior player he could play centre half or centre forward. Simon played for Warwickshire Schools, Norton Lindsay and Coten End Colts. He signed schoolboy forms for Birmingham City and progressed into the first team. Simon made one league appearance and one in the Anglo-Italian Cup for the Blues. He is best remembered for his time with Peterborough United between 1999 and 2005, during which time Simon helped them win the Third Division play offs in 2000. Simon also played for a few non-league teams including Nuneaton Borough, Redditch and Leamington. His father in law is Ian Walker who was a fine player in Warwickshire football. Simon's son is now on Birmingham City's books.

Julian Alsop

Julian was born in Nuneaton on 28th May 1973. The striker began his career with local team Nuneaton Borough then played for VS Rugby, Racing Club Warwick, Tamworth and Halesowen. Julian made his breakthrough with Bristol Rovers. He is best remembered for his time with Cheltenham Town and Swansea City. A big strong centre forward he also played for Oxford United and Northampton Town. Julian played for a number of non-league teams well into his 40s. Danny Finlay played with Julian at VS Rugby and he told me that big and strong, Julian used to frighten defenders.

Memorable Match

Swansea City 1-0 West Ham United -FA Cup 3rd round replay, 13th January 1999.

Third Division Swansea City knocked out Premiership West Ham United out of the FA Cup at the Vetch Field. Martin Thomas scored the winning goal for the Welsh side. Julian was up against Rio Ferdinand and Neil Ruddock to whom he gave a rough time. Swansea also included Steve Watkin who scored against Arsenal seven years earlier.

Swansea City – Freestone, Jones, Bound, Smith, Howard, Coates, Cusack, Roberts,Thomas, Alsop, Watkin

West Ham United – Hislop, Breacker (Hall) Dicks, Ferdinand, Ruddock, Lampard,Laziridis, Lomas, Omoyinmi (Berkovic) Hartson

Steve Bicknell

Steve was born in Stockton, Warwickshire on 28th November 1959. A left winger, he began his career with Leicester City and made his full debut on 9th April 1977 against Newcastle United. Steve made 7 senior appearances for the Foxes and played alongside Brian Alderson and Frank Worthington. He joined Torquay United in 1978 making 3 league appearances then played for VS Rugby and Southam United.

Trefor West

Trefor played at right half or inside forward and joined West Bromwich Albion aged fifteen in May 1960. A pupil of Whitley Abbey School he had offers from Coventry City, Birmingham City, Wolverhampton Wanderers, Aston Villa and Nottingham Forest. Trefor joined Walsall in May 1964 by then playing at full back. He didn't play for the Saddlers long before moving to Nuneaton Borough. Trefor has become a well-known name in fishing and written a book and had his own range of fishing equipment.

David Foy

David was born on 20th October 1972 in Coventry. He played in the football league for Birmingham City and Scunthorpe United. He was a midfielder who played as a forward in his junior days. David grew up in Radford, Coventry and attended Coundon Court School. As a junior David played for successful teams Allesley Sports, Stoke Heath and Mount Nod. David scored 10 goals on his debut for Stoke Heath scoring 75 in the season. He also played for

Coventry Schools in the same age group as Warren Bufton, Craig Dutton and Boyd Young.

David got spotted by Birmingham City by John Halford and progressed through youth/ YTS ranks to earning a professional contract. Blues were managed by Dave Mackay when he was first at the club then Lou Macari and Terry Cooper. David played a few first team games for Blues making his debut v Portsmouth on 13th February 1993. Another Coventry born player James Quinn also made his debut against a Pompey side that included Paul Walsh and Guy Whittingham. David played a couple more matches, against Leicester City and Grimsby Town. David Sullivan and Karen Brady took over at Birmingham City and David was offered a contract but wouldn't have much first team action. David has good memories of playing with Louie Donowa, John Frain, Dean Peer and Paul Peschisolido at Birmingham City. David joined Scunthorpe United under Richard Money but was played out of position as a holding midfielder he was more of a box to box midfielder.

David had a trial at Doncaster Rovers and Coventry City. The Sky Blues were managed by Bobby Gould then Phil Neal. Coventry had a lot of midfielders and Phil Neal liked him but he didn't stay at Highfield Road. Brendan Phillips who was manager of Stafford Rangers came in for David. He spent two seasons at Stafford Rangers playing alongside Paul Shepstone, Martin Bodkin and Dave Crowley. David joined Tamworth on loan then signed permanently for the Lambs. He enjoyed success at Tamworth as they won the Beazer Homes Midland Division and had some good FA Cup runs playing against Bury, Exeter City and Rochdale. David suffered a cruciate ligament injury as he went in for a tackle with Mark Cooper and was out for a season. He also played for Worcester City, Halesowen, Moor Green, Stratford Town and

Bedworth United. David played for Monica Star over 35s with top players like Lee Hendrie, Paul Devlin and Lee Carsley. He really enjoyed playing in this team and with those players. David played in Frank Worthington's testimonial when he was at Birmingham City and it was a fantastic experience playing against legends George Best and Kevin Keegan. David now lives in Nuneaton and is a coach for Nuneaton Borough under 15s' team. Outside football he worked a Triumph motorcycles and in tiling.

Chapter Fourteen – Footballing People

In this chapter we are going to look at local footballing people who have done well in coaching, managing, refereeing and administration.

George Reader

George was born in Chilvers Coton, Nuneaton on 22nd November 1896. According to the 1901 census there was a George Reader of Coton Road, Nuneaton. George attended King Edward Grammar School in Nuneaton. A promising young centre forward, George played for Nuneaton Town during the 1914/15 season. George played 21 times and scored 13 goals as Nuneaton Town won the Birmingham Combination. On 5th of April he scored four goals in the final of the Atherstone Nursing Cup as Nuneaton Town beat Atherstone 6-0. George made 4 appearances and scored 3 goals in the 1919/20 season before moving to St Luke's College in Exeter. He made a few appearances for Exeter City and Southampton. George then played in non-league football up until 1930 whilst working as a schoolmaster in Southampton. He took up refereeing in 1930 progressing to becoming a Football League Linesman in 1936. In 1939 he became a Football League referee then eventually becoming a FIFA listed referee. In 1950 at the age of 53 George referred the opening match of the World Cup between Brazil and Mexico. He took charge of Uruguay and Bolivia. George would then referee the decisive match of the final group stage which Uruguay beat Brazil 2-1. He retired from refereeing to concentrate on his teaching career. In 1963 he returned to Southampton FC as a director then later chairman. In 1976 George saw Southampton beat Manchester United 1-0 in the FA Cup final. He sadly passed away on 13th July 1978 aged 81.

Roy Evans

Roy was a football coach and teacher in Coventry for a number of years. I had the pleasure of speaking to him on the phone. He was born in the Coventry suburb of Whoberley and lived in a few areas of the city growing up. Roy attended Bablake School and studied at the City of Leeds and Carnegie College. He taught in Wolverhampton then worked at Caludon Castle School in Wyken. Back then teachers from all departments were running teams, Roy ran the Hockey team. Roy played a bit of Sunday League football for the Painted Lady and the Devonshire Arms. He talked about a few players in local football at the time in the 1970s like Pete Scanlon (good goalkeeper) Roy Slade, Lol Cairns, Jimmy and Robbie McGovern. Roy is well known and respected in Coventry for his time as coach of Coventry Schoolboys. He also wrote a column for the Coventry Evening Telegraph called Schoolboy Scene. Roy also had other roles - Overseas Secretary, General Secretary and Chairman of Coaches. Roy is well known and respected in Coventry for his time as coach of Coventry Schoolboys.

Roy talked about the fine McGinty footballing family – Mick, John, Tom and Gez were all great players. In 1977-78 he coached Ian Muir and Peter Hormantschuk who were part of a very good side. Abbey Kelly was a great athlete, John Lee represented England at youth level, Clive Deslandes had fantastic pace. Roy also mentioned Terry Gow, Peter Meggitt and Roy Deakin from that late 1970s side. Into the 1980s the class of 1982 reached the English Schools final against Sheffield Wednesday. Two years previously his team lost in the Semi-finals to Middlesbrough. The team of 1982 played without centre forwards as they had so much goal threat from midfield. Gareth Evans and Peter Shearer became professionals, both quality players Roy told me. Moz Harnett, Kenny Trickett and Don Gethfield all had decent non-league careers. Mark Crick, Gary Hardwick, Simon Wilkinson, Darren Reilly, Sean Crowley and Rob O'Brien were all mentioned. Andy Harvey was also in the team: he would go on to have a long association with Coventry City in various roles - assistant physio, first team kit man operations manager and player liaison officer. Roy talked about players in the late 1980s – Gez Carr, Paul Shepstone, Michael Burrows. Steve Phelps (now a superb author) and Michael Stephenson.

In 1992 Roy got a phone call to see Bobby Gould at Coventry City and he signed a five year contract to become Youth Development Officer which he never saw. He was sacked after thirteen months which was very disappointing. Roy went back into teaching and worked at Whitley Abbey, Blue Coat, Foxford and Kenilworth Schools. It was fantastic to speak to Roy who coached some really good players. Roym along with other stalwarts Keith Newbold, Les Harris and Geoff Chatwin to name a few, has done a lot for junior football in Coventry.

Roy coached a lot of great players. I asked him if he could name a best XI.

I've been fortunate to have had some great players to choose from between 1972 and 1992. At the risk of upsetting a few people I have the greatest respect for I'm going for this team in a 4-4-2 formation - Maurice Harnett (Cardinal Newman); John Lee (Ernesford Grange), Sean Crowley (Cardinal Newman), Gez Carr (Cardinal Wiseman), Mick McGinty (Bishop Ullathorne); Gareth Evans (Woodlands), John McGinty (Bishop Ullathorne, captain), Peter Shearer (Cardinal Wiseman), Peter Hormantschuk (Caludon Castle); Michael Stephenson (Cardinal Newman), Ian Muir

(Caludon Castle). Subs: Dean Reid (Cardinal Wiseman), Roy Deakin (President Kennedy), Terry Gow (Bishop Ullathorne), John Halford (Coundon Court), Abbey Kelly (Woodlands) and Steve Clews (Sidney Stringer). So five internationals in the starting XI, two USA soccer scholarships, and seven who earned pro contracts at some stage. I stress that these are just selections from teams I coached. The likes of Pete Scanlon, Ian Crawley, Danny Conway, Neville Bulpitt, Derek Owen, Robbie Jones, John McCloskey and a whole host of others would have been under consideration had they qualified.

I asked Roy about John Gray who played for Coventry Schools over 15s in the late 1960s. John became an international rugby player and a fine cricketer. He was a pupil at Woodlands School and played for Coventry RFC. In 1973 he switched codes to play Rugby League for Wigan. John played as a forward and represented England and Great Britain at Rugby League. He then went onto have a great career in Australia where he still lives. John played first class cricket for Warwickshire. He was a left-arm medium-fast bowler. Roy described him as Coventry's own Ian Botham, a larger than life character with a great sense of humour.

Keith Newbold

Keith was given the name Mr. Ullathorne for his devotion to Bishop Ullathorne School where he coached generations of footballers to outstandingly high levels. He is mentioned in a number of chapters of this book, remembered by many as a great teacher and coach, a wonderful motivator and a dedicated leader in Coventry Schools' Football. Keith not only ran school and city teams but was Chairman of the Schools' FA for many years, taking the association to nationally recognised levels. Keith held similar posts in the Birmingham County FA. He worked tirelessly to promote skill and sportsmanship.

Keith trained for his teaching at St. Paul's College, Cheltenham, a specialist PE college, and went on to teach at Barker Butts School and then Ullathorne. A skilled footballer and cricketer, Keith received his coaching badges from the FA and the MCC. No single person did more for local football than Keith Newbold, a truly great Coventry kid.

As an innovator Keith pioneered school football tours to Europe. On one such tour "Mr. Ullathorne" was given a table setting prepared for "Bishop Ullathorne", the staff thinking that Keith was the Bishop himself! When Keith's assistant left to join Cardinal Newman School the first letter that he received was addressed to "Cardinal Newbold." After 'retiring' Keith became the dedicated and creative Education Officer at Coventry City FC ensuring that the apprentices went to college for further education thus giving them a back-up should their football not lead to professional contracts.

Coventry has been blessed with great servants to local football, none greater then Keith.

Keren Barratt

Keren was born in Coventry in 1946. He became a Football League linesman in 1978. From 1981 to 1992 he was a referee in the Football League. 1992 to 1994 Keren was a Premier League referee. The first match he took charge of in the new league was Manchester United v Everton. The Toffees won this match 3-0 on 19th August 1992. Keren took charge of the 1993 FA Cup Final between Arsenal and Sheffield Wednesday. He also referred the replay. Since 1994 he has worked as a referee assessor and on the Premier League referee select group.

Stuart Attwell

Stuart was born in Nuneaton on 6th October 1982. In 2007 he was the National List of Referees. A year later Stuart became the youngest person to referee in the Premier League, as he took charge of a match between Blackburn Rovers and Hull City. Stuart studied at Staffordshire University and progressed through non-league football to the Premier League. In September 2008 he refereed a match between Reading and Watford which became infamous for the 'Ghost Goal.' Reading took the lead in the Championship match, the ball having passed wide of the goal, but the assistant flagged for a goal rather than a corner kick! The goal was awarded and Stuart sent Watford boss Aidy Boothroyd to the stands for protesting. Stuart was dropped from duties after that error, but came back to referee in the Football League, Premiership and Japanese J League.

Laura Harvey

Laura is currently head coach of the United States under 20s women's national soccer team. She was born in Nuneaton on 15th May 1980 and grew up in Bulkington. Laura went to George Eliot School in Nuneaton and is a former Coventry City Ladies' player. Her dad and brother have also coached. Laura used to watch Coventry City when they were at Highfield Road. As a teenager she played for Coventry City Ladies before moving to Wolverhampton to study. Laura played for Wolverhampton Wanderers and Birmingham City but at twenty- two she suffered an ACL which ended her playing career.

In 2002 Laura began her coaching career with Birmingham City. She was appointed assistant coach then later became team manager. In 2008 Laura began a four year successful association with Arsenal Ladies FC. Laura was initially appointed as First team coach then Assistant Academy Director, Reserve Team manager and then First Team manager. During her time at Arsenal they won three consecutive league titles, two Continental Cups and an FA Women's Cup. Laura managed Seattle Reign and twice won the NSWL Shield.

In November 2017 Laura was appointed head coach of Utah Royals. At International level Laura has coached England at Under 17, 19 and 23 levels as well as USA under 23 (interim) and in January 2020 she was appointed USA Under 20 head coach. On an individual basis she has won NWSL Coach of the Year, FA WSL Coach of the Year and FA Pro Game Female Elite Coach of the Year. Now aged forty Laura still has plenty of time to achieve even more in the Ladie's game. Laura, her family, friends should be very proud of what she has achieved.

Jamie Harvey

I asked Laura's brother Jamie a few questions. He has been a successful coach in the USA.

What teams did you play for in Bulkington and Nuneaton?

I played for Chetwynd Harriers (with Peter Whittingham) I was in the CCFC academy from 10 yrs old till 16 years old. I went to Henley College and studied sports then went to Edge Hill University to get a sports degree.

How did you get into coaching and what teams have you coached?

I got into coaching early doing work experience whilst at Henley College (age seventeen). Then I came out to the states with UK International Soccer Camps age nineteen in the summer holidays. When I graduated from university I got offered a full-time position with UKISC for a year in Los Angeles then worked for a soccer club in LA.

What would you say your greatest achievement was in Soccer (football)?

Greatest achievement was playing for Coventry City academy and being selected to go to regional sessions at Lilleshall. Coaching - Being LA Galaxy Academy U17 head coach and working with some of the best players in the United States. Achieved the A License also.

Your dad I believe worked for Coventry City for a number of years did he inspire you both to get into football?

Yes a huge inspiration for both of us. A great technical coach and he coached a lot of good players. He would always talk to us about the game the technically and tactically at the dinner table most weeks! Dad was a very good player also he played the Semi Pro circuit around the area.

Tony Elliott

Tony is currently goalkeeping coach for the England Blind and Deaf football teams. He is also lead goalkeeping coach for Birmingham City Women's FC. Tony was born in Nuneaton on

30th November 1969. He was a professional goalkeeper in the 1980s and 1990s. He played for Birmingham City, Hereford United, Huddersfield Town, Cardiff City, Carlisle United and Scarborough. Tony has become an accomplished coach and worked for England Men's Futsal team, England Women's Deaf Futsal team, England Cerebral Palsy team. He has also worked for Liverpool, Manchester City, Darlington and Bristol City. Tony won FA Disability Coach of the Year in 2015 and is the Author of 'A Modern Approach to Goalkeeping.'

Bryan Klug

Bryan was born in Coventry on 8th October 1960 but grew up Grimsby. The midfielder played for Lincolnshire team Louth United Juniors before joining Ipswich Town. Bryan never played a first team game for Ipswich and spent time on loan with Wimbledon. In 1983 he joined Chesterfield then played for Peterborough United, Sudbury Town and Chelmsford City. Bryan played in the 1989 FA Vase final for Sudbury, the first match ended 1.1 but Tamworth won the replay 3.0. From 1987 to the present day he has had a long association with Ipswich Town. Between 2010 and 2012 he worked for Tottenham Hotspur but returned to Portman Road. Bryan has held various coaching roles and is now Head of Coaching and Player Development. In 2005 Ipswich won the FA Youth Cup. He has also been caretaker manager of the first team on four occasions.

Marcus Law

Marcus is a well-respected manager at non-league level, having twenty years of experience. He was born in Coventry on 28th September 1975 and attended Ernesford Grange School. Marcus played in goal for Coventry Schoolboys but began his career with Bristol Rovers making two senior appearances. He played for Stafford Rangers and Sacramento Knights in the USA, however a hip injury ended his playing career. Marcus has managed Coventry Sphinx, Racing Club Warwick, Quorn, Barwell, Tamworth, Chasetown and Kettering Town. In 2012 Marcus led Tamworth to the FA Cup Third Round, going out of the competition following a 2-0 defeat to Everton at Goodison Park. Marcus was Kettering manager when the won the Southern League Premier Central division in 2019. Outside football he has been a Senior Quantity Surveyor, Director and a Project Manager.

Mick Brady

Sir Mick as he is known among Leamington FC fans, sadly passed away on 25th September 2020 aged 76.The club's life president and former chairman Mick and others like David Hucker kept the club going in the wilderness years from 1988 to 2000. In the mid-1980s Leamington's old ground on Tachbrook Road was sold for housing. After the 1987/88 season Leamington FC went into an abeyance they had no ground to play on so the decision was made to mothball the team. The annual fee was paid to Companies' House and In the 1990s land was purchased on Harbury Lane, in 2000 Leamington FC reformed. The club has progressed through the leagues and are now in the Nationwide League North. Brakes' fans and the town of Leamington owe so much to him, RIP Mick.

A Tribute to Mick Brady by Nigel Murray

Nigel's best memories of Mick were in the years after the club was mothballed in 1988. Mick had such passion and enthusiasm for Leamington FC Nigel told me. He worked tirelessly in the 1990s to keep the club alive. Mick wasn't a typical chairman: he was more like a regular supporter, a people person who mixed with supporters. He was a modest man who didn't want the limelight, very much an approachable man who would speak to anyone. Mick wasn't afraid to voice his opinions. In the early days before the club reformed in 2000 he would do things steady, not to make any mistakes which may have been done in the past. Nigel remembers Mick walking around the ground with his hands behind his back, talking to fans and watching the game. Sir Mick, as he has been affectionately known by Leamington fans, was the drive to get the club back in business. Nigel recalls the magic of the first match after reforming in 2000. It was a memorable occasion. Nigel told me that other people played big parts in the club reforming but Mick was seen as the leader and the inspiration behind it. "Leamington Fans will always be grateful for Mick's efforts," Nigel added.

Martin Ashcroft

Martin is the manager of newly formed Kenilworth Sporting FC; I asked him a few questions about his football career.

Could you tell me a little bit about yourself who you played and managed previously?

I played for local teams such as Folly Lane, Alvis, GPT, and Coventry Sphinx. I always enjoyed playing our wonderful game but a back injury / operation put a halt to me playing at a decent level.

How did the manager's job at Kenilworth Sporting come about?

It was my old friend the late Willie Knibbs who offered me role as his assistant at Sphinx, which gave me the taste for management. It wasn't long before a decent job opportunity came up with a return to Alvis as the manager. We won the League Cup and finished in the top five which was a great achievement. In my second season we pushed the eventual League One winners all the way to finish runners up. Sphinx at the time we're not having the best of seasons and I agreed to take over the reins with them flirting with relegation. I managed to settle the ship and went in to become one of the most successful managers in the history of the club. I will always hold the Sphinx in very high regard, It had the backing of a very supportive committee and chairman that I will always be grateful for and I hope the feeling is mutual. After standing down due to family commitments I had five months completely away from the hassle of managing, but when Jimmy Ginnelly asked me to join him at Atherstone I felt it was right for me and my family, we won the league and got Atherstone promoted in the our first season together. Most of the next years were taken up coaching and managing my son's team at Coventry Sphinx Juniors, and we put together the most successful junior team in the history of the club, capping it all in our final season as U16s winning the County Cup at Birmingham County Headquarters. With feeling that enough was enough and was very happy to relax and watch for change the phone call came from Mark Eyden the secretary of the newly formed Kenilworth Sporting FC. Mark asked me to come over for a chat at the rebuilt and highly improved facilities at Gypsy Lane. I met the owner and sole keeper of the ground in Geoff Harris, he said he wanted to take the club to the next level on and off the field. Both Geoff and Mark's enthusiasm was exciting and after a couple of hours of talking I agreed to take the job. We were already a month behind every other team with getting a squad together and preseason training. I asked one of my previous players at Sphinx and another ex-Sphinx manager in Luke Hopkins to come in as my assistant. Luke jumped at the chance and we both worked tirelessly to get Friendly matched arranged and more importantly get in players. We managed to get a squad together and we played some very competitive games to see where we were as a squad. To say we are over the moon with our start is an understatement we have played 8 won 7 lost 1 and sitting at the top of the league. Kenilworth Sporting FC is a sleeping giant and I'm delighted to be playing my part in getting this club to a level of football it, and the owner deserves. If we can generate a buzz within Kenilworth as the only non-league team there and get the locals through the gate regularly it would be fantastic for my young exciting team.

Richard Aston

Richard is chairman of the Coventry Charity Cup, I asked him a few questions about his time in football.

It must have been a great honour to be chairman, how long have you been chairman and how did it come about?

I have been involved in football all of my life. I played football all through school, and in to adult life, then I became a referee quickly progressing to be a Class One Referee, referring in local leagues. I was asked to join the Coventry Charity Football Cup in 1999, by Keren Barratt, who was Secretary at the time. In 2002 I was asked to become Chairman when the Incumbent Chairman, Ray Fox, retired, but I turned down the role as I believed that I had not been on the committee long enough at that time. Jimmy James (a name you may know, as well as Ray) took over as Chairman but in 2003 retired through ill health, and I was asked to be Chairman again. This time I decided to take on the role and have been Chairman ever since. It has been a great honour, meeting many people over the years, but more importantly raising well over £150,000 for local Charities since I became Chairman.

Which are your favourite charity cup finals over the years?

The highlights of our finals have been Coundon Court Old Boys winning the first Charity Cup Final to be played at the Ricoh Arena. It was very good to see Woodlands WMC win the Charity Cup for the first time in 2018, after being beaten in the final the previous two years. I often don't see much of the actual game as I am too busy running around organizing everything. All of our finals played at Highfield Road were also excellent occasions as the final was always held "courtesy of Coventry City FC" who never charged is for hosting the final. This is the only disappointment of holding the final at the Ricoh Arena as we are charged in excess of £2,000.00 for holding the final there, a lot of money that we would prefer to donate to charity. The Coventry Charity Football Cup has a wonderful committee, most of whom have been involved in local football for many years, and are all on the committee for the same reason, to support local football and raise lots of money for local charities.

I believe that David Kite and Keren Barratt we're both involved with the Charity Cup. What are your memories of David and Keren?

Keren was an excellent Secretary, especially with his contacts in football. He resigned after we had Alan Wiley from the FA Premier League referee one of our Cup Finals. This did not go down well with the local Referees Association so Keren felt that he should resign. He still supports the Charity Cup by attending our Sportsman's Evening every year, whilst last year he was Guest of Honour at our Cup Final at the Ricoh Arena.

David was a massive part of the Charity Cup and will be very sadly missed following his death at the start of April. He was Chairman of the Charity Cup Sportsman's Evening Committee for 29 years, even running it when he lived in the Lake District for many years. Through this evening David raised many thousands of pounds for local Charities as well as having some of the biggest names in football as the Guest Speaker. For many years David also selected the Player of the Match at our Cup Final. Hopefully later in the year there will be a celebration of David's life which I know will be attended by the great and good in local football.

What teams did you play for?

I played for Parkhill Primary and Woodlands Schools, Callow United in the Coventry Minor League, then Equity & Law (where I worked) on a Sunday. Saturday's were either watching Coventry City or refereeing when I had qualified. I also started to referee on a Sunday.

Mark "Curly" O'Callaghan

It is not often in life that you find someone so inspiring. I have known Curly for a couple of years through our mutual interest in football. Curly is well known in local football through his time coaching and managing Stockton, Southam, Racing Club Warwick, Woodford, Redditch and Leamington. A Leamington kid, Curly was a big AP Leamington fan and particularly enjoyed the Jimmy Knox and Graham Allner teams. Curly's favourite all time player was Roger Brown. For a number of years he battled cancer and everyone who knew him was touched by upbeat personality, drive and determination. Curly loved reading about his AP Leamington heroes on a Facebook group of which several former players are members. He had beaten cancer but in January 2021 he suffered an infection and Veno Occlusive Disease. Sadly on 27th February he passed away aged 56. Curly will always be remembered in local football and for the kind, inspiring man that he was.

Nigel Murray

Nigel is one of Leamington Spa's most successful sportsmen. He is a former World and Paralympian gold medallist in the sport of Boccia. In the Sydney Paralympics in 2000 he won the individual gold medal and was a team gold medallist in Beijing 2008. Nigel has won many more medals and in 2013 he was awarded an MBE. I first met Nigel a couple of years ago, I was going to a Leamington match and I had arrived into Leamington train station late. I got chatting to Nigel's brother on the train who said his brother won't mind giving me a lift too. I then became friends with Nigel through our mutual interest of Leamington FC on Facebook. Nigel is a massive Brakes fan who first started watching AP Leamington under Jimmy Knox in the 1970s. He remembers great players like Tommy Gorman, Roger Brown and Kim Casey. Nigel enjoys watching Leamington in the modern era and is proud of how the club has progressed over the years. A local sporting hero and a very nice guy, Nigel will I'm sure continue to enjoy watching his beloved Brakes for many years to come.

Chapter Fifteen - Family Connections

In this chapter we are going to look at footballing families from Coventry and Warwickshire.

Edwards

Harry and Bill Edwards were brothers from Coventry who played for Small Heath (Now Birmingham City) in the 1890s. Bill was an outside left who also played for Singer's FC and Rugby. Harry was an Inside forward who played for Singer's FC, Leicester Fosse and Watford. Singer's FC enjoyed success in 1891 and 1892 winning the Birmingham Junior Cup, Harry was part of the team.

Mason

George Mason is one of Coventry City's greatest ever players: the centre half is a club legend. He was born in Birmingham on 5th September 1913. He joined Coventry City from Redhill Amateurs in November 1931.George made his Bantams' debut against Bristol Rovers in March 1932 but didn't become a regular until the 1935/36 season. The same season Coventry City won the Third Division South championship, the next three seasons City did well in Division Two. Like many players of that era George was in his prime during World War Two. He continued to play for Coventry City. George played until the 1951/52 season then joined Nuneaton BoroughIn total he made 350 official appearances plus over 170 war time matches. On 18th April 1942 he became the first Coventry City player to play for England, in a thrilling 5-4 win for Scotland at Hampden Park. England included Stanley Matthews, Tommy Lawton and Eddie Hapgood (who is buried in Leamington cemetery). Scotland had a couple of famous future managers in their team, Bill Shankly and Matt Busby. George played in the next match against Wales where he faced Bantams' team mate George Lowrie. Regular centre half Stan Cullis then returned to the team and George would make only the two appearances for England. Unfortunately war time internationals do not count as official matches. George became a publican in Coventry and he passed away on 12th August 1993.

George had twin sons John and Peter, both of whom attended Whitley Abbey School and played for Coventry Boys. In December 1957 John and Peter were selected for a Birmingham County XI against Shropshire. At the time Peter was a centre half and John was an inside forward. Their father George had played for Birmingham County in 1927. The twins were good athletes too, participating in relay and sprint races. John was a fine goal scorer for Close Athletic a Coventry Junior club and he was also a member of Coventry Godiva Harriers. In 1965 John was scoring goals for Alvechurch as they had a fine run in the FA Amateur Cup. John then spent time with Peterborough United, Coventry Amateurs, Nuneaton Borough and played in South Africa. In October 1970 Bedworth United manager Gordon Dougall signed John after a brief spell with Nuneaton Borough. He would become a great signing and formed a strike partnership with David Eades for the Greenbacks. In July 1977 John was appointed Nuneaton Borough second team player-manager. John represented England schools at athletics and England Amateurs at football. Peter played for Coventry City youth 'A' and Reserves from 1958 to 1961, Rootes, Coventry Amateurs and Sphinx.

Jephcott

Paul was an inside forward who was on Coventry City's books as a young player. His dad Joffre and uncle Fred Jephcott played for successful Coventry Amateur team Coventry Tile in the 1940s. Joffre was an inside forward and Fred played in goal. Team mates included Alf Setchell who also played for Coventry City and prolific centre forward Leslie Harkus. Paul played for Wyken Croft and Caludon Castle schools. I asked him about his football career.

Could you tell me about your playing days?

I joined Coventry City in 1964, I had a good school boy career. I played for Coventry schoolboys at u13, u14 and u15 levels and I also played for Warwickshire schoolboys. Stan Cullis the Wolves manager wanted me and WBA wanted to sign me but I chose Coventry City. But felt I got treated very badly at Coventry and left after a year. I played for Wood End and we won the Midlands Youth Cup, under a great character manager called Jock Donaldson. We often beat the good teams from Birmingham. I had a spell with Coventry Amateurs, but became disillusioned and packed up playing when I was about twenty. I played football all through school with Trevor Gould brother of Bobby who I was with at Coventry. Their dad use to drive us to games, but he became blind. Bobby encouraged me to stay at Coventry but felt very bitter and I left. When I left the City, I played for Ken Mathews who had a hairdresser's team and he had a shop on Ball Hill. I think he then had a car sales garage on Swan Lane.

Who did you play with at Coventry City?

Ian Walker lived in Leamington and we used to be loaned out when we were at Coventry City to play for the Co-op in the Thursday's league. Ian joined Coventry City at the same time as Mick Coop, they were both Leamington lads. John Burkitt who I went to school with at Caludon Castle. Paddy Morrissey, Bill Tedds was another good player who was kept out of the first team because the team kept winning and were on the up. I spoke to Dennis Oakes a while back, another good half back who told me about Alan Turner another good player who was kept out because city kept winning. Dennis told me Alan Turner married into the third richest family in England so he did all right!

Ian Walker sadly passed away in 1995 aged forty-six. He was a well-respected player for Westlea Wanderers and Racing Club Warwick.

Oakes

A footballing family from Bedworth, Jack was a full back for Lockheed Leamington, Nuneaton Borough, Bedworth Town and Hinckley Athletic in the 1940s and 1950s. A good cricketer, he was a batsman for Newdigate Colliery and Bedworth Cricket Club. Jack was born in Wolvey but lived most of his life in Bulkington. He had four sons – Dennis, Alan, Malcolm and Keith who would all become good sportsmen. Many thanks to Leamington FC historian Paul Vanes: this information was obtained from Brakes' Trust website.

Dennis, his eldest son, made five first-class appearances for Warwickshire in 1965. He was also a good footballer who could play in defence or midfield He was on Coventry City's books but never played for the first team. Dennis also played for Notts County, Peterborough United, Chelmsford City and Nuneaton Borough. Alan and Malcolm played football for Bedworth Town. Keith had the most success in football, the defender playing for

Bedworth, Peterborough United, Gillingham, Fulham, Newport County and Boston United. In the 1980/81 season Newport County reached the European Cup Winners' Cup quarter-final narrowly getting beat by Carl Zeiss Jana 3-2 on aggregate. Third Division Newport had won the Welsh Cup in 1980 and had a good team with players like John Aldridge, Tommy Tynan and Keith who made the Fourth Division team of the year in 1980. Since finishing playing Keith has worked as a physiotherapist at Peterborough United. Sadly Jack passed away in 2012 aged eighty-nine.

Kelly-Evans

Twin brothers Dion and Devon Kelly-Evans were born in Coventry on 21st September 1996. They attended Holy Family and Cardinal Newman Schools and both spent time with Coventry Sphinx as youngsters. Dion plays at right back whereas, Devon is a right sided / attacking midfielder. Both players came through the Sky Blues youth team, but it was Dion who broke into the senior team first making his debut on 8th May 2016 against Oldham Athletic. In the 2016/17 season he became a regular making thirty three appearances in all competitions including the 2017 EFL Trophy Final at Wembley. The next season in League Two he only made two league appearances but did play in the same side as Devon as Coventry City beat West Bromwich Albion under 21 in the Football League Trophy on 7th November 2017. Dion joined Kettering Town in 2018 and a year later signed for Notts County.

Devon made his debut on 23rd August 2016 in a League Cup defeat against Norwich City. He made fourteen appearances in League Two, scoring in a 2-0 win over Exeter City in September 2017. Devon had a couple of loan spells with Nuneaton Borough then moved to Liberty Way permanently in 2018. Both Dion and

Devon are doing well for their current clubs and at only twenty-four they both have a great future in the game. Hopefully they can reach a higher level again as both of them did well in League One and Two. Devon and Dion are celebrated at their old school, I attended an open day at Cardinal Newman and both of them are in lots of photos about the school. I'm sure all Coventry fans will wish them all the best as they were both popular players at the club.

Middleton

Twins Craig and Lee Middleton were born in Nuneaton on 10th September 1970. They both came through the Sky Blues' YTS scheme and were members of the FA Youth Cup winning team in 1987. Lee was a central defender and made his senior debut as a substitute against Chelsea on 23rd September 1989, he made one more first team appearance. Unfortunately Lee suffered a back injury which would end his professional career. He had an unsuccessful trial with Swindon Town then had spells with Corby Town, Cambridge United, Atherstone Town and Bedworth United. Craig was a midfielder and made his debut against Tottenham Hotspur on 14th April 1990. He made three other appearances for the first team. His last Sky Blues appearance was in the Premier League on 7th November 1990 against Arsenal. Craig partnered another former youth team player Lee Hurst in midfield but the Gunners won comfortably 3-0. In the summer of 1993 Craig joined Cambridge United, then had a long career with Cardiff City, Plymouth Argyle, Halifax Town and Bedworth United. Craig and Lee both recently celebrated their 50th birthday and are members of the CCFPA.

Kelly

A fine footballing family from Coventry, the Kelly brothers, who attended Woodlands School, were talented footballers. Errington was a forward with Triumph Athletic, AP Leamington, VS Rugby, Ledbury Town, Lincoln City, Bristol City and Bristol Rovers prior to joining Coventry City in 1983. Despite scoring on a regular basis for the reserves he was never given a first team chance. Terry Gibson was first choice striker and Bobby Gould preferred to play him alongside a target man like Dave Bamber or Graham Withey. Errington joined Peterborough United in 1984 and became a fans favourite at London Road. He finished his career playing in Sweden and later became an English teacher.

Abbey was a talented midfielder for Coventry Schoolboys in the late 1970s. He was in the same team as Ian Muir and Peter Hormantschuk. He enjoyed a good non-league career with Leamington, Racing Club Warwick Triumph Athletic, Coleshill, Bedworth, Coventry Sporting, St Albans City and Stratford Town.

Tony was a winger best known for his time with Stoke City and Bristol City. He also played for Bury, Leyton Orient, Cardiff City and Hull City. Tony is now managing director and founder of Red card consultancy who help people with gambling addiction. Tony's book Red Card tells his own personal story of how his addiction affected his life and family. He is an inspirational person who has turned his life around and helping others.

Charlie and Mel (Tony's twin brother) also played non-league football. Leon is their cousin, he has had a long career which included playing for Cambridge United, Hinckley United and Worcester City.

A great footballing family, Abbey and Errington were not given a chance at Coventry City. I am certain both of them would have done well in the first team both were terrific players.

Guest

Father and son Stuart and Louis Guest have both been involved with Coventry Sphinx for a number of years. I asked them both some questions.

<u>Stuart</u>

What teams did you play for?

Growing up in Solihull, I played locally and for Solihull Schools.

Could you tell me what is your favourite match that you have seen Louis play in?

I think my favourite game was watching Louis play for Coventry Sphinx against Ilkeston Town last season. Ilkeston were the top of the league at the time and flying and we were mid-table and we went away in front of (600 fans) and beat them 4-0. It really epitomised the spirit of Coventry Sphinx and what they're all about.

How long have you been a match photographer for Coventry Sphinx?

I'm not officially a match day photographer, but I have taken my hobby away from football to take some shots whilst watching the sphinx and it is something that I thoroughly enjoy doing.

Louis

Congratulations on your 150 game milestone, a brilliant achievement. Could you tell me a bit about your university football career, what teams you played for and what you enjoyed about that standard of football?

This was certainly a highlight of my personal football career. I started in my first year in the second team before ending that season with the first team finishing mid table playing with some great players. In my second season we had another solid year, just falling short and finishing second in the league but had the great experience of working alongside Alessandro Barcherini who has now gone on to work with the Leeds United first team as GK coach. In my third year I was honoured to be offered the role of captaining the team where we managed to win the league for the first time in the universities history and get promoted to the Premier Division, alongside maintaining our six game unbeaten run in the varsity series against our rivals. In my fourth year (Masters) I was fortunate enough to be offered a sports scholarship by the university, where we competed in the premier division against 'the big boys' of university sport - This was a great stage for Nottingham Trent University to be competing on and up against universities that are well established at that level. We had a very strong team and we caused a huge upset beating all teams within the league and actually winning the premier division which had never been done before at the university - We had a great team alongside some unbelievable coaches (Tom Shaw ex pro for Cambridge United & Noel Whelan (I'm sure you know all about Noel ha ha) and it was the perfect way to sign off my university career.

Who would you say were the best players that you played with or against during your career?

Players I have played with I would say Jordan Graham (Winger, now at Gillingham) great feet and pace and superb delivery. Julian Joachim at the end of his career we overlapped for a while as I was just coming through at Shepshed, a great guy to learn from. There was many great non-league players, Jack Edwards (Leamington) Nathan Stainfield (Now at Newark, previously of Boston United) also learning a hell of a lot from some of the older Sphinx players as a youngster coming through. Players I have played against would be Dior Angus, Omar Bogle, Marcus Tudgay all established strikers that have all either been in the professional game or are still a pro now!

What is your favourite match during your time with Coventry Sphinx?

As a youngster we went away to Solihull Moors in the Birmingham Senior Cup and won 3-0, I think, trying to remember the score but this was a team that were four leagues above us at the time and it was again another great example of the approach of a Coventry Sphinx side. I think as my Dad mentioned the Ilkeston game last year was a big one but ultimately the Coventry derby is certainly my favourite that I remember, particularly holding onto our sevengame unbeaten run against them which was unfortunately ended this year!

Watkins

Father and son Ken and Kenny are the second and third generations from this footballing family. I contacted them both to ask them about their playing days.

Ken Watkins

Ken, like his dad Ken Watkins senior, was a good footballer and cricketer. Ken played football for Sphinx, Bulkington, Daytona Sports and Painted Lady. He began as a winger but later played at left back and sweeper. Ken played cricket for Coventry and North Warwickshire Cricket Club and Morris. He played with his dad for a couple of seasons. He was mainly an opening batsman, Ken went to Caludon Castle School and represented Coventry Schools. A team mate of Ken's was Neville Bulpitt who was a good player, Neville played for Warwickshire's 'A' team. Another good local player was Alan Gordon who also played for Warwickshire. Alan sadly passed away in 2007. Ken also talked about Dennis Oakes as a good player and a young Ian Bell who was destined to play at the top level of cricket. Ken played football till he was forty and cricket till he was fifty. Like his dad, Ken enjoyed playing football and cricket.

Kenny Watkins

Kenny was a midfielder/forward who has played for Barwell, Stratford Town, Coventry Copeswood, Potters Green, Highway and Brooklands Jaguar. As a youngster he spent time with three professional clubs. I asked Kenny a few questions about his career.

What was the favourite club you played for?

The best club I played for was Barwell. I was only there for a season, but the pitch was always in sublime condition which suited my game as a touch player.

Who were the best players that you played with at any club?

At Man City I played in a very good side with the likes of Joey Barton and Glenn Whelan who both went on to get international

*caps for England and the Republic of Ireland respectively. At Stoke
I played with Karl Henry who was the captain of Wolves in the mid
2000's, and Kris Commons who went on to be a Celtic hero!*

**You were at Coventry City academy too wasn't you? How long
were you there?**

*Yes I was at the Coventry academy from age ten to fourteen, but
was offered pro contracts at Manchester City, Leicester City and
Stoke City. Coventry couldn't match it so I signed a 5 1/2 year deal
with Manchester City. 2 years schoolboy forms a 2 year
apprenticeship and a 1 1/2 year professional contract.
Unfortunately I got seriously injured at 16 and was a bit homesick.
So I made a mutual decision with Man City to be released from my
contract and move closer to home with Stoke City.*

Stewart Rushton

Stewart is Ken's brother in law. They played together for the
Painted Lady.

Hi, Stewart. What teams did you play for?

*I went to Caludon and played for Coventry schools with the likes of
Steve Raybould, John McCluskey and Gez McGinty. I went on to
work and play for the Standard and I think Ken Brown was
manager. My training officer took me to Atherstone but a certain
Jeff Astle kept me out the team. I then went on to play for the
Sphinx where Cos Lee and Dave Reznick formed a formidable
sweeper centre half combo. I had a spell Bedworth mostly reserves
because Les Ebrey and Danny Conway were up front. I had some
success at Massey Ferguson and went to play at the colliery with
all five Downing brothers and their dad was manager. I had a spell
at Jaguar while working for them and played a while at Coventry*

Sporting and Kenilworth Rangers. Played for Folly lane as a kid but my earliest memories are playing up front with Steve Ross for the Highwaymen as juniors. I only really played any decent football for one side on a Sunday the Painted Lady but played for many over 35s Folly Lane, Jaguar and VS Rugby just a flash back and remembered I had 2 fantastic seasons at the old Matrix and a brief spell at the Alvis. Lived for football

McGinty

A talented footballing family from Coventry, the McGinty brothers are a local football family of whom to be proud. John McGinty was a defender who attended Bishop Ullathorne School. He played for Coventry Sporting with his brother Mick in the early 1980s. In 1983 he was part of the VS Rugby team which won the FA Vase at Wembley. Five years later John returned to the famous old stadium with Telford United in the FA Trophy Final. Telford and Enfield drew the first game 0-0 then both sides played in a replay at The Hawthorns. Enfield won 3-2 with two goals from future Coventry City striker Paul Furlong, Steve Norris scoring for Telford. John also played for Hednesford Town, Racing Club Warwick, J.F.Kennedy and a second spell with VS Rugby teaming up with his brother Tom. Mick McGinty was a midfielder who spent time with Coventry City and played for Leamington He later joined the Police force. Mick played for England Schools and he was part of an excellent Coventry Schools' team that reached the English Schools' Cup semi-final against Middlesbrough. Mick's team mates for Coventry included – Wayne Mumford, John Matthews, Robbie Jones and Kevin Kane. Tom McGinty was a defender who played for Coventry Sporting, Moor Green, VS Rugby, Nuneaton Borough and Sutton Coldfield. Gez McGinty tragically passed away at a young age playing for Massey Ferguson.

Chapter Sixteen – In the News

A random look at which teams and players were making the headlines.

22nd October 1949

Bill Molloy Makes Southampton Debut

Bill Molloy from Coventry made his Saints debut in a 3-1 win over Blackburn Rovers in Division Two. It would be Bill's only appearance for Southampton. In 1950 he joined Lockheed Leamington. Bill made a few appearances for Newport County and was on Millwall's books. Bill played for a few local non-league teams then became a painter and decorator in Coventry.

27th April 1968

Jet Blades Reserves Win Cup

Folly Lane Reserves were beaten 1-0 at Burnaby Road in Radford as Jet Blades Reserves win the West Bromwich Albion Cup. Dixon scored the only goal in this tight match. Jet Blades also had Pitt sent off.

14th May 1979

J.F.Kennedy Win Birmingham Junior Sunday Cup

JFK beat Keresley End 3-2 to win the cup in Sutton Coldfield, Tom Kilmurray scored the winner in extra-time. Brian Rankin and Martin McGrogan scored for JFK then Keresley fought back with goals from John Brooks and Paul Upton. Rankin was sent off for JFK but Kilmurray got the winner from a free-kick.

27th April 2012

Christ the King Win Coventry Charity Cup

Christ the King from the Coventry Alliance League beat Racing Club Warwick from the Midland Alliance Premier Division 1-0 at the Ricoh Arena. Andy Morris scored a last minute free kick to earn the Coventry team the win. Sean Gormley of Christ the King was named Man of the match.

22nd March 1965

Eddy Brown Shines for Bedworth

New Bedworth player-manager and former Coventry City forward Eddy Brown had a great game at inside-right as Bedworth beat Bilston 3-2. Johnson and Ken Brown (no relation) with the goals for Bedworth.

22nd March 1965

Lockheed Leamington in Entertaining Draw

The Brakes drew 4-4 with Ilkeston at the Windmill Ground. Jimmy Knox scored twice and goals from Syd Hall and Ernie Ward. Lockheed had a strong team, Knox and Ward had been on Coventry City's books.

4th March 1976

Chris Prophet Has Trial at Derby County

Twenty one year old Racing Club Warwick striker Chris Prophet has joined Tommy Docherty's Derby County on trial. Chris joined RCW from GEC and also plays for top Sunday team Sweeney Todd.

13th May 1978

Boro Win Birmingham Senior Cup

Redditch United v Nuneaton Borough – Birmingham Senior Cup Final replay at Fellows Park, Walsall FC

Nuneaton won the replay 1-0 thanks to a goal from Tim Smithers. The first match at Coventry City's Highfield Road was a 1-1 draw. The match would be Kirk Stephens' last for the club before a move to Luton Town. Trevor Peake and Tim Smithers would soon follow Kirk into league football. Wayne Thomas would soon depart for a successful career in Germany.

Nuneaton Borough: Knight, Stephens, Smith, Peake, Tysall, Thomas, Lewis (Chinn), Smithers, Dale, Vincent (Nardiello), Fleet.

15th May 1979

Greenbacks' Cup Glory

AP Leamington 0-2 Bedworth United – Birmingham Senior Cup Final replay at Manor Park, Nuneaton Borough

Danny Conway is the hero as Bedworth won the cup for the first time in their history. Danny, who joined The Greenbacks from AP Leamington, scored both goals.

31st March 1955

Coventry Charity Cup Win

Coventry City B 2-1 Walsgrave – Highfield Road

Ken Brown gave Coventry City "B" the lead, then Crisp equalised for Walsgrave. Coventry's winner came via a Tracey own goal.

Coventry City"B" -Sillito, Easterlow, Cole, Umbers, Dadge, Jones, Bates, Cramp, Sheppard, Upton, Brown

Walsgrave – Challis, Gardner, Parker, Bennett, Mitchell, Tracey, Falloon, Smith, Crisp, Chater, Newbold

27th May 1978

Willenhall Social Win Treble

The Chace Avenue team completed a superb treble after they retained the Coventry and North Warwickshire Premier Division.

They recently won the Coventry Charity Cup and Coventry Evening Telegraph Cup.

12th November 1977

Roy Slade Signs for Racing Club Warwick

Racing Club boss George Anderson has signed forward Roy Slade from Coventry Sporting. George said that he has always rated Roy and been impressed since he played for Massey Ferguson.

12th October 1974

Sweeney Todd Score Sixteen

Sweeney Todd showed no mercy as they hammered Sky Blue Rangers 16-0. Duffy, C Howarth and B Howarth all got hat tricks.

7th April 1966

Mason in FA Amateur squad

John Mason, a striker of Alvechurch FC, is in the FA Amateur squad to play against Queens Park Rangers at Loftus Road. John is the son of former Coventry City legend George Mason. John also played for Nuneaton Borough and Bedworth.

7th April 1966

Canley Social Club Win Cup

Canley beat Shilton 2-1 to win the Coventry Benelovent Cup. Bryan and Beaufoy scored for Canley, Shilton scored via an own goal.

31st January 1976

GEC Hammer Folly Lane

Anderson and Prophet scored two goals each as GEC beat Folly Lane in the Telegraph Cup. GEC goalkeeper was Pete Scanlon, a long serving teacher at Cardinal Newman School.

15th of April 1963

Bermuda Win Telegraph Cup Final

Ray Smart scored the only goal as Bermuda WMC won the cup for the first time in their history beating Rootes Athletic 1-0 at Highfield Road. Bermuda who are Nuneaton Amateur league leaders did well to beat a strong Rootes team who included former Football League forward Ken Chapman.

4th May 1968

GEC Win Telegraph Cup

Fred Robinson scored the only goal as GEC beat Rootes Athletic 1-0 to win the Evening Telegraph Challenge Cup final at Highfield Road.

7th May 1966

Bristol City Watching Ray Holmes

Bristol City have shown an interest in Lockheed Leamington centre-forward Ray Holmes. He is the leading scorer for Lockheed in the Midland League, The Robins are looking for a successor to John Ateyo. Ray who was at Coventry City earlier in his career has benefited from playing with superb wide players in Syd Hall and Ernie Ward. Syd an outside-left spent time at Leicester City and Ernie an Outside-Right was at Coventry City. Neither Ray, Ernie or Syd made it into league football but came close, but it was to Lockheed's benefit as they won the Midland League in 1965.

29th May 1988

Coventry Kid Runner up at Wembley

Former Coventry City youth and reserve left back Shaun McGrory was part of the Burnley team that at Wembley against Wolverhampton Wanderers. It was the Associate Members' Cup Final, known as the Sherpa Van Trophy Final, a competition between Third and Fourth Division teams in its fifth year. Wolves won the match 2-0 thanks to goals from Andy Mutch and Robbie Dennison. Shaun played Sixty one minutes of the match. He joined Burnley in 1987 after being released by Coventry City. Predominantly a left back, Shaun was born in Coventry on the 29th February 1968. A regular at Turf Moor he was released by Burnley in May 1990 and subsequently played for VS Rugby, Shepshed Dynamo, Bedworth United and Nuneaton Borough.

22nd October 1976

Harry Redknapp Joins AP Leamington

Famous now for his appearances on television programme I'm a Celebrity... Get Me Out Of Here! and his various adverts. Harry had a very good career in football as a player for West Ham United and later as a manager. For a brief time in 1976 he played for

Southern League Premier Division team AP Leamington. Harry was in between spells with North American Soccer League team Seattle Sounders. He played for AP during the NASL close season. Harry's time at the Old Windmill was ruined by injuries and one time he refused his wages stating that he didn't earn it! After his time in Warwickshire he played in North America for three years then embarked on a great career in coaching. Harry was a coach at Seattle Sounders, Oxford City and AFC Bournemouth with whom he got his first management role. From 1994 to 2017 he managed West Ham United, Portsmouth, Tottenham Hotspur, Southampton, Queens Park Rangers, Birmingham City and Jordan National team. AP Leamington manager Jimmy Knox pulled of a coup signing Harry, although his spell was brief I'm sure players and fans alike enjoyed having him in Warwickshire.

4th May 2005

Sphinx Win Last Ever Telegraph Cup at Highfield Road

Coventry Sphinx beat Brooklands Jaguar 5-0 in the Coventry Evening Telegraph Cup Final. The last ever final at the famous old ground, Sphinx captained by Danny McSheffrey ran out comfortable winners. Jamie Towers scored twice, Robbie Stephenson, Paul Woods and Wayne Pulford also scored.

13th December 1990

Adders' Cup Run Over

Atherstone United of the Beazer Homes League pushed Third Division Crewe Alexandra all the way in this FA Cup Second Round replay. Alex edged past Atherstone thanks to a goal from Andy Sussex. Ron Bradbury's team caused their hosts lots of problems. Ian Gorrie in particular played very well. Crewe were a decent outfit in the early 1990s under Dario Gradi. This team included many well-known players. Kenny Swain had previously won trophies with Aston Villa. Neil Lennon and Craig Hignett would go on to have great careers.

Crewe Alexandra – Edwards, Swain, Lennon, Callaghan, Carr, Smart, Hignett, Rose, Sussex, Gardiner (Edwards) Clayton (Jasper)

Atherstone United – Starkey, Abell, Upton, Whetton, Randle, Olner, Parker (Lewis) Green
(Landan), Bradder, Bodkin, Gorrie

26th April 1975

Ernie Hunt Wins Cup Medal

Former Coventry City and Wolves player Ernie Hunt won his first ever cup final medal. Ernie has won the Birmingham Senior Cup with Atherstone Town after they beat AP Leamington 1-0. Now at the end of his career the inside forward will always be remembered for the famous 'Donkey kick goal' against Everton in 1970. Ernie's full name is Roger Patrick Hunt but he used Ernie to avoid any confusion with Liverpool and England forward Roger Hunt. Ernie was a fans favourite at Highfield Road where he spent five years with the Sky Blues after signing from Everton in 1967.

26th May 1985

Wayne Thomas Wins German Cup with Bayer Uerdingen

Former Nuneaton Borough midfielder Wayne Thomas came on as an 82nd minute substitute as Bayern Munich were beaten 2-1 in the DFB-Pokal final. Bayern were the favourites to win the match. They had star players like Soren Lerby, Lothar Matthaus and Klaus Aughtenhaler. Bayer though had good players too in Friedhelm Funkel and Matthais Herget. It was Bayern who took the lead through West Germany striker Dieter Hoesness. Bayer soon equalised through a goal from Feilzer. In the second half Schafer scored the winning goal. Wayne replaced Icelandic striker Larus Gudmundsson to help see the game out. Wayne enjoyed a good career in Germany playing for KSV Baunatal, Alem Aachen, Hannover 96 and Kickers Offenbach.

4th February 1978

Gallagher Set for Cup Debut

Top local non-league forward Stewart Gallagher is set for a debut for J.F Kennedy Athletic against Coundon Social in the Birmingham Junior Cup. Stewart has played Saturday football for Coventry Sporting, VS Rugby and AP Leamington. In May 1978 he scored a hat trick as J.F Kennedy beat Bubbenhall 4-0.

13th May 1978

Morris at the Double

Morris Motors have won the Coventry Alliance Premier I after getting a point at defending champions Nuneaton Griff. Morris Reserves also clinched the Alliance II Championship.

26th April 1997

Player from Rugby Scores Last Ever Goal at Famous Old Ground

Stuart Storer who is from Rugby, scored the only goal of the game as Brighton and Hove Albion beat Doncaster Rovers 1-0. It was the last ever match at the Goldstone Ground and also kept the Seagulls in the Football League. Stuart has also played for Birmingham City, Bolton Wanderers and Wigan Athletic. He did join Everton in 1987 but didn't play for the first team. Stuart is well known in local non-league football having played for and managed Hinckley United and he is now manager of Bedworth United.

28th April 1984

Leamington Kid Makes Debut in Black Country Derby

Paul Dougherty from Royal Leamington Spa made his Wolverhampton Wanderers debut against local rivals West Bromwich Albion in a 0-0 draw. It was a season of struggle for Wolves as they finished bottom of the First Division. Team mates of Paul were Kenny Hibbitt and Billy Livingstone who was born in Coventry but represented Scotland at Under 18 level winning the 1982 European Championship. The Baggies had a few familiar faces to Coventry City fans – Cyrille Regis, Garry Thompson and Steve Hunt. Paul played regularly in the next season in the Second

Division, scoring against Manchester City and Leeds United. Tim Flowers from Kenilworth broke into the first team after relegation. Another team mate was Mark Buckland who was signed from AP Leamington. Paul stayed with Wolves until January 1987 before having a successful career in the USA. At 5 feet 2 inches tall, Paul was suited for indoor soccer and became a prolific goal scorer for Buffalo Blizzard and San Diego Soccers.

20th January 1976

Coventry Sporting Sign Geoff Brassington

Geoff is a twenty five year old striker who is a former Coventry City Junior. He has previously played for Massey Ferguson and Hinckley Athletic having been released by the Sky Blues in April 1967.

29th October 1975

We Want Crystal Palace in the First Round of the FA Cup

Skipper Bobby Mundy said, "We don't intend to lose on Saturday we want to win and draw Crystal Palace the glamour team of the Third Division."

Match secretary Frank Jeavons father of goalkeeper Howard Jeavons said, "The fourth qualifying round of the FA Cup might not be everyone's idea of Utopia. But to Coventry Sporting it is something of a dream"

Sporting beat Spalding to set up a First Round tie against Tranmere Rovers.

30th October 1978

Sporting Win in FA Vase

Sporting beat Gornal Athletic 2-0 thanks to two goals from Geoff Brassington. Howard Jeavons made a great save for Sporting when it was 0-0 and they now progress to the Third Round of the FA Vase.

22nd October 1977

"We will pull through," says Tony Dunk

Tony who has been with the club for eleven years has twice near left the club. Sporting have been on a slump on the field and financially but are looking to turn the corner after a good result against VS Rugby. Tony scored twice against VS Rugby. Two weeks previously they got thrashed 5-0 by Willenhall. Caretaker manager Dick McKinnon looks set to replace George Awde.

11th November 2017

Leamington Kid Breaks World Record

Paul Bastock made his 1,250th senior appearance beating Peter Shilton's world record. Paul, who was born in Leamington, began his career with Coventry City winning the FA Youth Cup in 1987. He made his record breaking appearance for Wisbech Town in the FA Vase against Thetford Town. Paul left Coventry City in 1988 without making a senior appearance, he joined Cambridge United. He played for quite a few clubs during his career, his longest spell was with Boston United between 1992 and 2004. Paul is now assistant manager for Kings Lynn Town FC, he continued to play until he was in his late 40s.

29th November 2006

Former Nicholas Chamberlain Pupil Captains England to Victory

Craig Stanley was born in Nuneaton on 3rd March 1983. The midfielder has enjoyed a long football career. He is still playing for Lymington Town at the age of 37 and recently completed his 700th match. Craig who has type 1 diabetes has played for many teams including Morecambe, Bristol Rovers and Lincoln City. One of his finest moments was when England C won the 2005–06 European Challenge Trophy. England C or England Semi-pro team won the competition after winning all three matches of a four team tournament. Craig captained the team as they clinched the trophy with a 4-1 win over Netherlands Amateurs under 23s. Craig Mackail-Smith, George Boyd, Steve Morison and Kieran Charnock scored the goals. Ironically Craig (Mackail-Smith) and George would both win full caps for Scotland, Steve would play for Wales. Craig's cousin is Jai Stanley who was a talented midfielder for a number of local non-league teams.

24th October 2020

Coventry Connections Help Banbury United Win Famous FA Cup Tie

Banbury United reached the FA Cup First Round Proper after beating Bury Town 2-1. One of Banbury's players is experienced Coventry born defender Kelvin Langmead who has played in the Football League for Shrewsbury Town, Northampton Town and

Peterborough United. Jack Finch also plays for Banbury. The midfielder played for the Sky Blues in League One. Banbury United are managed by Andy Whing who needs no introduction to Coventry City fans. The right back was a fans' favourite making over 100 appearances and famously scoring the last ever goal at Highfield Road. Banbury lost in the next round against Canvey Island.

26th October 2009

Greenbacks' Cup Run Comes to an End

Bedworth United were beaten 2-0 by York City in the FA Cup Fourth round qualifying. Leek Town, Causeway United, Rainworth Miners Welfare and Coventry Sphinx were beaten in previous rounds. Bedworth's cup run came to an end at Bootham Crescent with Rankine and Brodie scoring the goals for York City.

Bedworth: Bevan, Moran, Squire, Cummins, Shilton (Petty), Allen (Kabango), Connolly, Lenton, Blair, Robinson (Beard), Moore.

7th January 1967

Nuneaton Borough Knock Swansea Town out of FA Cup

Nuneaton Borough knocked Third Division Swansea Town out of the FA Cup Second round 2-0 at Manor Park. A Tommy Crawley goal and an own goal won it for the non-league side. Swansea included Ivor Allchurch a Welsh football legend and former Coventry City forward Billy Humphries but they were no match for Nuneaton. In the next round Borough drew 1-1 with Rotherham but would lose the replay 1-0.

Nuneaton Borough: Crump, Jones, Wilson, Davis, Watts, Allen, Ashe, Cutler, Richards, Crawley, Hails.

Swansea Town : Hayes, Gommersall, R. Evans, Williams, Purcell, Coughlin, B. Evans, Allchurch, McLaughlin, Todd, Humphries.

24th March 1979

Coventry Schools' Under 15s in Big Win

Peter McDonald of Binley Park got a hat trick as Banbury Schools under 15s were beaten by Coventry 6-2. Steve Thomas, Greg Murphy and Michael McGinty also scored for Coventry Schools.

4th May 1967

Coventry Boys Win Cup

Coventry Boys beat Aston 3-1 to win the Warwickshire Schools under-14 Cup. Joyce, Howard and Swords scored for Coventry.

7th October 1978

Sweeney Todd Do Well in Birmingham Junior Cup

Jackie Manning got a hat trick and Stu Fisher also scored as Birmingham team Siviter Sports were beaten 4-0.

17th September 1977

Super Mac!

Bernie McErlane scored four goals as Willenhall Social beat Shilton 4-2

26th November 1977

Tommy Gorman Impressing AP Leamington Boss Jimmy Knox

Midfielder Tommy who also plays for top Sunday League side J F Kennedy, has impressed Brakes' manager Knox. Tommy has previously played for Willenhall Social. Jimmy said, "Tommy has no airs and graces. He just puts his head down and plays." A player in fine form, he scored three goals in four games.

24th March 1974

Coventry Schools' Under 13s Achieve Excellent Win

Coventry's youngsters beat South Birmingham 4-1 with Steve Kimberley impressing. Steve scored and assisted Michael Macbeth for one of his goals. Muldoon also scored for Coventry. South Birmingham scored from a penalty.

4th December 1993

Nuneaton Borough Earn Replay Against AFC Bournemouth in FA Cup

Boro got a great 1-1 draw against League Division Two side AFC Bournemouth in the FA Cup second round. Alex Watson gave the Cherries the lead but Kim Green got the equaliser. Nuneaton Borough of the Southern League Premier Division knocked Swansea City out in the previous round lost the replay 1-0 at Manor Park.

Bournemouth: Bartram, Chivers, Masters, Morris, Watson, Parkinson, O'Connor, McGorry, Beardsmore (Cotterill), Wood, Leadbetter.

Nuneaton Borough: Attwood, Byrne, McGrory, Keogh, Tarry, Wade (Symond), Simpson, Bradder, Green, Rosegreen, Shearer.

11th May 1987

GEC Win the Coventry Evening Telegraph Cup

GEC (Coventry) beat Jaguar / Daimler at Highfield Road 2-1. Daryl Finch gave Jaguar the lead then GEC scored two goals from Paul Blain and Paul Luckett to give GEC the lead at half time. Jaguar's John Docherty hit a good shot which forced keeper Paul Haynes into a good save in the second half but GEC held on. GEC captain Derek Jones once played for Coventry Sporting as did David Heal. Steve Kimberley had played for Leamington FC, Paul Luckett was once on Coventry City's books.

Jaguar / Daimler – McDonald, Hudson, Byrne, Howard, Miles (Davies) Saunders, Milbourn, Guest, Docherty, McDonald, Finch.

GEC – Haynes, Heal, Luckett, Jones, Clarke, Atkinson, Kimberley, McDermott, Gillings, Quinn, Blain

12th August 2015

Coventry United in Comfortable Win

Hinckley AFC lost 4-0 at home to Coventry United. Josh O'Grady scored two goals and Josh Blake and Jean Dakouri also scored.

22nd October 2005

Brakes Reach FA Cup First Round Proper

Leamington beat Ossett Town 3-2 in the FA Cup Fourth round qualifying to set up a first round match against Colchester United. Walshaw gave the home team the lead. Josh Blake equalised for Leamington. Jon Adams put the Brakes ahead then his brother Richard added a third in the second half. Ossett scored a penalty which resulted in Leamington captain Leon Morgan being sent off. Leamington held on to win and could look forward to a trip to Layer Road. Colchester would thrash Leamington 9-1, but Richard Adams scored a stunning goal for Leamington to give the visiting Brakes fans some cheer.

2nd May 1983

Greenbacks Win Midland Floodlit Cup

Leading 2-1 from the first leg at The Oval, Bedworth United came out on top in the second leg thanks to a Les Ebrey goal therefore winning 3-1 on aggregate.

Nuneaton Borough: Dulleston, Hall, Dixey, Glover, Gibson, Hendry, Parker, Phillips, Morley, Dale, Lowe.

Bedworth United: Martin, Brookes, Peacock, Taylor, Halton, Jackson, Carmichael, Gorman, Downes, Smith, Ebrey.

17th November 1984

VS So Close to Causing Cup Shock

Jimmy Knox's VS Rugby team made the short journey to play Northampton Town. VS gave their Division Four hosts a good game and had looked like winning. Ian Crawley scored twice for VS Rugby and Ian Benjamin scored for the Cobblers. Ray Train scored a last minute equaliser to deny VS a great win. Northampton Town won the replay 1-0 at Butlin Road. VS Rugby had a good team

Northampton Town – Gleasure, Cavaner, Lewis, Gage, Barnes, Train, Lee, Hayes, Mann, Benjamin, Belfon

VS Rugby – Marsden, McGinty, Webb, Knox, Harrison, Ingram, Gorman, Gardner, Carmichael, Conway, Crawley

7th September 2020

Great Start for Kenilworth Sporting FC

Newly formed Kenilworth Sporting won 5-0 at WLV Sport FC to record their first ever win. Luke Steer got a hat trick and Tyrone Wilson and Archie Ashcroft also scored.

7th March 1983

George Best Stars for Boro

Football legend George Best makes a guest appearance for Nuneaton Borough. He helped Boro beat a Coventry City XI 2-1 in a Borough appeal fund match. Best rolled back the years to assist

Paul Culpin for the first goal then scored a penalty. Paul Dyson scored for the Sky Blues who fielded a strong team but played a lot of players out of position.

11th May 2000

Stratford Town Win Final Match of a Fine Season

Stratford Town beat Bridgnorth Town 2-1 at Masons Road. They had a fine season finishing second in the Midland Alliance under manager Lenny Derby. Jon Brant and Peter McBean scored the goals, Marcus Hamill had a good game on the right wing. Scott Darroch finished top scorer with 20 goals, followed by Peter McBean on 18 and Craig Martin on 11.

It was a great era for Stratford Town, I asked fans Jim Connolly and Doug Armstrong about their memories of those days.

Jim

It was a good time to be watching the Town as we always had good teams even if they never quite managed to get promoted. Andy Beechey was a great player and servant, and great guy who we still see at games now and again and keep in contact with on Twitter. Marcus Hamill had great ability, a real throwback winger who would leave fullbacks on the seat of their pants and then go back and beat them again just for fun. Peter McBean was a big favourite as he was very much the rugged centre forward and brave with it.

Doug

Lenny (Derby) attracted decent players and he encouraged them to play football. He was a three at the back man.

Morley had a massive tan and coiffured hair. He was still quick even in his early 40s. He helped Town out when it nearly collapsed and players had to be brought in. He was very direct. Andy Beechey played at left back then returned from Evesham and played centre or left of the back three. He never give less than 100%, was a real trier with a good left foot. He was also a great guy and interacted with the supporters always. Hamill played wide right up from and wing back a few times. He was quick, not short on skill and like Andy always gave 100%. He was also a lovely bloke and great with the supporters. Ian Muir was still skilful although his legs had a gone a bit. He played in centre midfield and could set the tempo. He also coached and looked pretty decent. I was told by other players that he was always passing on tips and sharing his valuable experience. Stephenson played at centre forward when he arrived bu he then played just behind front two which allowed him to drift around: he had a huge amount of skill. When he came back a second time he played in centre midfield. He was always talking a lot on the pitch. My favourite player was Warren Ayres. I remember him playing for several games with a dead leg: now that is commitment.

Sadly Peter McBean passed away in 2019. He played for a lot of teams including Coventry Sporting, Atherstone, Bedworth, VS Rugby, Nuneaton Borough, Aylesbury and Racing Club Warwick.

A Tribute to Peter by Lincoln Liburd

Beany, a true gentleman in the eyes of bothteammates and opponents, an accolade I could never reach.

Pete made the most of his ability and was a sought after striker and played at many semi pro clubs for many years with that killer smile of his. I have many fond memories of Beany winning the telegraph cup at Highfield Road with Massey Ferguson. Always had your back a memory I will share with you. We played for Albany Social and I got punched in the face from behind. Before I could react Beany had decked the player that had punched me, a true and loyal friend till the end. A super human being who is missed every day.

Dedication

In recent times we have lost Curly O'Callaghan, Gordon Simms, Johnny Matthews, Mick Brady, Peter McBean, Peter Wyer, Jack Lovering, Nick Kirk, Ian McConville, David Kite, Howard Jeavons, Joy Barry, Cliff Morby, Pep Gill, Gordon Dougall, Hugh Morrow, Bobby Hancocks, Nick Morgan, Bernard Jones and Peter Whittingham who are all local footballers or footballing people. This book is dedicated to them and to the many other footballers and footballing people from Coventry and Warwickshire who have passed away over the years.

Acknowledgements

I would like to thank the following people who have helped make this book possible. Thank you all for your help and time.

I would like to thank Tony Kiely my proof-reader who is also my old school teacher and a friend. It has been great that I have been able to share this journey of the book with you.

Jim Brown, Dietmar Bruck, Gloria Lines, Geoff Lines, Steve Lines, Chris Goodwin (England online), Nigel Murray, Garry Thompson, Steve Green, Alan Green, Jim Holmes, Graham Smith, Tony Sheridan, Leigh Burdett, Deborah Pritchard, Ken Watkins, Kenny Watkins, Craig Herbert, Chris Dangerfield, Clive Deslandes, Dior Angus, Terry Angus, Alan Harkus, Paul Jephcott, Dennis Taylor, Frank Houston, Tom Kilkelly, Tommy Gorman, David Smith, John Docker, Dean Thomas, John Curtis, Warren Bufton, Alun French, Matty Blair, Andy Blair, Kelvin Langmead, Frank Pritchard, Dean Nelson, Roy Evans, Martin Ashcroft, Jamie Harvey, Rikki Bains, Willie Boland, Paul McCrink, Reis Ashraf, Paul O'Brien, Richard Aston, Roy Slade, Brendan Phillips, Stewart

Rushton, Louis Guest, Stuart Guest, Mark Edwards, Jack Edwards, John Setchell, Scott Garner, Nikki Miles, Leon James, Michael Brady, Bernie James, Luke Rowe, Chris Dawson, Daniel Nardeillo, Roland Matthews, Kerrie Field, Graham Walker, Sue Burdett, Lesley Kleztenbauer, Shane Murphy, Natalie Downes, Chris Downes, Steve Norris, Marie McConville,Josh O'Grady, Edwin Greaves, Brian Ndlovu, Ian Goodwin, Gary Bradder, Matty Fowler(Burt), Craig Dutton, Marcus Hamill, Richard Landon, Andy Beechey, Kenneth Puffett, Bob Abercrombie, Mel Davis, Derek Jones, Steve Gibbs, Peter McInulty, David Hudgell, Les Ebrey, Adrian Metcalf, Jack Manning, Nigel Bunt, Wayne Mumford, Ryan Gallagher, Stewart Gallagher, Peter Hormantschuk, Marcus Hall, Gary McSheffrey, Boyd Young, Steve Montgomery, Paul Luckett, Gary Hardwick, Sean Crowley, Don Gethfield, Tommy English, Luke English, Darren Dickson, Adam Willis, Iyseden Christie, Jamie Lenton, Kyle King, Jamie Barnwell-Edinboro, Connor Gudger, Tom Bates, Vijay Sidhu, Brett Healy, Rory Linnie, Michael Stephenson, Gerry Carr, Gavin O'Toole, Barry Quinn, Mike Young, Alex Hudson, Andy Taylor, Jessica Sephton-Bray, Yvonne-Pamela Brady, Nigel Bridge-Wilkinson, Lincoln Liburd, Duncan Holley, Danny Finlay, Peter Lee, Nuneaton Borough – from to town to town, e book. Jim Connolly, Doug Armstrong, Adam Walker, Allan Dolby, Michelle Livingstone, Billy Livingstone, Alan Thompson, Sharon Turner, Gary Hannam, Adam Walker, Scott Darroch, David Foy, Martin and Paul O'Conner (Coventry City Footballers book published in 1993)

Cover photos courtesy – Dean Nelson and David Featherstone.

Printed in Great Britain
by Amazon

63082553R00210